Alexander Jacob Schem

The American Ecclesiastical and Educational Almanac

Alexander Jacob Schem

The American Ecclesiastical and Educational Almanac

ISBN/EAN: 9783337336592

Printed in Europe, USA, Canada, Australia, Japan

Cover: Foto ©Lupo / pixelio.de

More available books at **www.hansebooks.com**

THE AMERICAN

ECCLESIASTICAL

LMANAC,

FOR MINISTERS AND LAYMEN,

FOR

1868.

BY

PROF. ALEXANDER J. SCHEM.

New York:

FREDK. GERHARD, Agt., 15 Dey St.,

POST BOX 4001.

A Magnificent Engraving!

AN ORNAMENT FOR EVERY CHRISTIAN HOME!

On February 1st 1868, will be published a splendid Engraving of

designed and engraved by H. CLAUSSEN.

SIZE, 24 × 30 INCHES, PRICE, TWO DOLLARS.

This beautiful engraving, the finest work of the kind ever published, is certain to become a favorite with Christian families, and ought to find its way into every Christian home. The design is appropriate, executed in the best style of art, and harmonizes in the most striking and symbolical manner with the spirit of the divine instruction,

How to Pray.

The attention of ministers is invited to this magnificent work, and they are requested, if they see fit, to introduce it to the notice of their church-members.

Ministers and other Gentlemen, desiring to act as agents, will be allowed a very liberal discount, which will enable them to sell it at a very handsome profit.

Agents wanted in every City and County. Canvassers can make easily from 10 to 20 Dollars a day.

Circulars stating the terms for agents &c., sent on application to the Publisher. Those, wishing at the same time to receive a sample-copy will please enclose Two Dollars.

FREDK. GERHARD,

No. 15 Dey St., New York,

POST OFFICE BOX 4001.

1st MONTH. # JANUARY, 1868. **31 DAYS.**

MOON'S PHASES	D.	BOSTON. H. M.	NEW YORK. H. M.	WASH'TON H. M.	CHARLES'N H. M.	Sun on Merid. or noon mark. D.	H.	M.	S.
First Quarter	2	11 18 ev.	11 6 ev.	10 54 ev.	10 42 ev.	1	12	3	43
Full Moon	9	6 9 ev.	5 57 ev	5 45 ev.	5 33 ev.	9	12	7	17
Third Quarter	16	0 20 ev.	0 8 ev.	11 56 mo	11 44 mo.	17	12	10	17
New Moon	24	2 34 ev	2 22 ev.	2 10 ev	1 58 ev.	25	12	12	33

Day of Year.	Day of Month.	Day of Week	Sun's decl S.	CALENDAR FOR Boston; New England, N. York State, Michigan, Wiscons., Iowa and Oregon. Sun ris's	Sun sets	Moon sets.	H. W. B'stn.	CALENDAR FOR N. York City; Philadph., Conn.; New-Jersey, Pen'la, Ohio, Indiana & Ilinois. Sun ris's.	Sun sets	Moon sets.	H W. N.Yk.	Calendar for Washington; Mary'd, V'g'a, Ken'y, M ss'ri, & California. Sun. ris's	Sun sets	Moon sets.	CALENDAR FOR Charles'n: North Carolin., Tennes ee, Geo., Alabama, Miss's'pi, & Louisiana. Sun ris's.	Sun sets	Moon sets.	H. W. Ch't'n
			° ′ ″	H.M.	H M.	H M.	H. M.	H.M.	H.M.	H M	H. M.	H M.	H.M.	H. M.	H.M.	H M.	H. M.	H. M.
1	1	W	23 1 39	7 30	4 38	11 13	3 28	7 25	4 43	11 13	0 14	7 19	4 49	11 14	7 3	5 5	11 15	morn.
2	2	Th	22 56 32	7 30	4 39	morn.	4 13	7 25	4 44	morn.	1 1	7 19	4 50	morn	7 3	5 6	morn	0 13
3	3	Fr	22 50 58	7 30	4 40	0 13	5 5	7 25	4 45	0 13	1 51	7 19	4 51	0 12	7 3	5 7	0 11	1 5
4	4	Sa	22 44 57	7 30	4 41	1 14	5 58	7 25	4 46	1 13	2 43	7 19	4 52	1 11	7 3	5 7	1 7	1 58
5	5	1	22 38 28	7 30	4 42	2 18	6 59	7 25	4 47	2 16	3 44	7 19	4 52	2 14	7 3	5 8	2 7	2 59
6	6	M	22 31 33	7 29	4 43	3 26	8 1	7 25	4 48	3 23	4 46	7 19	4 53	3 20	7 4	5 9	3 10	4 1
7	7	Tu	22 24 11	7 29	4 44	4 33	9 4	7 25	4 49	4 30	5 49	7 19	4 44	4 26	7 4	5 10	4 14	5 4
8	8	W	22 16 22	7 29	4 45	5 40	10 4	7 24	4 50	5 36	6 50	7 19	4 55	8 32	7 4	5 11	5 19	6 4
9	9	Th	22 8 7	7 29	4 46	rises.	11 4	7 24	4 51	rises.	7 47	7 19	4 56	rises.	7 4	5 12	rises	7 4
10	10	Fr	21 59 27	7 29	4 47	6 8	11 56	7 24	4 52	6 12	8 40	7 19	4 47	6 16	7 4	5 12	6 27	7 56
11	11	Sa	21 50 20	7 29	4 48	7 20	ev. 48	7 24	4 53	7 23	9 34	7 19	4 58	7 26	7 3	5 13	7 35	8 48
12	12	2	21 40 48	7 28	4 50	8 31	1 40	7 23	4 54	8 33	10 25	7 18	4 59	8 35	7 3	5 14	8 41	9 40
13	13	M	21 30 51	7 28	4 51	9 40	2 29	7 23	4 55	9 41	11 12	7 18	5 0	9 42	7 3	5 15	9 45	10 29
14	14	Tu	21 20 29	7 28	4 52	10 40	3 18	7 23	4 56	10 48	ev. 3	7 18	5 1	10 48	7 3	5 16	10 48	11 18
15	15	W	21 9 42	7 27	4 53	11 51	4 7	7 22	4 57	11 50	0 54	7 18	5 2	11 49	7 3	5 17	11 46	ev. 7
16	16	Th	20 58 30	7 27	4 54	morn	5 0	7 22	4 59	morn.	1 47	7 17	5 3	morn	7 3	5 18	morn.	1 0
17	17	Fr	20 46 55	7 26	4 55	0 54	5 56	7 21	5 0	0 52	2 42	7 17	5 5	0 50	7 2	5 19	0 45	1 58
18	18	Sa	20 34 56	7 26	4 56	1 53	6 53	7 21	5 1	1 51	3 38	7 16	5 6	1 48	7 2	5 20	1 40	2 53
19	19	3	20 32 34	7 25	4 58	2 52	7 48	7 21	5 2	2 49	4 33	7 16	5 7	2 45	7 2	5 21	2 35	3 48
20	20	M	20 9 48	7 24	4 59	3 47	8 43	7 20	5 3	3 44	5 28	7 15	5 8	3 40	7 2	5 21	3 28	4 43
21	21	Tu	19 56 40	7 24	5 0	4 41	9 33	7 19	5 4	4 37	6 19	7 15	5 9	4 33	7 1	5 22	4 20	5 33
22	22	W	19 43 10	7 23	5 1	5 32	10 20	7 18	5 5	5 28	7 6	7 14	5 10	5 23	7 1	5 23	5 10	6 20
23	23	Th	19 29 17	7 22	5 3	6 17	11 4	7 17	5 7	6 13	7 47	7 14	5 11	6 9	7 0	5 24	5 56	7 4
24	24	Fr	19 15 3	7 22	5 4	sets.	11 44	7 17	5 8	sets.	8 6	7 13	5 12	sets.	7 0	5 25	sets.	7 44
25	25	Sa	19 0 28	7 21	5 5	6 12	morn.	7 16	5 9	6 15	9 7	7 12	5 13	6 18	7 0	5 26	6 28	8 20
26	26	4	18 45 32	7 20	5 6	7 9	0 21	7 16	5 10	7 11	9 46	7 12	5 15	7 14	6 59	5 27	7 21	9 0
27	27	M	18 30 15	7 19	5 8	8 7	1 0	7 15	5 11	8 8	10 23	7 11	5 16	8 10	6 58	5 28	8 15	9 38
28	28	Tu	18 14 39	7 18	5 9	9 5	1 38	7 14	5 13	9 6	11 0	7 10	5 17	9 6	6 58	5 29	9 9	10 18
29	29	W	17 58 43	7 17	5 10	10 4	2 18	7 13	5 14	10 4	11 41	7 9	5 18	10 4	6 57	5 30	10 3	10 57
30	30	Th	17 42 27	7 16	5 12	11 5	2 57	7 12	5 15	11 4	morn	7 8	5 19	11 3	6 57	5 31	10 59	11 40
31	31	Fr	17 25 53	7 15	5 13	morn	3 40	7 12	5 16	morn.	0 26	7 8	5 20	morn.	6 56	5 32	11 57	morn.

SECURITY LIFE INSURANCE

AND

ANNUITY COMPANY,

NO. 31 PINE STREET, NEW YORK.

ASSETS..$700,000

DIRECTORS:

EDWARD HAIGHT,
EDWARD WOOD,
CHARLES L. SWORDS,
JOHN F. UNDERHILL,
ROBERT LINDLEY MURRAY,
FRANCIS F. WALKER,
WILLIAM HUBBARD,
THOMAS W. BIRDSALL,
JOSEPH F. KNAPP,
JAMES M DRAKE,
JAMES BRETT,
FRANCIS PAYSON,
AUGUSTUS TABER,
JOHN W. GRAYDON,
ROBERT BOWNE,
CHARLES T. GOODWIN,
SIDNEY WINTRINGHAM,
EDWARD MARSHALL,
ROBERT L. CASE,
THEODORE R. WETMORE,
WALTER M. FRANKLIN,
J. NELSON TAPPAN,
EDMUND TITUS,
CHARLES BELLOWS,
REUBEN H. UNDERHILL,
JOHN T. WILLETS,
A. B. WETMORE,
ROBERT B. HOWLAND.

ISAAC W. BUSHMORE, Brooklyn, L. I.
NATH B. WEED, Darien, Ct.
WM. HENRY CHASE, Union Springs, N. Y.
WM. B. WILLIS, New Hamburgh, N. Y.
GEORGE INNIS, Poughkeepsie, N. Y.
SANDFORD A. KNAPP, Peekskill N. Y.
JAMES BIGLER, Newburgh, N. Y.
DAVID MOORE " "

ROBT. L. CASE. Pres. THEO. R. WETMORE, Vice Pres. ISAAC H. ALLEN, Secy.

STEPHEN WOOD, M. D.,
WM. HENRY CHURCH, M. D., } Medical Examiners, at the Office daily, from 1 to 3 P. M.

REUBEN H. UNDERHILL, Counsel.

NEW AMSTERDAM FIRE INSURANCE COMPANY,

CAPITAL,................$300,000.

OFFICE: NO. 173 BROADWAY, COR. OF CORTLANDT ST. N. Y.

DIRECTORS.

DAVID S. MANNERS, PRESIDENT.

DAVID S. MANNERS
A. H. WALLIS,
FRANCIS MANY,
JOHN WESTFALL,
WM. F. BEARNS,
PETER DURYEE,
JAMES G. POWERS,
JOHN WHEATON,
WILLIAM T. HALL,
NICHOLAS D HERDER,
ANDREW HOOGLAND,
HERMAN H. BRUNJES,
JAMES S. BEARNS,
H. H. KATTENHORN,
E. C. KORNER,
FRANCIS BOLTING,
HENRY J. BEERS,
HENRY A. BOOREAM,
JOHN C. KOHLSAAT,
LEANDER DARLING,
CALEB BARSTOW,
ABRAHAM VOORHIS,
MICHAEL LIENAU,
DAVID JONES,
LEANDER B. SHAW,
R. H. LAIMBEER,
JNO. G. LINNEMANN,
OTTO LOESCHIGK,
JAMES R. BOUCK,
H. BLYDENBURGH.

D. R. DOREMUS, SURVEYOR.
ISAAC D. COLE JR., SECRETARY.

EDWARD J. EVANS & CO.,

NURSERYMEN AND SEEDSMEN.

YORK, PENN.

FRUIT, SHADE AND ORNAMENTAL TREES,

GRAPES, SMALL FRUITS,

Ornamental Shrubs, Roses, Hedge Plants, &c.

In full assortment;

CHOICE GARDEN SEEDS,

in great variety,

all *carefully tested before sending out*, and

WARRANTED TO GROW.

The following Catalogues are issued, and mailed to any address, on receipt of stamp:

1. Amateur's Price List of Fruit and ornamental Trees, Grape-Vines, Small Fruits, &c.
2. Descriptive Strawberry Catalogue, with Supplement.
3. Wholesale Catalogue of Fruit and ornamental Trees, &c.
4. Descriptive Seed Catalogue.
5. " Circular of New Seeds.
6. " Catalogue of Bedding Plants, &c.

2d MONTH. # FEBRUARY, 1868. 29 DAYS.

MOON'S PHASES.	D	BOSTON. H. M.	NEW YORK. H. M.	WASH'TON. H. M.	CHARLES'N. H. M.	Sun on Merid. or noon Mark D.	H.	M.	S.
First Quarter......	1	1 32 ev.	1 20 ev.	1 6 ev.	0 56 ev.	1	12	13	41
Full Moon........	8	4 51 mo.	4 39 mo.	4 27 mo.	4 15 mo.	9	12	14	28
Third Quarter....	15	4 33 mo.	4 21 mo.	4 9 mo.	3 57 mo	17	12	14	16
New Moon........	22	9 36 mo.	9 24 mo.	9 12 mo.	9 0 mo.	25	12	13	20

Day of Year.	Day of Month.	Day of Week.	Sun's decl. S. ° ′ ″	CALENDAR FOR Boston, New England, N York State, Michigan, Wiscon. Iowa & Oregon. Sun r's's. H.M	Sun sets. H.M.	Moon sets. H. M.	H. W. B'st'n. H. M.	CALENDAR FOR N. York City, Philadelphia, Conn. N. Jersy, Penn'ia, Ohio Indiana & Illinois. Sun ris's H.M.	Sun sets. H.M.	Moon sets. H. M.	H. W. N.Yk. H. M.	CALENDAR FOR Washington, Maryl'd Virg'a, Ken'y, Misso'r., and California. Sun r's's H M.	Sun sets. H.M.	Moon sets. H M.	CALENDAR FOR Charles'n, North Carolin., Tennessee Geo., Alabama, Mis-s'ippi & Louisiana. Sun r's's. H.M	Sun sets H.M.	Moon sets H. M.	H. W. Ch't'n. H. M.
32	1	Sa	17 9 1	7 14	5 14	0 7	4 30	7 11	5 18	0 5	1 17	7 7	5 21	0 3	6 55	5 33	morn.	0 30
33	2	5	16 51 50	7 13	5 15	1 9	5 25	7 10	5 19	1 7	2 14	7 6	5 23	1 4	6 55	5 34	0 55	1 25
34	3	M	16 34 22	7 12	5 16	2 15	6 28	7 9	5 20	2 12	3 14	7 5	5 24	2 8	6 54	5 34	1 58	2 28
35	4	Tu	16 16 35	7 11	5 18	3 20	7 37	7 7	5 21	3 16	4 22	7 4	5 25	3 12	6 53	5 35	2 59	3 37
36	5	W	15 58 34	7 10	5 19	4 23	8 45	7 6	5 22	4 19	5 30	7 3	5 26	4 15	6 52	5 36	4 2	4 45
37	6	Th	15 40 15	7 9	5 21	5 22	9 48	7 5	5 23	5 18	6 34	7 2	5 27	5 13	6 52	5 37	5 1	5 48
38	7	Fr	15 21 40	7 8	5 22	rises.	10 43	7 4	5 25	rises	7 32	7 1	5 28	rises	6 51	5 38	rises.	6 48
39	8	Sa	15 2 50	7 6	5 23	6 4	11 40	7 3	5 26	6 7	8 22	7 0	5 29	6 9	6 50	5 39	6 17	7 40
40	9	6	14 43 44	7 5	5 24	7 17	ev.28	7 2	5 27	7 18	9 15	6 59	5 30	7 20	6 49	5 40	7 24	8 28
41	10	M	14 24 24	7 4	5 25	8 26	1 16	7 1	5 28	8 27	10 2	6 58	5 32	8 27	6 48	5 41	8 29	9 16
42	11	Tu	14 4 49	7 2	5 26	9 35	2 4	7 0	5 30	9 35	10 46	6 57	5 33	9 34	6 47	5 42	9 33	10 4
43	12	W	13 45 1	7 1	5 28	10 40	2 48	6 58	5 31	10 39	11 32	6 55	5 34	10 38	6 47	5 43	10 33	10 48
44	13	Th	13 24 58	7 0	5 29	11 43	3 35	6 57	5 32	11 41	ev.21	6 54	5 35	11 39	6 46	5 44	11 32	11 35
45	14	Fr	13 4 43	6 59	5 30	morn.	4 25	6 56	5 34	morn	1 12	6 53	5 36	morn.	6 45	5 45	morn.	ev. 25
46	15	Sa	12 41 15	6 57	5 32	0 43	5 18	6 55	5 35	0 40	2 4	6 52	5 38	0 37	6 44	5 46	0 28	1 18
47	16	7	12 23 34	6 56	5 33	1 41	6 18	6 53	5 36	1 38	3 3	6 51	5 39	1 34	6 43	5 47	1 23	2 18
48	17	M	12 2 42	5 54	5 35	2 35	7 14	6 52	5 37	2 31	4 0	6 49	5 40	2 27	6 42	5 48	2 15	3 14
49	18	Tu	11 41 38	6 53	5 36	3 27	8 11	6 51	5 39	3 23	4 55	6 48	5 41	3 19	6 41	5 48	3 6	4 11
50	19	W	11 20 23	6 52	5 38	4 13	9 3	6 49	5 40	4 9	5 48	6 47	5 42	4 5	6 40	5 49	3 52	5 3
51	20	Th	10 58 57	6 50	5 39	4 57	9 51	6 48	5 41	4 53	6 37	6 46	5 44	4 49	6 39	5 50	4 36	5 51
52	21	Fr	10 37 21	6 48	5 40	5 37	10 36	6 46	5 43	5 33	7 21	6 44	5 45	5 30	6 37	5 51	5 19	6 36
53	22	Sa	10 15 35	6 47	5 42	6 12	11 17	6 45	5 44	6 9	7 59	6 43	5 46	6 6	6 36	5 52	5 57	7 17
54	23	8	9 53 40	6 45	5 43	sets.	11 55	6 44	5 45	sets.	8 38	6 42	5 47	sets	6 35	5 53	sets.	7 55
55	24	M	9 31 36	6 44	5 45	6 59	morn.	6 42	5 46	7 0	9 19	6 40	5 48	7 1	6 34	5 54	7 4	8 32
56	25	Tu	9 9 23	6 42	5 46	7 58	0 32	6 41	5 48	7 58	9 56	6 38	5 49	7 58	6 33	5 55	7 59	9 10
57	26	W	8 47 2	6 41	5 47	8 59	1 10	6 39	5 49	8 58	10 33	6 37	5 51	8 58	6 32	5 56	8 55	9 45
58	27	Th	8 24 34	6 39	5 49	10 0	1 49	6 38	5 50	9 58	11 13	6 36	5 52	9 57	6 31	5 57	9 52	10 30
59	28	Fr	8 1 58	6 38	5 50	11 1	2 30	6 37	5 51	10 59	11 59	6 31	5 53	10 56	6 30	5 58	10 49	11 14
60	29	Sa	7 39 15	6 37	5 50	morn.	3 14	6 36	5 52	morn.	morn.	6 34	5 53	11 59	6 29	5 58	11 49	morn.

THE MUTUAL
Life Insurance Company
OF NEW YORK.

144 and 146 Broadway.

FREDERICK S. WINSTON, PRESIDENT.

THIS COMPANY offers the following peculiar advantages to persons intending to insure their lives:—

ITS ASSETS are *larger* than those of any other Life Insurance Company in the United States, amounting to

$22,000,000.

and are *exclusively cash*.

ITS RATES OF PREMIUM are *lower* than those of the majority of other Life Insurance Companies—yet its Dividends have been *greater*; the result of a very low rate of mortality among the insured, consequent on a most careful and judicious selection of lives.

THE MORTALITY AMONG ITS MEMBERS has been proportionally *less* than that of any other Life Insurance Company in either America or Europe whose experience has been made known—a result in the highest degree favorable to Policy-holders.

ITS DIVIDENDS are made annually, and may be used either to increase the amount insured, or to decrease the premium.

EVERY POLICY has a dividend, which may be so used at the end of the first and every subsequent year that he remains insured.

THE ASSETS of the Company are invested exclusively on Bond and Mortgage on Real Estate in the City and State of New York, worth in each case at least *double* the amount loaned, and bearing interest at seven per cent: the solidity and security of this disposition of the Company's funds cannot be over-rated.

Note.—The business of this Company is conducted on the MUTUAL principle in the strictest sense of the term; the entire surplus, *deducting necessary expenses alone*, being equitably divided among the assured.

RICHARD A. McCURDY, *Vice-President.*
SHEPPARD HOMANS, *Actuary.*

ISAAC ABBATT,
JOHN M. STUART, } *Secretaries.*

WILLIAM BETTS, LL.D.,
HON. LUCIUS ROBINSON, } *Counsel.*

MINTURN POST, M.D.,
ISAAC L. KIP, M.D., } *Medical Examiners.*

3d MONTH. # MARCH, 1868. **31 DAYS.**

MOON'S PHASES.	D.	BOSTON. H. M.	NEW YORK. H. M.	WASH'TON. H. M.	CHARLES'N. H. M
First Quarter	1	0 5 mo.	11 53 ev.	11 41 ev	11 29 ev.
Full Moon	8	3 38 ev.	3 26 ev.	3 14 ev.	3 2 ev.
Third Quarter.....	15	10 45 ev.	10 33 ev.	10 21 ev.	10 9 ev.
New Moon	24	2 15 mo.	2 3 mo	1 51 mo.	1 39 mo.
First Quarter	31	7 41 mo.	7 29 mo.	7 17 mo	7 5 mo.

Sun on Merid. D.	H.	M.	S
	12	12	25
9	12	10	32
17	12	8	18
25	12	5	53

Day of Year.	Day of Month.	Day of Week.	Sun's decl. S.	CALENDAR FOR Boston; New England, N. York State, Michigan, Wiscons. Iowa and Oregon. Sun ris's.	Sun sets.	Moon sets.	H. W. B'stn.	CALENDAR FOR N. York City; Philadph., Conn. New-Jersey, Pen'la, Ohio, Indiana & Illinois. Sun ris's.	Sun sets.	Moon sets	H. W. N. Yk.	CALENDAR FOR Washington. Mar'ld, Virg'a. Ken'y, Miss'ri and California. Sun ris's.	Sun sets.	Moon sets.	CALENDAR FOR Carleston; North Carolin., Tennessee, Geo., Alabama, Mis-sis'pi, & Louisiana Sun ris's.	Sun sets	Moon sets	H. W. Ch't'n
			° ' "	H. M.	H M	H M.	H. M	H. M.	H M.	H. M	H. M.	H. M.	H. M.	H. M.	H. M.	H. M.	H. M	H. M
61	1	**9**	7 16 25	6 36	5 51	0 5	4 4	6 35	5 53	0 2	0 51	6 33	5 54	morn.	6 28	5 59	morn	0 4
62	2	M	6 53 30	6 35	5 52	1 8	5 4	6 34	5 53	1 5	1 50	6 32	5 55	1 1	6 27	5 59	0 49	1 4
63	3	Tu	6 30 29	6 33	5 53	2 11	6 9	6 32	5 54	2 7	2 55	6 30	5 56	2 3	6 26	6 0	1 50	2 9
64	4	W	6 7 22	6 31	5 54	3 10	7 20	6 30	5 55	3 8	4 5	6 29	5 57	3 2	6 25	6 0	2 49	3 2
65	5	Th	5 44 11	6 30	5 55	4 5	8 29	6 29	5 56	4 1	5 14	6 27	5 57	3 57	6 23	6 1	3 44	4 29
66	6	Fr	5 20 55	6 28	5 56	4 55	9 33	6 27	5 57	4 52	6 19	6 26	5 58	4 48	6 22	6 1	4 37	5 33
67	7	Sa	4 57 35	6 26	5 57	5 39	10 29	6 25	5 58	5 37	7 14	6 24	5 59	5 34	6 21	6 2	5 26	6 29
68	8	**10**	4 34 11	6 25	5 58	rises.	11 21	6 24	5 59	rises.	8 2	6 23	6 0	rises.	6 20	6 3	rises	7 21
69	9	M	4 10 43	6 23	5 59	7 11	ev. 6	6 22	6 0	7 11	8 51	6 21	6 1	7 11	6 19	6 3	7 11	8 6
70	10	Tu	3 47 12	6 21	6 0	8 19	0 49	6 20	6 1	8 18	9 36	6 20	6 2	8 18	6 17	6 4	8 14	8 49
71	11	W	3 23 39	6 20	6 2	9 27	1 34	6 19	6 2	9 25	10 19	6 18	6 3	9 23	6 16	6 5	9 17	9 34
72	12	Th	3 0 3	6 18	6 3	10 29	2 0	6 17	6 3	10 26	11 2	6 17	6 4	10 24	6 15	6 6	10 15	10 0
73	13	Fr	2 36 26	6 16	6 4	11 30	3 3	6 16	6 4	11 26	11 48	6 15	6 5	11 23	6 13	6 6	11 12	11 3
74	14	Sa	2 12 46	6 14	6 5	morn	3 51	6 14	6 5	morn	ev.37	6 13	6 6	morn.	6 12	6 7	morn.	11 51
75	15	**11**	1 49 6	6 13	6 6	0 27	4 43	6 12	6 6	0 24	1 30	6 12	6 7	0 19	6 11	6 8	0 7	ev.43
76	16	M	1 25 24	6 11	6 7	1 20	5 40	6 11	6 8	1 16	2 26	6 10	6 8	1 12	6 10	6 9	0 59	1 40
77	17	Tu	1 1 42	6 9	6 9	2 9	6 37	6 9	6 9	2 5	3 23	6 9	6 9	2 1	6 8	6 9	1 48	2 37
78	18	W	0 37 59	6 7	6 10	2 54	7 35	6 7	6 10	2 50	4 20	6 7	6 10	2 45	6 7	6 10	2 33	3 35
79	19	Th	S. 14 17	6 6	6 11	3 35	8 29	6 6	6 11	3 31	5 14	6 6	6 11	3 28	6 6	6 11	3 16	4 29
80	20	Fr	N. 9 25	6 4	6 12	4 11	9 18	6 4	6 12	4 8	6 4	6 4	6 12	4 5	6 4	6 12	3 55	5 18
81	21	Sa	0 33 6	6 2	6 13	4 45	10 3	6 2	6 13	4 42	6 49	6 3	6 13	4 40	6 3	6 12	4 32	6 3
82	22	**12**	0 56 46	6 0	6 14	5 17	10 47	6 1	6 14	5 15	7 31	6 1	6 14	5 13	6 1	6 13	5 8	6 47
83	23	M	1 20 24	5 59	6 15	5 47	11 25	5 59	6 15	5 46	8 8	5 59	6 15	5 45	5 59	6 14	5 42	7 25
84	24	Tu	1 44 0	5 57	6 17	sets.	morn.	5 58	6 16	sets.	8 48	5 58	6 16	sets.	5 58	6 14	sets.	8 3
85	25	W	2 7 33	5 55	6 18	7 52	0 3	5 56	6 17	7 51	9 28	5 56	6 17	7 49	5 57	6 15	7 45	8 42
86	26	Th	2 31 4	5 53	6 19	8 56	0 42	5 54	6 18	8 54	10 11	5 54	6 18	8 51	5 56	6 16	8 45	9 25
87	27	Fr	2 54 32	5 52	6 20	9 39	1 25	5 52	6 19	9 56	10 50	5 53	6 19	9 53	5 55	6 16	9 44	10 8
88	28	Sa	3 17 56	5 50	6 21	11 3	2 8	5 51	6 20	10 59	11 39	5 51	6 19	10 55	5 54	6 17	10 44	10 55
89	29	**13**	3 41 16	5 48	6 22	morn.	2 55	5 49	6 21	morn.	morn.	5 50	6 20	11 56	5 52	6 18	11 44	11 48
90	30	M	4 4 32	5 46	6 23	0 5	3 48	5 47	6 22	0 1	0 34	5 48	6 21	morn.	5 51	6 19	morn.	morn.
91	31	Tu	4 27 44	5 45	6 24	1 5	4 49	5 46	6 23	1 1	1 36	5 47	6 22	0 56	5 50	6 19	0 43	0 49

203, 399, 511 & 756 BROADWAY,

AND FOURTH AVENUE, cor. of 17th St.

DRUGS, MEDICINES, FANCY ARTICLES, &C.

Hegeman & Co.'s Benzine,

For the instant removal of Paints, Grease Spots, etc.

Hegeman & Co.'s Camphor Ice, with Glycerine,

A certain cure for Chapped Hands, Sunburn. Sore Lips, Chilblains, etc.

Hegeman & Co.'s Genuine Cod Liver Oil,

Warranted pure, and prepared from the fresh Livers, without bleaching or any chemical preparation. This article has stood the test of fifteen years' experience, with increasing reputation, for Consumption, Scrofula, etc.

Hegeman & Co.'s Cordial Elixir of Calisaya Bark,

Prepared from the Calisaya (or King's) Bark, being the best variety of Peruvian Bark. It is an agreeable cordial to the taste, and possessing the valuable tonic properties of the bark—an excellent preventive to Fevers, Fever and Ague, etc , for residents in malarious districts.

Hegeman & Co.'s Velpeau's Diarrhea Remedy and Cholera Preventive.

Used with unfailing success during and since the cholera of 1845. A single dose will usually check or cure the Diarrhea. No family should be without it.

Hegeman's Ferrated Elixir of Bark, the Most perfect Iron Tonic in Use.

This Elixir is composed of the active principles of Calisaya Bark, combined with Pyrophosphate of Iron, and in all cases where an efficient Iron Tonic is required will prove very valuable.

Hegeman's Odonto or Pearl Dentifrice.

A most agreeable and economical Powder for cleaning and preserving the teeth.

Hegeman & Co's Bronchial Pastilles.

They allay irritation of the mucous membrane, cure Catarrh, Cough, and Incipient Bronchitis. Particularly valuable for Clergymen and Public Speakers, as they keep the throat moist, etc.

THE ABOVE PREPARATIONS ARE SOLD BY DRUGGISTS GENERALLY,

In the United States and Canadas.

4th MONTH. # APRIL, 1868. **30 DAYS.**

MOON'S PHASES	D	BOSTON. H.	M.	NEW YORK. H.	M.	WASH'TON. H.	M.	CHARLES'N. H.	M.
Full Moon	7	2	23 mo.	2	21 mo.	2	9 mo.	1	57 mo.
Third Quarter	14	5	51 ev.	5	39 ev	5	27 ev.	5	15 ev.
New Moon	22	3	36 ev.	3	24 ev.	3	12 ev.	3	0 ev.
First Quarter	29	1	34 ev	1	22 ev.	1	10 ev	0	58 ev.

Sun on Merid. or noon mark. D.	H.	M.	S.
1	12	3	45
9	12	1	25
17	11	59	23
25	11	57	47

Day of Year.	Day of Month.	Day of Week	Sun's decl. N.	CALENDAR FOR Boston; New England, N. York State, Michigan, Wisconsin, Iowa and Oregon. Sun ris's	Sun sets	Moon sets.	H. W. B'stn.	CALENDAR FOR N. York City; Philadph., Conn.; New-Jersey, Pen'la, Ohio, Indiana & Illinois. Sun ris's.	Sun sets	Moon sets.	H. W. N.Yk.	Calendar for Washington; Mary'd, V'g'a, Ken'y, Miss'ri, & California. Sun. ris's	Sun sets	Moon sets	CALENDAR FOR Charles'n: North Carolin., Tennessee, Geo., Alabama, Mis-sis'pi, & Louisiana. Sun ris's.	Sun sets	Moon sets.	H. W. Ch't'n
			° ′ ″	H.M.	H.M.	H. M.	H. M.	H.M.	H.M.	H M	H. M.	H M.	H.M.	H. M	H.M.	H M.	H M	H M.
92	1	W	4 50 51	5 43	6 25	1 59	5 56	5 44	6 24	1 55	2 42	5 46	6 23	1 50	5 48	6 20	1 38	1 56
93	2	Th	5 13 52	5 41	6 27	2 49	7 6	5 42	6 26	2 45	3 51	5 44	6 24	2 41	5 47	6 21	2 30	3 6
94	3	Fr	5 36 48	5 40	6 28	3 34	8 14	5 41	6 27	3 31	4 58	5 42	6 25	3 28	5 46	6 21	3 19	4 14
95	4	Sa	5 59 38	5 38	6 29	4 14	9 14	5 39	6 28	4 12	6 0	5 41	6 26	4 10	5 45	6 22	4 3	5 14
96	5	**14**	6 22 22	5 36	6 30	4 51	10 8	5 37	6 29	4 50	6 54	5 39	6 27	4 49	5 43	6 23	4 46	6 8
97	6	M	6 44 59	5 35	6 31	rises	10 57	5 36	6 30	rises.	7 40	5 37	6 28	rises.	5 42	6 23	rises	6 57
98	7	Tu	7 7 29	5 33	6 32	7 6	1 41	5 34	6 31	7 4	8 23	5 36	6 29	7 3	5 41	6 24	6 58	7 41
99	8	W	7 29 52	5 31	6 33	8 11	ev.22	5 33	6 32	8 8	9 9	5 34	6 30	8 6	5 39	6 25	7 59	8 42
100	9	Th	7 52 7	5 30	6 34	9 14	1 6	5 31	6 33	9 11	9 52	5 33	6 31	9 8	5 38	6 26	8 58	9 6
101	10	Fr	8 14 14	5 28	6 36	10 15	1 50	5 30	9 34	10 11	10 34	5 31	6 32	10 8	5 37	6 26	9 56	9 50
102	11	Sa	8 36 13	5 26	6 37	11 11	2 34	5 28	6 35	11 7	11 16	5 30	6 33	11 2	5 36	6 27	10 50	10 34
103	12	**15**	8 58 4	5 25	6 38	morn	3 21	5 26	6 36	11 59	ev. 6	5 28	6 34	11 54	5 34	6 28	11 41	11 21
104	13	M	9 19 45	5 23	6 39	0 3	4 9	5 25	6 37	morn	0 56	5 27	6 35	morn	5 33	6 28	morn.	ev. 9
105	14	Tu	9 41 18	5 21	6 40	0 50	5 3	5 24	6 38	0 46	1 50	5 25	6 36	0 42	5 32	6 29	0 29	1 3
106	15	W	10 2 41	5 20	6 41	1 32	5 58	5 22	6 39	1 29	2 41	5 21	6 37	1 24	5 31	6 30	1 12	1 58
107	16	Th	10 23 54	5 18	6 42	2 10	6 56	5 20	6 40	2 7	3 41	5 23	6 38	2 3	5 30	6 31	1 53	2 56
108	17	Fr	10 44 57	5 16	6 43	2 45	7 48	5 19	6 41	2 42	4 33	5 21	6 39	2 39	5 28	6 31	2 31	3 48
109	18	Sa	11 5 50	5 15	6 45	3 16	8 41	5 17	6 42	3 15	5 25	5 20	6 40	3 13	5 27	6 32	3 6	4 41
110	19	**16**	11 26 32	5 13	6 46	3 47	9 26	5 16	6 43	3 45	6 12	5 18	6 41	3 44	5 26	6 33	3 40	5 26
111	20	M	11 47 2	5 12	6 47	4 17	10 12	5 14	6 44	4 16	6 58	5 17	6 42	4 16	5 25	6 33	4 15	6 12
112	21	Tu	12 7 21	5 10	6 48	4 47	10 56	5 13	6 45	4 48	7 39	5 16	6 42	4 48	5 24	6 34	4 50	6 56
113	22	W	12 27 28	5 9	6 49	sets	11 36	5 11	6 46	sets.	8 18	5 14	6 43	sets.	5 23	6 35	sets.	7 36
114	23	Th	12 47 23	5 7	6 50	7 47	morn.	5 10	6 47	7 45	9 4	5 13	6 44	7 42	5 21	6 36	7 34	8 18
115	24	Fr	13 7 5	5 6	6 51	8 43	0 18	5 8	6 48	8 40	9 50	5 11	6 45	8 36	5 20	6 36	8 26	9 3
116	25	Sa	13 26 31	5 4	6 52	9 58	1 3	5 7	6 49	9 54	10 36	5 10	6 46	9 50	5 19	6 37	9 38	9 52
117	26	**17**	13 45 50	5 3	6 53	11 0	1 52	5 6	6 59	10 56	11 26	5 9	6 47	10 51	5 18	S 38	10 38	10 44
118	27	M	14 4 53	5 1	6 55	11 57	2 44	5 4	6 51	11 53	morn	5 8	6 48	11 49	5 17	6 38	11 36	11 38
119	28	Tu	14 23 41	5 0	6 56	morn	3 38	5 3	6 52	morn	0 21	5 6	6 49	morn	5 16	6 39	morn	morn.
120	29	W	14 42 15	4 58	6 57	0 49	4 39	5 2	6 53	0 45	1 26	5 5	6 50	0 41	5 15	6 40	0 29	0 39
121	30	Th	15 0 35	4 57	6 58	1 33	5 45	5 0	6 55	1 30	2 30	5 4	6 51	1 27	5 14	6 41	1 17	1 45

HOUSEHOLD BLESSINGS.

The Celebrated

UNION WASHING MACHINE

AND

CLOTHES WRINGER.

COMBINED OR SEPARATE.

Over 40,000 Sold and now Used in Hotels, Families etc.

UNIVERSALLY ADMITTED TO BE THE BEST MACHINE IN THE WORLD.

FIRST PRIZE MEDAL AWARDED IN EUROPE AND AMERICA.

Warranted to wash perfectly without soaking, rubbing or boiling and without injury to the most tender fabric. Soap, labor and health saved. No drudgery, no steam, no slops. The Union Wringer will fit any kind of tub and is the best and most durable in use. Clergymen of all denominations, Physicians and Philantrophists have written in the most glowing terms of the merits of these machines. Ladies who have them, say, they would not be without them for hundreds of dollars.

We keep on hand the largest assortment in the United States of mangles for ironing all kinds of plain clothes without heat. Suitable for hotels, laundries and families.

The Washer Womans Friend!

No Further Use for a Wash Board!

Hand Rubbing and Back Breaking Abolished

WARD'S

FAMILY WASHING MACHINE

PRICE, (*without wringer*) **ONLY $10.**

It is so simple in construction and so easily operated that a mere child can understand and work it. *SERVANT GIRLS* adopt it at once, and are quite willing to throw aside their wash board in favor of it.

Every Family can afford to get one.

IT WILL WASH CLOTHES PERFECTLY.

WITHOUT ANY HAND RUBBING WHATEVER,

Saving Three-Fourths in Time, Labor and Soap.

Excepting the celebrated

"UNION WASHING MACHINE"

It is the Best, Simplest and Cheapest Washer now before the Public.

ANY KIND OF WRINGFR

Can be Attached to it.

J. WARD & CO.

23 CORTLANDT ST., NEW YORK,
AND 102 SUMMER ST., BOSTON.

VAN NAME & Co., St. Louis and Cincinnati.
HARRY DUVALL, 164 Lake St., Chicago.

5th MONTH. **MAY, 1868.** 31 DAYS.

MOON'S PHASES.	D.	BOSTON. H. M.	NEW YORK. H. M.	WASH'TON. H. M.	CHARLES'N. H. M.
Full Moon	6	1 53 ev.	1 41 ev.	1 29 ev	1 17 ev.
Third Quarter.....	14	0 31 ev.	0 19 ev.	0 7 ev.	11 55 mo.
New Moon	22	1 52 mo.	1 40 mo.	1 28 mo.	1 16 mo.
First Quarter	28	6 58 ev.	6 46 ev	6 34 ev	6 22 ev.

Sun on Merid or noon mark. D.	H.	M.	S
1	11	56	54
9	11	56	14
17	11	56	11
25	11	56	44

Day of Year.	Day of Month.	Day of Week.	Sun's decl. N.	Boston; New England, N. York State, Michigan, Wiscons, Iowa and Oregon. Sun ris's.	Sun sets.	Moon sets.	H. W. B'stn.	N. York City; Philadph., Conn. New-Jersey, Pen'la, Ohio, Indiana & Illinois. Sun ris's.	Sun sets.	Moon sets.	H. W. N. Yk.	Washington. Mar.l'd, Virg'a, Ken'y, Miss'ri and California. Sun ris's.	Sun sets.	Moon sets.	Carleston; North Carolin., Tennessee, Geo., Alabama, Missis'pi. & Louisiana. Sun ris's.	Sun sets.	Moon sets.	H. W. Ch't'n
			° ′ ″	H. M.	H. M.	H. M.	H. M.	H. M.	H. M.	H. M.	H. M.	H. M.	H. M.	H. M.	H. M.	H. M.	H. M.	H. M.
122	1	Fr	15 18 40	4 56	7 0	2 15	6 51	4 59	6 56	2 13	3 37	5 2	6 52	2 10	5 13	6 42	2 3	2 51
123	2	Sa	15 36 29	4 54	7 1	2 52	7 54	4 58	6 57	2 50	4 30	5 1	6 53	2 49	5 12	6 43	2 41	3 54
124	3	**18**	15 54 3	4 53	7 2	3 26	8 52	4 56	6 58	3 26	5 37	5 0	6 54	3 25	5 11	6 44	3 24	4 52
125	4	M	16 11 22	4 52	7 3	4 0	9 44	4 55	6 59	4 0	6 30	4 59	6 55	4 0	5 10	6 45	4 2	5 44
126	5	Tu	16 28 24	4 51	7 4	4 32	10 32	4 54	7 0	4 33	7 17	4 58	6 56	4 35	5 9	6 45	4 40	6 32
127	6	W	16 45 9	4 49	7 5	rises.	11 17	4 53	7 1	rises.	8 0	4 57	6 57	rises.	5 8	6 46	rises	7 17
128	7	Th	17 1 38	4 48	7 6	8 0	11 57	4 52	7 2	7 57	8 42	4 55	6 58	7 53	5 7	6 47	7 43	7 57
129	8	Fr	17 17 50	4 47	7 7	8 59	ev.40	4 51	7 3	8 55	9 26	4 54	6 59	8 51	5 7	6 47	8 38	8 40
130	9	Sa	17 33 45	4 46	7 8	9 54	1 24	4 49	7 4	9 50	10 10	4 53	7 0	9 45	5 6	6 48	9 32	9 24
131	10	**19**	17 49 22	4 44	7 9	10 44	2 7	4 48	7 5	10 39	10 50	4 52	7 1	10 35	5 5	6 49	10 21	10 7
132	11	M	18 4 41	4 43	7 10	11 28	2 51	4 47	7 6	11 24	11 35	4 51	7 2	11 19	5 4	6 49	11 7	10 51
133	12	Tu	18 19 42	4 42	7 11	morn	3 37	4 46	7 7	morn.	ev.23	4 50	7 2	morn.	5 3	6 50	11 50	11 37
134	13	W	18 34 25	4 41	7 12	0 9	4 26	4 45	7 8	0 5	1 13	4 49	7 3	0 2	5 2	6 51	morn.	ev.26
135	14	Th	18 48 49	4 40	7 13	0 44	5 16	4 44	7 9	0 41	2 2	4 49	7 4	0 38	5 2	6 51	0 28	1 16
136	15	Fr	19 2 54	4 39	7 14	1 16	6 10	4 43	7 10	1 14	2 40	4 48	7 5	1 11	5 1	6 52	1 4	2 10
137	16	Sa	19 16 40	4 38	7 15	1 47	7 4	4 42	7 11	1 46	3 49	4 47	7 6	1 44	5 0	6 53	1 38	3 4
138	17	**20**	19 30 7	4 37	7 16	2 16	7 56	4 41	7 12	2 16	4 41	4 46	7 7	2 15	5 0	6 54	2 12	3 56
139	18	M	19 43 13	4 36	7 17	2 46	8 48	4 40	7 13	2 46	5 33	4 45	7 8	2 46	4 59	6 54	2 47	4 48
140	19	Tu	19 56 0	4 35	7 18	3 17	9 37	4 39	7 14	3 18	6 23	4 44	7 9	3 19	4 58	6 55	3 22	5 37
141	20	W	20 8 26	4 34	7 19	3 52	10 26	4 39	7 15	3 54	7 11	4 43	7 10	3 56	4 58	6 55	4 2	6 26
142	21	Th	20 20 32	4 33	7 20	4 29	11 13	4 38	7 16	4 32	7 55	4 43	7 10	4 35	4 57	6 56	4 43	7 13
143	22	Fr	20 32 17	4 32	7 21	sets.	11 58	4 37	7 17	sets.	8 43	3 42	7 11	sets.	4 57	6 57	sets.	7 58
144	23	Sa	20 43 41	4 31	7 22	8 50	morn.	4 36	7 18	8 46	9 34	4 41	7 12	8 41	4 56	6 57	8 28	8 48
145	24	**21**	20 54 43	4 31	7 23	9 50	0 48	4 36	7 19	9 46	10 25	4 41	7 13	9 42	4 56	6 58	9 28	9 39
146	25	M	21 5 24	4 30	7 24	10 45	1 39	4 35	7 20	10 41	11 15	4 40	7 14	10 37	4 55	6 59	10 25	10 33
147	26	Tu	21 15 43	4 29	7 25	11 33	2 33	4 34	7 20	11 30	morn.	4 39	7 14	11 26	4 55	7 0	11 16	11 27
148	27	W	21 25 40	4 29	7 26	morn.	3 27	4 34	7 21	morn.	0 13	4 39	7 15	morn	4 54	7 0	morn.	morn.
149	28	Th	21 35 15	4 28	7 27	0 17	4 26	4 33	7 22	0 15	1 13	4 38	7 16	0 12	4 54	7 1	0 3	0 26
150	29	Fr	21 44 27	4 27	7 28	0 55	5 27	4 32	7 23	0 53	2 12	4 38	7 17	0 51	4 54	7 1	0 46	1 27
151	30	Sa	21 53 17	4 27	7 28	1 30	6 28	4 32	7 23	1 30	3 14	4 37	7 17	1 29	4 53	7 2	1 26	2 28
152	31	**22**	22 1 44	4 26	7 29	2 2	7 30	4 31	7 24	2 2	4 14	4 37	7 18	2 2	4 53	7 2	2 3	3 30

Exposition Universelle, Paris, 1867.

Wheeler & Wilson, 625 Broadway, N. Y.

Awarded over Eighty-two Competitors, the Highest Premium,

A GOLD MEDAL,

FOR THE PERFECTION OF

SEWING MACHINES AND BUTTON-HOLE MACHINES,

The only GOLD MEDAL for this Branch of Manufacture.

Paris Exposition.—Sewing Machine Awards.

There was recently published a brief telegram from Paris, announcing the award, over eighty-two competitors, to Messrs. Wheeler & Wilson, of the Highest Premium, a Gold Medal for the perfection of Sewing Machines and Button-Hole Machines. The following are copies of the official documents confirming the announcement:

Exposition Universelle, Paris, 1867.
Commission Imperiale, Champ-de-mars, July 16, 1867.

Mr. R. Hunting, No. 139 Regent Street, London;

Dear Sir —Replying to your inquiry, I beg to state that the only Gold Medal for the manufacture and Perfection of Sewing Machines and Button-Hole Machines was awarded to Messrs. Wheeler & Wilson, of New-York.

Yours respectfully,

HENRY F. Q. D'ALIGNY,
Member of International Jury and Reporter of same.

Another letter of the same date says:

Dear sir,—Replying to your inquiry, I herewith give you the list of Gold-Medals awarded to my class: Dupuis et Dumery, for Screw Shoe Machines; Wheeler & Wilson, New York, for the manufacture and perfection of their Sewing Machines and Button-Hole Machines. There is, also, in the list of "Co-operators," a Gold-Medal granted to Mr. Elias Howe, Jr., personally, as Promoter of the Sewing Machine.

Respectfully yours,

HENRY F. Q. D'ADIGNY.
Reporter of Class No. 57, (Group No. 6.) Member of International Jury at the Exposition Universelle.

Extract from Le Moniteur Universel, official journal of the French Empire:

"The Wheeler & Wilson Company, of New York, manufacturers of American Sewing Machines have just received the Gold Medal at the Exposition Universelle, for the good construction of their Machines; the new improvement for making Button Holes, applicable to their Sewing Machines; also, for their Machine especially for making Button Holes. This award is accorded for the great development that Messrs. Wheeler & Wilson have given to the Sewing Machine industry, in bringing their Machine to the doors of all, by their cheapness and solid construction, which allows their employment with satisfaction in families, and with great advantage in workrooms."

6th MONTH. **JUNE, 1868.** 30 DAYS.

MOON'S PHASES	D.	BOSTON. H	M	NEW YORK H.	M.	WASH'TON. H.	M	CHARLES'N H.	M.	Sun on Merid. or noon mark. D.	H.	M.	S.
Full Moon........	5	2	11 mo.	1	59 mo.	1	47 mo	1	35 mo.	1	11	57	38
Third Quarter.....	13	5	29 mo.	5	17 mo.	5	5 mo.	4	53 mo	9	11	59	2
New Moon	20	10	1 mo.	9	49 mo.	9	37 mo.	9	25 mo.	17	12	0	42
First Quarter......	27	1	6 mo.	0	54 mo	0	42 mo.	0	20 mo	25	12	2	26

Day of Year.	Day of Month.	Day of Week	Sun's decl. N.	CALENDAR FOR Boston; New England, N. York State, Michigan, Wisconsin, Iowa and Oregon. Sun ris's	Sun sets	Moon sets.	H. W. B'stn.	CALENDAR FOR N. York City; Philadph., Conn.; New-Jersey, Pen'la, Ohio, Indiana & Illinois. Sun ris's.	Sun sets	Moon sets.	H. W. N.Yk.	Calendar for Washington; Mary'd, V'g'a, Ken'y, Miss'ri, & California. Sun ris's.	Sun sets	Moon sets	CALENDAR FOR Charles'n: North Carolin., Tennessee, Geo., Alabama, Miss'pi, & Louisiana. Sun ris's.	Sun sets.	Moon sets.	H. W Ch't'n
			° ′ ″	H.M.	H M.	H M.	H. M.	H.M.	H.M.	H M	H. M.	H M.	H.M.	H. M	H.M.	H M.	H M.	H M
153	1	M	22 9 48	4 25	7 30	2 34	8 26	4 31	7 24	2 36	5 11	4 36	7 19	2 37	4 52	7 3	2 40	4 26
154	2	Tu	22 17 28	4 25	7 30	3 7	9 17	4 30	7 25	3 9	6 3	4 36	7 19	3 11	4 52	7 3	3 18	5 17
155	3	W	22 24 46	4 25	7 31	3 42	10 6	4 30	7 26	3 45	6 52	4 3[illegible]	7 20	3 47	4 52	7 4	3 56	6 6
156	4	Th	22 31 39	4 24	7 32	rises	10 54	4 30	7 26	rises	7 38	4 35	7 21	rises.	4 52	7 4	rises.	6 54
157	5	Fr	22 38 9	4 24	7 32	7 46	11 35	4 29	7 27	7 42	8 17	4 3[illegible]	7 21	7 38	4 52	7 5	7 25	7 35
158	6	Sa	22 44 16	4 24	7 33	8 37	ev.17	4 29	7 28	8 33	9 3	4 35	7 22	8 2[illegible]	4 51	7 5	8 15	8 17
159	7	23	22 49 58	4 23	7 33	9 24	1 0	4 29	7 28	9 19	9 46	4 34	7 23	9 1[illegible]	4 51	7 6	9 3	9 0
160	8	M	22 55 16	4 23	7 34	10 7	1 41	4 29	7 29	10 3	10 27	4 34	7 23	9 5[illegible]	4 51	7 6	9 46	9 41
161	9	Tu	23 0 11	4 23	7 35	10 44	2 23	4 28	7 30	10 41	11 6	4 34	7 24	10 37	4 51	7 7	10 27	10 23
162	10	W	23 4 41	4 23	7 36	11 18	3 5	4 28	7 30	11 15	11 50	4 34	7 24	11 1[illegible]	4 51	7 7	11 4	11 5
163	11	Th	23 8 47	4 22	7 36	11 50	3 49	4 28	7 31	11 48	ev.35	4 34	7 2[illegible]	11 4[illegible]	4 51	7 8	11 39	11 49
164	12	Fr	23 12 28	4 22	7 37	morn.	4 36	4 28	7 31	morn	1 23	4 34	7 25	morn	4 51	7 8	morn.	ev.36
165	13	Sa	23 15 45	4 22	7 37	0 18	5 25	4 28	7 32	0 17	2 12	4 34	7 2[illegible]	0 16	4 51	7 8	0 12	1 25
166	14	24	23 18 37	4 22	7 38	0 46	6 19	4 28	7 32	0 46	3 4	4 34	7 2[illegible]	0 4[illegible]	4 51	7 9	0 45	2 19
167	15	M	23 21 4	4 22	7 38	1 16	7 14	4 28	7 32	1 17	3 58	4 34	7 2[illegible]	1 17	4 51	7 9	1 19	3 14
168	16	Tu	23 23 7	4 22	7 38	1 47	8 9	4 28	7 33	1 48	4 55	4 34	7 2[illegible]	1 50	4 51	7 9	1 55	4 9
169	17	W	23 24 46	4 22	7 39	2 23	9 5	4 28	7 33	2 25	5 50	4 34	7 2[illegible]	2 28	4 51	7 10	2 35	5 5
170	18	Th	23 25 59	4 22	7 39	3 3	9 58	4 28	7 33	3 6	6 44	4 34	7 2	3 9	4 51	7 10	3 19	5 58
171	19	Fr	23 26 48	4 22	7 39	3 49	10 55	4 28	7 34	3 53	7 39	4 34	7 2[illegible]	[illegible] 57	4 52	7 10	4 9	6 55
172	20	Sa	23 27 12	4 23	7 40	sets	11 46	4 29	7 34	sets.	8 28	4 34	7 2[illegible]	sets.	4 52	7 11	sets	7 46
173	21	25	23 27 11	4 23	7 40	8 35	morn.	4 29	7 34	8 31	9 21	4 34	7 2[illegible]	8 26	4 5[illegible]	7 11	8 13	8 36
174	22	M	23 26 45	4 23	7 40	9 28	0 3[illegible]	4 29	7 34	9 24	10 14	4 35	7 2[illegible]	9 20	4 52	7 11	9 8	9 21
175	23	Tu	23 25 54	4 23	7 40	10 16	1 29	4 29	7 34	10 13	11 4	4 35	7 2	10 16	4 52	7 11	10 0	10 21
176	24	W	23 24 39	4 23	7 40	10 57	2 21	4 29	7 35	10 54	11 58	4 35	7 29	10 52	4 5[illegible]	7 11	10 46	11 13
177	25	Th	23 22 59	4 24	7 41	11 32	3 13	4 30	7 35	11 31	morn	4 35	7 29	11 30	4 5[illegible]	7 11	11 26	morn
178	26	Fr	23 20 54	4 24	7 41	morn	4 5	4 30	7 35	morn.	0 52	4 36	7 29	morn.	4 5[illegible]	7 12	morn.	0 5
179	27	Sa	23 18 25	4 24	7 41	0 6	5 1	4 30	7 35	0 6	1 48	4 36	7 29	0 6	4 54	7 12	0 5	1 1
180	28	26	23 15 31	4 25	7 40	0 39	5 59	4 29	7 35	0 39	2 46	4 37	7 29	0 40	4 54	7 12	0 43	1 59
181	29	M	23 12 13	4 25	7 40	1 10	6 59	4 29	7 35	1 12	3 44	4 37	7 29	1 14	4 54	7 12	1 19	2 59
182	30	Tu	23 8 30	4 26	7 40	1 45	7 56	4 29	7 35	1 47	4 41	4 37	7 29	1 50	4 55	7 12	1 58	3 56

WATERS'

1st Premium Piano-Fortes,

GRAND SQUARE AND UPRIGHT.

Melodeons, Parlor, Church & Cabinet Organs,

THE BEST MANUFACTURED; WARRANTED FOR SIX YEARS.

SECOND-HAND PIANOS, MELODEONS AND ORGANS,

At Great Bargains. Prices from $50 to $200.

Any of the above instruments to let, and rent applied if purchased; monthly instalments received for the same. Old Pianos taken in exchange, or bought for cash.

ILLUSTRATED CATALOGUES SENT TO ANY ADDRESS.

TESTIMONIALS.

The Horace Waters Pianos are known as among the very best.—*N. Y. Evangelist.*

We can speak of the merits of the Horace Waters Pianos from personal knowledge as being of the very best quality.—*Christian Intelligencer.*

The Horace Waters Pianos are built of the best and most thoroughly seasoned material—*Advocate and Journal.*

Waters' Pianos and Melodeons challenge comparison with the finest made anywhere in the country.—*Home Journal.*

Our friends will find at Mr. Waters' store the very best assortment of Music and Pianos to be found in the United States.—*Grahams Magazine.*

Manufactory and Warerooms,

No. 481 Broadway, New York,

HORACE WATERS & CO.

7th MONTH. # JULY, 1868. **31 DAYS.**

MOON'S PHASES.	D	BOSTON. H. M.	NEW YORK. H. M.	WASH'TON. H. M.	CHARLES'N. H. M.
Full Moon	4	3 55 ev.	3 43 ev.	3 31 ev.	3 19 ev.
Third Quarter.....	12	7 56 ev.	7 44 ev.	7 32 ev.	7 31 ev.
New Moon	19	5 12 ev.	5 0 ev.	4 48 ev.	4 36 ev.
First Quarter	26	9 7 mo.	6 55 mo	8 43 mo.	8 31 mo.

Sun on Merid. or noon mark. D.	H.	M.	S.
1	12	3	38
9	12	4	5[illegible]
17	12	5	53
25	12	6	14

				CALENDAR FOR Boston; New England, N. York State, Michigan, Wiscons. Iowa and Oregon.				CALENDAR FOR N. York City; Philadph., Conn. New-Jersey, Pen'la, Ohio, Indiana & Illinois.				CALENDAR FOR Washington. Maryl'd Virg'a, Ken'y, Miss'ri and California.			CALENDAR FOR Carleston; North Carolin., Tennessee, Geo., Alabama, Missis'pi, & Louisiana.			
Day of Year.	Day of Month.	Day of Week.	Sun's decl. N.	Sun ris's.	Sun sets.	Moon sets.	H. W. B'stn.	Sun ris's.	Sun sets.	Moon sets	H. W. N.Yk	Sun ris's.	Sun sets	Moon sets	Sun ris's.	Sun sets	Moon sets	H. W. Ch't'n
			° ' "	H. M	H. M	H M.	H. M	H. M.	H M	H. M.	H. M.	H. M.	H. M.	H M	H. M.	H M.	H M	H. M
183	1	W	23 4 33	4 26	7 40	2 21	8 51	4 32	7 35	2 24	5 36	4 38	7 29	2 27	4 55	7 12	2 38	4 51
184	2	Th	22 59 52	4 26	7 40	3 0	9 42	4 32	7 35	3 3	6 28	4 38	7 29	3 8	4 55	7 12	3 20	5 42
185	3	Fr	22 54 57	4 27	7 40	rises.	10 29	4 33	7 34	rises.	7 14	4 39	7 29	rises.	4 56	7 12	rises.	6 29
186	4	Sa	22 49 38	4 28	7 40	7 21	11 14	4 33	7 34	7 17	7 56	4 39	7 28	7 13	4 56	7 11	6 59	7 14
187	5	**27**	22 43 55	4 29	7 39	8 5	11 55	4 34	7 34	8 1	8 39	4 40	7 28	7 56	4 57	7 11	7 44	7 55
188	6	M	22 37 48	4 29	7 39	8 44	ev.36	4 35	7 34	8 40	9 22	4 41	7 28	8 36	4 57	7 11	8 25	8 36
189	7	Tu	22 31 18	4 30	7 39	9 19	1 14	4 35	7 33	9 16	10 0	4 41	7 28	9 13	4 58	7 11	9 3	9 14
190	8	W	22 24 21	4 30	7 38	9 51	1 54	4 36	7 33	9 49	10 36	4 42	7 27	9 16	4 58	7 11	9 39	9 54
191	9	Th	22 17 7	4 31	7 38	10 20	2 33	4 37	7 33	10 19	11 15	4 42	7 27	10 17	4 59	7 11	10 13	10 33
192	10	Fr	22 9 27	4 32	7 38	10 49	3 14	4 37	7 32	10 48	11 59	4 43	7 27	10 47	4 59	7 10	10 45	11 14
193	11	Sa	22 1 25	4 33	7 37	11 17	3 56	4 38	7 32	11 17	ev.42	4 44	7 26	11 17	5 0	7 10	11 18	11 56
194	12	**28**	21 52 59	4 33	7 37	11 47	4 43	4 39	7 31	11 48	1 29	4 44	7 26	11 49	5 0	7 10	11 52	ev.43
195	13	M	21 44 11	4 34	7 36	morn.	5 34	4 39	7 31	morn.	2 20	4 45	7 26	morn.	5 1	7 9	morn.	1 34
196	14	Tu	21 35 1	4 35	7 36	0 20	6 31	4 40	7 30	0 22	3 19	4 46	7 25	0 24	5 2	7 9	0 30	2 31
197	15	W	21 25 28	4 36	7 35	0 55	7 34	4 41	7 30	0 58	4 19	4 46	7 24	1 1	5 2	7 9	1 9	3 34
198	16	Th	21 15 34	4 37	7 34	1 37	8 38	4 42	7 29	1 41	5 22	4 47	7 24	1 44	5 3	7 8	1 55	4 38
199	17	Fr	21 5 18	4 37	7 34	2 26	9 38	4 43	7 29	2 30	6 24	4 48	7 23	2 35	5 3	7 8	2 47	5 38
200	18	Sa	20 54 41	4 38	7 33	3 21	10 36	4 44	7 28	3 25	7 21	4 49	7 23	3 29	5 4	7 7	3 43	6 36
201	19	**29**	20 43 42	4 39	7 32	sets.	11 30	4 44	7 27	sets.	8 13	4 50	7 22	sets.	5 5	7 7	sets.	7 30
202	20	M	20 32 23	4 40	7 31	8 5	morn	4 45	7 26	8 2	9 8	4 51	7 21	7 58	5 5	7 6	7 48	8 21
203	21	Tu	20 20 43	4 41	7 30	8 51	0 21	4 46	7 26	8 48	10 0	4 52	7 21	8 45	5 6	7 6	8 37	9 13
204	22	W	20 8 42	4 42	7 30	9 31	1 13	4 47	7 25	9 30	10 47	4 52	7 20	9 28	5 6	7 5	9 23	10 5
205	23	Th	19 56 21	4 43	7 29	10 6	2 5	4 48	7 24	10 5	11 35	4 53	7 19	10 5	5 7	7 5	10 3	10 51
206	24	Fr	19 43 40	4 44	7 28	10 41	2 51	4 48	7 23	10 41	morn.	4 54	7 18	10 42	5 8	7 4	10 43	11 41
207	25	Sa	19 30 40	4 45	7 27	11 12	3 41	4 49	7 23	11 16	0 27	4 55	7 18	11 17	5 8	7 4	11 20	morn.
208	26	**30**	19 17 20	4 46	7 26	11 47	4 33	4 50	7 22	11 49	1 20	4 56	7 17	11 51	5 9	7 3	11 59	0 33
209	27	M	19 3 41	4 47	7 25	morn.	5 29	4 51	7 21	morn.	2 15	4 57	7 16	morn.	5 10	7 2	morn.	1 29
210	28	Tu	18 49 43	4 48	7 24	0 22	6 27	4 52	7 20	0 25	3 13	4 58	7 15	0 28	5 10	7 1	0 38	2 27
211	29	W	18 35 27	4 49	7 23	1 0	7 25	4 53	7 19	1 4	4 10	4 58	7 14	1 7	5 11	7 1	1 19	3 25
212	30	Th	18 20 52	4 50	7 22	1 41	8 24	4 54	7 18	1 45	5 9	4 59	7 13	1 49	5 12	7 0	2 2	4 24
213	31	Fr	18 6 0	4 51	7 21	2 27	9 16	4 55	7 17	2 31	6 2	4 59	7 12	2 35	5 12	6 59	2 49	5 16

EMPIRE
SEWING MACHINE CO.

PRINCIPAL OFFICE,
616 Broadway, New York.

AGENCIES in ALL the PRINCIPAL TOWNS of the Union.

The EMPIRE SHUTTLE MACHINE, patented February 14, 1860, is constructed on a new principle of mechanism, possessing many rare and valuable improvements, and having been examined by the most profound experts, has been pronounced to be

SIMPLICITY AND PERFECTION COMBINED.

The EMPIRE SEWING MACHINE has a *Straight Needle, Perpendicular Action,* makes the *Lock or Shuttle Stitch,* which will neither *rip* or *ravel,* and is alike on both sides; performs perfect sewing on every description of material, from leather to the finest Nansook muslin, with cotton, linen or silk thread, from the coarsest to the finest number. ☞ It Hems, Fells, Binds, Braids, Tucks, Quilts, Plaits and Gathers.

Having neither *cam* or *cog wheel,* and the least possible friction, it runs as smooth as glass, and is

EMPHATICALLY A NOISELESS MACHINE.

We make three sizes of all degrees of finish. The No. 1, or Family Machine, can be had with either Iron or Walnut Table, half cabinet, folding top, or full cabinet enclosed, and is alike a handsome, useful piece of furniture.

The No. 2, for small manufacturing purposes, are all fitted up alike with large extension table of walnut and drawer. This Machine for tailoring work, heavy cloth, light leather, or family sewing, has no superior.

Our No. 8, New Leather and Coach Trimming Machine, is the same as our No. 3, Cloth Manufacturing Machine, which can be adapted to the Heaviest or Finest Leather Work, by removing the flat foot and substituting the roller foot in its place. This is especially desirable in *Sewing Patent Leather,* and is highly recommended to

SHOEMAKERS, LEATHER FITTERS, HARNESS MAKERS, &c.

AGENTS WANTED. APPLY FOR TERMS TO THE COMPANY.

PRINCIPAL OFFICE,

616 *BROADWAY, NEW YORK.*

8th MONTH. **AUGUST, 1868.** 31 DAYS.

MOON'S PHASES.	D	BOSTON. H. M.	NEW YORK. H. M.	WASH'TON. H. M.	CHARLES'N. H. M.	Sun on Merid. or noon Mark. D.	H.	M.	S.
Full Moon	3	7 6 mo.	6 52 mo.	6 44 mo.	6 32 mo.	1	12	6	1
Third Quarter	11	7 44 mo.	7 32 mo.	7 20 mo.	7 8 mo.	9	12	5	10
New Moon	18	0 27 mo.	0 15 mo.	0 3 mo.	11 51 ev.	17	12	3	43
First Quarter	24	8 3 ev.	7 51 ev.	7 39 ev.	7 27 ev.	25	12	1	45

Day of Year.	Day of Month.	Day of Week.	Sun's decl. S.	CALENDAR FOR Boston, New England, N York State, Michigan, Wiscon., Iowa & Oregon. Sun r's's	Sun sets.	Moon sets.	H. W. B'st'n	CALENDAR FOR N York City, Philadelphia, Conn. N. Jers'y Penn'ia, Ohio, Indiana & Illinois. Sun ris's.	Sun sets.	Moon sets.	H. W. N.Y'k.	CALENDAR FOR Washington; Mary'd Virg'a, Ken'y, Miss'o'ri and California. Sun r's's	Sun sets.	Moon sets.	CALENDAR FOR Charles'n, North Caroln., Tennessee Geo., Alabama, Mis-s'ippi & Louisiana. Sun r's's	Sun sets	Moon sets.	H. W. Ch't'n.
			° ′ ″	H. M	H. M.	H. M.	H. M.	H. M	H. M.	H. M.	H. M.	H. M.	H. M.	H. M.	H. M	H. M	H. M.	H. M.
214	1	Sa	17 50 49	4 52	7 20	3 17	10 5	4 56	7 16	3 21	6 51	5 0	7 11	3 26	5 13	6 58	3 39	6 25
215	2	**31**	17 35 22	4 53	7 18	rises.	10 52	4 57	7 14	rises.	7 36	5 1	7 10	rises.	5 14	6 58	rises.	6 52
216	3	M	17 19 37	4 54	7 17	7 20	11 30	4 58	7 13	7 17	8 12	5 2	7 9	7 14	5 15	6 57	7 3	7 30
217	4	Tu	17 3 35	4 55	7 16	7 54	ev.10	4 59	7 12	7 51	8 54	5 3	7 8	7 48	5 15	6 56	7 40	8 10
218	5	W	16 47 16	4 56	7 15	8 23	0 47	5 6	7 11	8 21	9 33	5 4	7 7	8 20	5 16	6 55	8 14	8 47
219	6	Th	16 30 42	4 57	7 14	8 53	1 25	5 1	7 10	8 52	10 11	5 5	7 6	8 51	5 17	6 54	8 48	9 25
220	7	Fr	16 13 51	4 58	7 12	9 21	2 3	5 2	7 9	9 21	10 45	5 6	7 5	9 21	5 17	6 53	9 20	10 3
221	8	Sa	15 56 44	4 59	7 11	9 50	2 41	5 3	7 7	9 51	11 23	5 6	7 4	9 51	5 18	6 52	9 54	10 41
222	9	**32**	15 39 22	5 0	7 10	10 19	3 22	5 4	7 6	10 20	ev. 7	5 7	7 2	10 22	5 19	6 51	10 27	11 22
223	10	M	15 21 45	5 1	7 8	10 54	4 6	5 5	7 5	10 56	0 53	5 8	7 1	10 58	5 19	6 50	11 6	ev. 6
224	11	Tu	15 3 54	5 2	7 7	11 30	4 59	5 6	7 4	11 33	1 46	5 9	7 0	11 37	5 20	6 49	11 47	0 59
225	12	W	14 45 47	5 3	7 6	morn.	5 59	5 7	7 2	morn.	2 46	5 10	6 59	morn.	5 21	6 48	morn.	1 59
226	13	Th	14 27 27	5 4	7 4	0 14	7 5	5 8	7 1	0 18	3 50	5 11	6 58	0 22	5 21	6 47	0 34	3 5
227	14	Fr	14 8 52	5 5	7 3	1 5	8 14	5 9	7 0	1 9	4 58	5 12	6 56	1 14	5 22	6 46	1 27	4 11
228	15	Sa	13 50 4	5 6	7 1	2 4	9 19	5 10	6 58	2 8	6 5	5 13	6 54	2 12	5 23	6 45	2 26	5 19
229	16	**33**	13 31 3	5 7	7 0	3 10	10 21	5 11	6 57	3 14	7 7	5 14	6 53	3 19	5 23	6 44	3 31	6 21
230	17	M	13 11 49	5 8	6 58	sets.	11 17	5 12	6 55	sets.	7 59	5 15	6 52	sets	5 24	6 43	sets.	7 17
231	18	Tu	12 52 22	5 10	6 57	7 22	morn.	5 13	6 54	7 20	8 51	5 16	6 51	7 18	5 25	6 42	7 11	8 6
232	19	W	12 32 43	5 11	6 55	8 0	0 6	5 14	6 53	7 59	9 39	5 17	6 50	7 58	5 25	6 41	7 55	8 53
233	20	Th	12 12 52	5 12	6 54	8 36	0 53	5 15	6 51	8 36	10 25	5 17	6 48	8 36	5 26	6 40	8 36	9 40
234	21	Fr	11 52 50	5 13	6 52	9 11	1 40	5 16	6 50	9 12	11 10	5 18	6 47	9 14	5 27	6 33	9 16	10 27
235	22	Sa	11 32 36	5 14	6 51	9 47	2 27	5 17	6 48	9 49	11 59	5 19	6 45	9 51	5 28	6 37	9 57	11 14
236	23	**34**	11 12 11	5 15	6 49	10 21	3 14	5 17	6 47	10 24	morn.	5 20	6 44	10 27	5 28	6 36	10 35	morn.
237	24	M	10 51 36	5 16	6 48	11 0	4 3	5 18	6 45	11 3	0 50	5 21	6 43	11 7	5 29	6 35	11 17	0 3
238	25	Tu	10 30 50	5 17	6 46	11 40	4 57	5 19	6 44	11 44	1 44	5 22	6 41	11 48	5 30	6 34	12 0	0 51
239	26	W	10 9 55	5 18	6 44	morn.	5 56	5 20	6 42	morn.	2 42	5 23	6 40	morn.	5 30	6 32	morn.	1 56
240	27	Th	9 48 50	5 19	6 43	0 25	6 57	5 21	6 41	0 29	3 42	5 24	6 38	0 34	5 31	6 31	0 47	2 57
241	28	Fr	9 27 35	5 20	6 41	1 13	7 54	5 22	6 39	1 17	4 39	5 25	6 37	1 21	5 32	6 30	1 35	3 54
242	29	Sa	9 6 12	5 21	6 39	2 4	8 49	5 23	6 37	2 8	5 34	5 26	6 35	2 12	5 32	6 29	2 25	4 49
243	30	**35**	8 44 40	5 22	6 38	2 58	9 38	5 24	6 36	3 1	6 24	5 26	6 34	3 5	5 33	6 28	3 17	5 38
244	31	M	8 22 59	5 23	6 36	3 54	10 23	5 25	6 34	3 57	7 9	5 27	6 32	4 0	5 33	6 27	4 10	6 23

D. APPLETON & CO.,

443 & 445 BROADWAY, NEW YORK.

THE

NEW AMERICAN CYCLOPAEDIA.

A POPULAR DICTIONARY OF USEFUL KNOWLEDGE.

EDITED BY GEORGE RIPLEY AND CHARLES A. DANA,

In Sixteen large volumes, 8vo. 750 double-column pages in each volume.

PRICE AND STYLE OF BINDING:

	PER VOL		PER VOL
EXTRA CLOTH	$5.00	HALF TURKEY MOROCCO, flex.	$7.00
LIBRARY LEATHER	6.00	HALF RUSSIA, extra gilt	7.50
HALF TURKEY MOROCCO, dark	6.50	FULL MOROCCO, antique, gilt edges	9.00

FULL RUSSIA $9.00

The NEW AMERICAN CYCLOPÆDIA surpasses all other works in the fullness and ability of the articles relating to the United States. No other work contains so many reliable biographies of the leading men of this and other nations. The best minds in this country have been employed in enriching its pages with the latest data and the most recent discoveries in every branch of manufacturers, mechanics, and general science. It is a library in itself, where every topic is treated, and where information can be gleaned which will enable a student, if he is so disposed, to consult other authorities, thus affording him an invaluable key to knowledge. It is neatly printed with readable type, on good paper, and contains a most copious index. It is the only work which gives any thing approaching correct descriptions of cities and towns of America, or embraces reliable statistics showing the wonderful growth of all sections.

The *Theological Department* of the NEW AMERICAN CYCLOPÆDIA is specially distinguished for its completeness and accuracy. The articles on the History and Doctrines of the Church have been prepared by theologians of the different denominations with most intimate relations with the topics under treatment. Among the contributors to this department are Rev. H. W. Bellows, D. D., Rev. Theo. H. Beveridge, Rev. Charles H Brigham, Rev. Dr. Edward Bright, D. D., Rev. John Newton Brown, D. D., Orestes A. Brownson, Rev. Geo. W. Burnap, D. D., Rev. J. W. Cummings, D. D., Rev D. Curry, D D., Rev. S. S. Cutting, D. D., Rev. David D. Demarest, D. D., Rev. O. D. Frottingham, Rev. E. W. Gilman, Rev. H Harbaugh, D. D., Rev. F. H. Hedge, D. D., Oliver Johnson, Arcabishop F. P. Keurick, Rev. J Starr King, Rev C. P. Krauth, D. D., Rev. Luther Lee, D. D., Rev. John M. Murdock, Prof. R. Richardson, Prof. Philip Schaff, D. D., Prof. Alexander J. Schem, Rev. E. de Schweinitz, D. D., Rev. Barnas Sears, D D., Prof. Henry B. Smith, D. D., Rev. W. B. Sprague, D. D., Rev. W. P. Strickland, D. D., Rev. W. L. Symonds, Rev. J. B. Thayer, Rev. Joseph P. Thompson D. D., Rev. John Thomson, D. D., Rev. John Weiss, Bishop W. M. Wightman D. D., Rev. W. D. Wilson, D. D.

THE AMERICAN

ANNUAL CYCLOPAEDIA

AND

Register of Important Events for the Year.

This work was commenced in the year 1861, and one volume is published annually, in the same style as the "New American Cyclopaedia." Each volume is intended to be a Cyclopaedia of the material and intellectual development of the year, and embraces the political, civil, military, and social affairs of all countries; important Public Documents; Biography; Statistics; Commerce Finance; Literature; Science; Agriculture; Mechanical Industry, etc. Special articles are given on nearly all the large religious denominations, carefully noticing their memberships, and the most notable events in their current history. No other publication in the English language contains so full information on recent church history as the volumes of the ANNUAL AMERICAN CYCLOPÆDIA.

PRICE AND STYLE OF BINDING:

Extra Cloth	per vol.	$5.00	Half Turk. Moroc. flex...	per vol.	$7.00
Library Leather	"	6.00	Half Russia, extra gilt	"	7.50
Half Turkey Morocco	"	6.50	Full Mrco. Ant. gilt edges	"	9.00

"Full Russia" .... $9.00.

9th MONTH. # SEPTEMBER, 1868. **30 DAYS.**

MOON'S PHASES.	D	BOSTON. H. M.	NEW YORK. H. M.	WASH'TON H. M.	CHARLES'N. H. M.	Sun on Merid. or noon mark. D.	H.	M	S
Full Moon	1	11 14 ev.	11 1 ev.	10 49 ev	10 37 ev.	1	11	59	39
Third Quarter.....	9	5 10 ev.	5 6 ev.	4 56 ev.	4 41 ev.	9	11	57	0
New Moon	17	8 35 mo.	8 23 mo	8 11 mo.	7 59 mo.	17	11	54	12
First Quarter	23	0 38 mo.	10 26 mo	10 14 mo.	10 2 mo.	25	11	51	25

Day of Year.	Day of Month.	Day of Week.	Sun's decl. N.	CALENDAR FOR Boston; New England, N. York State, Michigan, Wiscons. Iowa and Oregon. Sun ris's.	Sun sets.	Moon sets.	H. W. B'stn.	CALENDAR FOR N. York City; Philadph., Conn. New-Jersey, Pen'la, Ohio, Indiana & Illinois. Sun ris's.	Sun sets.	Moon sets.	H. W. N.Yk.	CALENDAR FOR Washington. Mar'l'd, Virg'a Ken'y, Missou'i and California. Sun ris's.	Sun sets.	Moon sets	CALENDAR FOR Carleston; North Carolin., Tennessee, Geo., Alabama, Miss'pi, & Louisiana. Sun ris's.	Sun sets	Moon sets	H W Ch't'n
			° ′ ″	H.M	H M	H. M	H. M.	H.M.	H M	H. M.	H. M.	H.M.	H.M.	H. M	H.M.	H M	H, M	H. M
245	1	Tu	8 1 10	5 24	6 35	rises.	11 4	5 26	6 33	rises.	7 47	5 28	6 31	rises.	5 34	6 25	rises	7 4
246	2	W	7 39 14	5 26	6 33	6 56	11 42	5 27	6 31	6 54	8 24	5 29	6 29	6 53	5 35	6 24	6 49	7 42
247	3	Th	7 17 10	5 27	6 31	7 24	ev. 17	5 28	6 29	7 24	9 3	5 30	6 28	7 23	5 35	6 22	7 22	8 17
248	4	Fr	6 54 59	5 28	6 29	7 52	0 54	5 29	6 28	7 53	9 40	5 31	6 26	7 54	5 36	6 21	7 55	8 54
249	5	Sa	6 32 42	5 29	6 28	8 22	1 32	5 30	6 26	8 23	10 17	5 32	6 25	8 25	5 37	6 20	8 29	9 32
250	6	36	6 10 17	5 30	6 26	8 54	2 11	5 31	6 25	8 57	10 53	5 33	6 23	8 59	5 37	6 19	9 5	10 11
251	7	M	5 47 47	5 31	6 24	9 30	2 53	5 32	6 23	9 33	11 37	5 34	6 22	9 36	5 38	6 17	9 45	10 53
252	8	Tu	5 25 10	5 32	6 22	10 10	3 40	5 33	6 21	10 14	ev. 26	5 35	6 21	10 18	5 39	6 16	10 29	11 40
253	9	W	5 2 29	5 33	6 21	10 65	4 35	5 34	6 20	11 0	1 22	5 35	6 20	11 4	5 39	6 15	11 17	ev. 35
254	10	Th	4 39 42	5 34	6 19	11 50	5 37	5 35	6 18	11 54	2 23	5 36	6 18	11 58	5 40	6 13	morn.	1 37
255	11	Fr	4 16 50	5 35	6 17	morn	6 45	5 36	6 16	morn.	3 31	5 37	6 17	morn.	5 41	6 12	0 12	2 45
256	12	Sa	3 53 53	5 36	6 15	0 51	7 56	5 37	6 15	0 54	4 41	5 38	6 15	0 59	5 41	6 11	1 12	3 36
257	13	37	3 30 52	5 37	6 14	1 59	9 4	5 38	6 13	2 2	5 49	5 39	6 14	2 6	5 42	6 9	2 18	5 4
258	14	M	3 7 47	5 38	6 12	3 8	10 2	5 39	6 11	3 11	6 48	5 40	6 12	3 14	5 43	6 8	3 24	6 2
259	15	Tu	2 44 39	5 39	6 10	4 23	10 57	5 40	6 9	4 25	7 40	5 41	6 10	4 27	5 43	6 7	4 34	6 57
260	16	W	2 21 27	5 40	6 8	sets.	11 45	5 41	6 8	sets.	8 27	5 42	6 9	sets.	5 44	6 5	sets.	7 45
261	17	Th	1 58 12	5 41	6 7	7 6	morn.	5 42	6 6	7 6	9 16	5 43	6 7	7 7	5 45	6 4	7 8	8 29
262	18	Fr	1 34 55	5 43	6 5	7 41	0 29	5 43	6 4	7 42	9 59	5 44	6 6	7 41	5 45	6 2	7 48	9 15
263	19	Sa	1 11 36	5 44	6 3	8 18	1 15	5 44	6 3	8 20	10 43	5 44	6 4	8 22	5 46	6 1	8 30	10 1
264	20	38	0 48 15	5 45	6 1	8 54	2 1	5 45	6 1	8 57	11 29	5 45	6 2	9 1	5 46	6 0	9 11	10 46
265	21	M	0 24 53	5 46	6 0	9 35	2 46	5 46	5 59	9 39	morn.	5 46	6 1	9 43	5 47	5 58	9 55	11 34
266	22	Tu	N. 1 29	5 47	5 58	10 21	3 34	5 47	5 58	10 25	0 20	5 47	5 59	10 29	5 48	5 57	10 42	morn.
267	23	W	S. 21 55	5 48	5 56	11 7	4 27	5 48	5 56	11 11	1 14	5 48	5 58	11 15	5 48	5 56	11 29	0 27
268	24	Th	0 45 29	5 49	5 54	11 57	5 23	5 49	5 54	morn.	2 8	5 49	5 56	morn.	5 49	5 54	morn.	1 23
269	25	Fr	1 8 44	5 50	5 53	morn	6 22	5 50	5 53	0 1	3 8	5 50	5 54	0 6	5 50	5 53	0 19	2 22
270	26	Sa	1 32 9	5 51	5 51	0 51	7 20	5 51	5 52	0 55	4 5	5 51	5 53	1 0	5 50	5 52	1 12	3 20
271	27	39	1 55 32	5 52	5 49	1 45	8 14	5 52	5 50	1 48	4 58	5 52	5 51	1 52	5 51	5 50	2 2	4 14
272	28	M	2 18 55	5 53	5 47	2 43	9 5	5 53	5 48	2 46	5 50	5 53	5 50	2 40	5 52	5 49	2 57	5 5
273	29	Tu	2 42 17	5 54	5 46	3 40	9 50	5 54	5 46	3 42	6 3[illegible]	5 54	5 48	3 44	5 52	5 48	3 50	5 50
274	30	W	3 5 36	5 56	5 44	4 37	10 31	5 54	5 44	4 38	7 16	5 55	5 46	4 39	5 53	5 46	4 43	6 31

"Unquestionably the best sustained work of the kind in the world."

HARPER'S MAGAZINE.

The most popular Monthly in the world.—*New York Observer.*

It meets precisely the popular taste, furnishing a pleasing and instructing variety of reading for all.—*Zion's Herald, Boston.*

"A complete Pictorial History of the Times."

HARPER'S WEEKLY.

AN ILLUSTRATED NEWSPAPER.

The model newspaper of our country.—*N. Y. Evening Post.*

The articles upon public questions which appear in HARPER'S WEEKLY form a remarkable series of brief political essays.—*North American Review.*

"An Illustrated Weekly Journal of Fashion, Pleasure, and Instruction."

HARPER'S BAZAR.

Besides the Fashions, it presents also the very best specimens of Household Literature. No subject of domestic interest is excluded from its columns.

TERMS FOR HARPER'S PERIODICALS.

HARPER'S MAGAZINE, One Year	$4 00
HARPER'S WEEKLY, One Year	4 00
HARPER'S BAZAR, One Year	4 00

HARPER'S MAGAZINE, HARPER'S WEEKLY, and HARPER'S BAZAR, to one address, for one year, $10 00

An Extra Copy of either the MAGAZINE, WEEKLY, *or* BAZAR *will be supplied gratis for every Club of* FIVE SUBSCRIBERS *at* $4 00 *each in one remittance; or, Six Copies for* $20 00.

BOOKS FOR

SCHOOLS AND COLLEGES

PUBLISHED BY

HARPER & BROTHERS, N. Y.

A New Descriptive Catalogue of HARPER & BROTHERS' PUBLICATIONS, and a List for Schools and Colleges, are now ready for distribution, and may be obtained gratuitously on application to the Publishers personally, or by letter, enclosing Five Cents.

The attention of Professors and Teachers, in town or country, is respectfully invited to these Catalogues of standard and most approved works in Educational Literature, which are offered on most liberal terms for examination and introduction.

To Librarians and others connected with Colleges, Schools, &c. who may not have access to a trustworthy guide in forming the true estimate of literary productions, it is believed these Catalogues will prove especially valuable for reference.

To prevent disappointment, it is suggested that, whenever books can not be obtained through any bookseller or local agent, applications with remittance should be addressed direct to the publishers, which will receive prompt attention.

HARPER & BROTHERS,
FRANKLIN SQUARE, NEW YORK.

10th MONTH. # OCTOBER, 1868. **31 DAYS.**

MOON'S PHASES	D	BOSTON. H. M.	NEW YORK. H. M.	WASH'TON H. M.	CHARLES'N. H. M.	Sun on Merid. D.	H.	M.	S
Full Moon	1	3 14 ev.	3 2 ev.	2 50 ev	2 38 ev.	1	11	49	27
Third Quarter	9	1 30 mo.	1 18 mo.	1 6 mo.	0 54 mo.	9	11	47	7
New Moon	15	6 17 ev.	6 5 ev.	5 53 ev.	5 41 ev.	17	11	45	17
First Quarter	23	4 58 mo.	4 46 mo.	4 84 mo.	3 22 mo.	25	11	44	6
Full Moon.	31	6 21 mo	6 9 mo	5 57 mo.	5 45 mo.				

Day of Year.	Day of Month.	Day of Week.	Sun's decl. S.	CALENDAR FOR Boston; New England, N. York State, Michigan Wiscons, Iowa and Oregon. Sun ris's.	Sun sets.	Moon rises.	H. W. B'stn.	CALENDAR FOR N. York City; Philadph., Conn. New-Jersey, Pen'la, Ohio, Indiana & Illinois. Sun ris's.	Sun set.	Moon ris's	H. W. N. Yk	CALENDAR FOR Washington. Maryl'd Virg'a Ken'y, Miss'ri and California. Sun ris's.	Sun sets.	Moon ris's	CALENDAR FOR Charleston; North Carolin., Tennessee, Geo., Alabama, Missis'pi, & Louisiana. Sun ris's.	Sun sets	Moon ris's	H. W. Ch't'n
			° ' "	H. M	H M	H M.	H. M	H. M.	H M	H. M.	H. M.	H. M.	H M.	H M	H. M.	H M	H M	H. M
275	1	Th	3 28 54	5 57	5 42	rises.	11 11	5 56	5 43	rises.	7 53	5 55	5 43	rises.	5 54	5 45	rises	7 11
276	2	Fr	3 52 10	5 58	5 40	6 25	11 48	5 57	5 41	6 26	8 31	5 56	5 42	6 27	5 54	5 44	6 30	7 48
277	3	Sa	4 15 22	5 59	5 39	6 57	ev. 24	5 58	5 39	6 59	9 11	5 57	5 40	7 1	5 55	5 42	7 7	8 24
278	4	**40**	4 38 32	6 0	5 37	7 30	1 5	5 59	5 38	7 33	9 51	5 58	5 39	7 36	5 56	5 41	7 44	9 5
279	5	M	5 1 38	6 1	5 35	8 9	1 47	6 0	5 36	8 13	10 31	5 59	5 37	8 16	5 57	5 40	8 27	9 47
280	6	Tu	5 24 41	6 2	5 33	8 53	2 32	6 1	5 35	8 57	11 15	6 0	5 35	9 1	5 57	5 39	9 13	10 32
281	7	W	5 47 40	6 3	5 32	9 44	3 22	6 2	5 33	9 48	ev. 7	6 1	5 34	9 52	5 58	5 37	10 6	11 22
282	8	Th	6 10 34	6 4	5 30	10 41	4 19	6 3	5 31	10 45	1 6	6 2	5 32	10 49	5 59	5 36	11 3	ev. 19
283	9	Fr	6 33 23	6 6	5 28	11 43	5 23	6 4	5 30	11 46	2 8	6 3	5 31	11 51	6 0	5 35	morn.	1 23
284	10	Sa	6 56 8	6 7	5 27	morn.	6 30	6 5	5 28	morn.	3 17	6 4	5 29	morn.	6 0	5 33	0 3	2 30
285	11	**41**	7 18 46	6 8	5 25	0 50	7 40	6 7	5 27	0 53	4 25	6 5	5 28	0 57	6 1	5 32	1 7	3 44
286	12	M	7 41 19	6 9	5 23	2 1	8 45	6 8	5 25	2 3	5 30	6 6	5 26	2 6	6 2	5 31	2 14	4 45
287	13	Tu	8 3 46	6 10	5 22	3 12	9 42	6 9	5 23	3 14	6 28	6 7	5 25	3 15	6 2	5 30	3 20	5 42
288	14	W	8 26 6	6 11	5 20	4 23	10 33	6 10	5 22	4 24	7 18	6 8	5 23	4 24	6 3	5 29	4 26	6 33
289	15	Th	8 48 18	6 13	5 19	sets.	11 22	6 11	5 20	sets.	8 3	6 9	5 22	sets.	6 4	5 27	sets.	7 22
290	16	Fr	9 10 24	6 14	5 17	6 10	morn	6 12	5 19	6 11	8 49	6 10	5 21	6 14	6 5	5 26	6 20	8 4
291	17	Sa	9 32 21	6 15	5 15	6 48	0 4	6 13	5 17	6 50	9 34	6 11	5 19	6 53	6 5	5 25	7 2	8 48
292	18	**42**	9 54 11	6 16	5 14	7 26	0 48	6 14	5 16	7 30	10 19	6 12	5 18	7 34	6 6	5 24	7 45	9 34
293	19	M	10 15 51	6 17	5 12	8 10	1 34	6 15	5 14	8 14	11 3	6 13	5 16	8 18	6 7	5 23	8 31	10 21
294	20	Tu	10 37 22	6 18	5 11	8 57	2 21	6 16	5 13	9 1	11 51	6 14	5 15	9 6	6 8	5 22	9 20	11 6
295	21	W	10 58 44	6 20	5 9	9 48	3 6	6 18	5 12	9 54	morn.	6 15	5 14	9 57	6 9	5 21	10 11	11 56
296	22	Th	11 19 56	6 21	5 8	10 41	3 56	6 19	5 10	10 45	0 42	6 16	5 13	10 49	6 9	5 19	11 2	morn.
297	23	Fr	11 40 58	6 22	5 6	11 36	4 49	6 20	5 9	11 40	1 37	6 18	5 11	11 44	6 10	5 18	11 55	0 49
298	24	Sa	12 1 49	6 23	5 5	morn.	5 45	6 21	5 7	morn	2 31	6 19	5 10	morn.	6 11	5 17	morn.	1 45
299	25	**43**	12 22 29	6 24	5 3	0 29	6 40	6 22	5 6	0 32	3 26	6 20	5 9	0 35	6 12	5 16	0 46	2 44
300	26	M	12 42 57	6 26	5 2	1 29	7 34	6 23	5 4	1 32	4 19	6 21	5 8	1 34	6 13	5 15	1 41	3 34
301	27	Tu	13 3 13	6 27	5 1	2 27	8 25	6 24	5 3	2 28	5 10	6 22	5 6	2 30	6 13	5 14	2 35	4 25
302	28	W	13 23 17	6 28	4 59	3 25	9 11	6 26	5 2	3 25	5 57	6 23	5 5	3 26	6 14	5 13	3 28	5 11
303	29	Th	13 43 8	6 29	4 57	4 25	9 56	6 27	5 1	4 25	6 42	6 24	5 4	4 24	6 15	5 12	4 24	5 58
304	30	Fr	14 2 47	6 31	4 57	rises	10 39	6 28	4 59	rises.	7 23	6 25	5 2	rises	6 16	5 11	rises	6 39
305	31	Sa	14 22 11	6 32	4 55	5 30	11 21	6 29	4 58	5 33	8 2	6 26	5 1	5 35	6 17	5 10	5 43	7 21

"It works like a Charm."

Use Renne's Pain Killing Magic Oil.

To my patrons respectfully.

I am introducing this remedy for Pain, all over the Country, as fast as I can. If it is not kept by the Druggist, or merchant, with whom you usually trade, they will send for the different sizes at your request, and sell at the manufacturers lowest price.

Renne's Magic Oil is put up in three different sized bottles, and called "TRIAL SIZE"—"MEDIUM SIZE"—and "LARGE SIZE"—It is not left for sale on Commission, but sold at uniform rates for cash.—Its use cures pain as water quenches fire.—It is safe, clean, and delicious to use, either externally or internally; and Physicians of all schools of practice say, it is the best, and safest remedy they have ever found used by families where they practice.—Try Renne's Magic Oil, reader!—Keep it in your house to use in case of sudden sickness, or accident, for Burns, Bruises, Sprains, Cholic, Fits, Cramps, Neuralgia, Rheumatism, Headache, Stings, Wounds, sore Eyes, &c. In the worst cases, after other remedies fail, we love to see Renne's Magic Oil used thoroughly. "It works like a charm." Orders should be addressed to

Wm. Renne, Proprietor.
Pittsfield, Mass.

Also sold by *all* wholesale Druggists.

LIFE AND FIRE INSURANCE
ROYAL INS. CO.
OF
LIVERPOOL AND LONDON.

Office 56 Wall Street.

Authorized Capital £2,000 000 Sterling, or $10,000,000

Paid up Capital and Surplus $4,535,000.

$1,000 invested in U. S. Stocks, held by the Superintendent of the Insurance Department on account of the Life Branch.
$216,000 do. do. on account of the Fire Branch.
$219,000 invested in U. S. stocks held by the New York Trustees and Committee of Management to meet losses.

$585,000 invested in New York.
Losses adjusted in New York and promptly paid.

IN ADDITION TO ITS FIRE BUSINESS THIS COMPANY IS PREPARED TO TRANSACT

LIFE INSURANCE
IN ALL ITS BRANCHES.

NEW YORK TRUSTEES:
ADAM NORRIE, RICH. IRVIN, ABIEL A. LOW

COMMITTEE OF ARRANGEMENTS.

WM. C. PICKERSGILL, ROYAL PHELPS.
ADAM NORRIE, THOS. RICHARDSON.
BENJ. R. SHERMAN, W. BUTLER DUNCAN
HENRY L. ROUTH, FRANCIS SKIDDY,
HENRY EYRE, HENRY A. SMYTHE,
GEORGE MOKE,
EDMUND HURRY, Surveyor.
A. B. McDONALD, Agent.

GERMANIA
FIRE INSURANCE CO.,
No. 175 Broadway, NEW YORK.

CASH CAPITAL..............................$500,000 00
SURPLUS..............................$312,180 56

Total Assets, July 1, 1867..............................$812,180 56

This company insures Property of all kinds against LOSS OR DAMAGE BY FIRE, on favorable terms.

Hugo Schumann, Secretary. **John E. Kahl,** Vice President. **Rudolph Garrigue,** President.

Principal Agencies; No. 357 Bowery and 518 8th Avenue.
F. MALIGNON.
" No. 32 Union Ave., between Montrose Ave. and Meserole Str., Williamsburgh,
G. KEHR.

Agency in Jersey City: No. 27 Montgomery St.
BUDENBENDER & MOLLER.
" Hudson City: Franklin St., Washington Village,
JOHN PETER VOLLHARDT.
" Union Hill: Cor. of Union St. and Palisade Av.
P. HEERBRANDT & CO.
" Hoboken: 135 & 137 Washington St.
BUDENBENDER & MOLLER.
" Staten Island: Cor. of Bay & Canal St.,
Stapleton, J. A. JANNIN,

Branch office in Newark, N. J.: 153 Market St. FRED. J. D. RUMPF, General Agent.

11th MONTH. **NOVEMBER, 1868.** 30 DAYS.

MOON'S PHASES.	D	BOSTON H. M.	NEW YORK. H. M.	WASH'TON. H. M.	CHARLES'N H. M.	Sun on Merid. or noon Mark D.	H.	M.	S.
Third Quarter	7	9 3 mo.	8 51 mo.	8 39 mo.	8 27 mo.	1	11	43	41
New Moon	14	6 11 mo.	5 59 mo.	5 47 mo.	5 55 mo	9	11	44	1
First Quarter	22	2 2 mo.	1 50 mo.	1 38 mo.	1 26 mo.	17	11	45	16
Full Moon	29	9 16 ev.	8 4 ev.	7 52 ev.	7 40 ev.	25	11	47	23

Day of Year.	Day of Month.	Day of Week.	Sun's decl. S.	CALENDAR FOR Boston, New England, N York State, Michigan, Wiscon., Iowa & Oregon. Sun. r's's	Sun sets.	Moon rises.	H W B'st'n	CALENDAR FOR N York City, Philadelphia, Conn. N. Jers'y Penn'ia, Ohio, Indiana & Illinois. Sun ris's.	Sun sets.	Moon rises.	H. W. N. Yk.	CALENDAR FOR Washington; Mary'd Virg'a, Ken'y, Mis'o'r. and California. Sun r's's	Sun sets.	Moon rises.	CALENDAR FOR Charles'n, North Carolin., Tennessee Geo., Alabama, Miss'ppi & Louisiana. Sun r's's	Sun sets	Moon rises.	H. W. Ch't'n.
			° ' "	H. M	H. M.	H. M.	H. M	H. M	H. M.	H. M	H. M.	H. M.	H. M.	H. M	H. M	H. M	H. M.	H. M.
306	1	44	14 41 22	6 33	4 54	6 8	11 59	6 30	4 57	6 10	8 44	6 27	5 0	6 14	6 18	5 9	6 25	7 59
307	2	M	15 0 18	6 34	4 53	6 50	ev. 43	6 31	4 56	6 54	9 28	6 28	4 59	6 58	6 19	5 9	7 11	8 43
308	3	Tu	15 19 0	6 36	4 51	7 40	1 30	6 32	4 54	7 44	10 17	6 29	4 58	7 48	6 19	5 8	8 2	9 30
309	4	W	15 37 27	6 37	4 50	8 35	2 20	6 34	4 53	8 39	11 2	6 31	4 57	8 44	6 20	5 7	8 58	10 20
310	5	Th	15 55 38	6 38	4 49	9 36	3 11	6 35	4 52	9 40	11 56	6 32	4 56	9 41	6 21	5 6	9 57	11 11
311	6	Fr	16 13 34	6 39	4 48	10 40	4 7	6 36	4 51	10 44	ev. 54	6 33	4 55	10 47	6 22	5 5	10 59	ev. 7
312	7	Sa	16 31 13	6 41	4 47	11 49	5 10	6 37	4 50	11 52	1 56	6 34	4 54	11 55	6 23	5 4	morn.	1 10
313	8	45	16 48 36	6 42	4 45	morn	6 17	6 38	4 49	morn.	3 2	6 35	4 53	morn.	6 24	5 4	0 4	2 17
314	9	M	17 5 41	6 43	4 44	0 57	7 20	6 40	4 48	0 59	4 5	6 36	4 52	1 1	6 25	5 3	1 8	3 20
315	10	Tu	17 22 29	6 44	4 43	2 7	8 21	6 41	4 47	2 7	5 4	6 37	4 51	2 9	6 26	5 2	2 11	4 21
316	11	W	17 38 59	6 46	4 42	3 15	9 16	6 42	4 46	3 15	6 2	6 38	4 50	3 15	6 27	5 2	3 15	5 11
317	12	Th	17 55 11	6 47	4 41	4 25	10 8	6 43	4 45	4 24	6 54	6 39	4 49	4 23	6 27	5 1	4 20	6 8
318	13	Fr	18 11 5	6 48	4 40	5 34	10 56	6 44	4 44	5 32	7 39	6 40	4 48	5 30	6 28	5 0	5 23	6 56
319	14	Sa	18 26 39	6 49	4 39	sets.	11 41	6 46	4 43	sets.	8 23	6 41	4 47	sets	6 29	5 0	sets.	7 41
320	15	46	18 41 54	6 51	4 39	6 0	morn.	6 47	4 42	6 4	9 10	6 43	4 47	6 8	6 30	4 59	6 21	8 23
321	16	M	18 56 49	6 52	4 38	6 47	0 23	6 48	4 41	6 51	9 56	6 44	4 46	6 5	6 31	4 59	7 9	9 10
322	17	Tu	19 11 23	6 53	4 37	7 37	1 10	6 49	4 40	7 41	10 40	6 45	4 45	7 46	6 32	4 58	8 0	9 56
323	18	W	19 25 37	6 54	4 36	8 29	1 56	6 50	4 39	8 33	11 22	6 46	4 44	8 37	6 33	4 58	8 51	10 40
324	19	Th	19 39 29	6 56	4 35	9 24	2 40	6 51	4 39	9 28	morn.	6 47	4 44	9 32	6 34	4 57	9 45	11 26
325	20	Fr	19 53 1	6 57	4 34	10 21	3 26	6 53	4 38	10 24	0 11	6 48	4 43	10 28	6 35	4 57	10 38	morn.
326	21	Sa	20 6 10	6 58	4 34	11 18	4 13	6 54	4 38	11 20	0 59	6 49	4 43	11 23	6 36	4 56	11 32	0 13
327	22	47	20 18 57	6 59	4 33	morn.	5 2	6 55	4 37	morn.	1 49	6 50	4 42	morn.	6 37	4 56	morn.	1 2
328	23	M	20 31 22	7 0	4 32	0 15	5 54	6 56	4 36	0 17	2 40	6 51	4 42	0 19	6 38	4 56	0 25	1 54
329	24	Tu	20 43 23	7 2	4 32	1 13	6 40	6 57	4 36	1 14	3 32	6 52	4 41	1 15	6 38	4 55	1 18	2 46
330	25	W	20 55 2	7 3	4 31	2 11	7 39	6 58	4 35	2 11	4 24	6 53	4 40	2 11	6 39	4 55	2 12	3 39
331	26	Th	21 6 17	7 4	4 31	3 10	8 29	6 59	4 35	3 9	5 14	6 55	4 40	3 9	6 40	4 55	3 6	4 29
332	27	Fr	21 17 8	7 5	4 30	4 11	9 18	7 0	4 35	4 10	6 4	6 56	4 40	4 8	6 41	4 55	4 3	5 18
333	28	Sa	21 27 35	7 6	4 30	5 14	10 5	7 2	4 34	5 12	6 51	6 57	4 40	5 9	6 42	4 54	5 1	6 5
334	29	48	21 37 37	7 7	4 30	rises.	10 54	7 3	4 34	rises	7 38	6 58	4 39	rises.	5 43	4 54	rises.	6 54
335	30	M	21 47 15	7 8	4 29	5 32	11 39	7 4	4 34	5 36	8 21	6 59	4 39	5 41	6 44	4 54	54	7 39

12th MONTH. # DECEMBER, 1868. **31 DAYS.**

MOON'S PHASES.	D	BOSTON. H. M.	NEW YORK. H. M.	WASH'TON. H. M.	CHARLES'N. H. M.	Sun on Merid. or noon Mark D.	H.	M.	S.
Third Quarter	6	4 5[illegible] ev.	4 38 ev.	4 26 ev.	4 14 ev.	1	11	49	29
New Moon	13	6 49 ev.	8 37 ev.	8 25 ev.	8 13 ev.	9	11	52	52
First Quarter	21	11 44 ev.	11 32 ev.	11 20 ev.	11 8 ev.	17	11	56	42
Full Moon	29	9 3 mo.	8 51 mo.	8 39 mo.	8 27 mo.	25	12	0	41

Day of Year.	Day of Month.	Day of Week.	Sun's decl. S. ° ' "	CALENDAR FOR Boston, New England, N York State, Michigan, Wiscon., Iowa & Oregon. Sun r's's H. M.	Sun sets. H. M.	Moon rises. H. M.	H. W. B'st'n H. M.	CALENDAR FOR N York City, Philadelphia, Conn. N. Jers'y Penn'a, Ohio, Indiana & Illinois. Sun ris's. H. M.	Sun sets. H. M.	Moon rises. H. M.	H. W. N. Yk. H. M.	CALENDAR FOR Washington; Mary'd Virg'a, Ken'y, Miss'ri and California. Sun r's's H. M.	Sun sets. H. M.	Moon rises. H. M.	CALENDAR FOR Charles'n, North Carolin., Tennessee Geo., Alabama, Miss'ppi & Louisiana. Sun r's's H. M.	Sun sets H. M.	Moon rises. H. M.	H. W. Ch't'n. H. M.
336	1	Tu	21 56 27	7 10	4 29	6 27	ev. 26	7 5	4 34	6 31	9 13	7 0	4 39	6 3[illegible]	6 45	4 54	6 50	8 20
337	2	W	22 5 14	7 11	4 29	7 27	1 17	7 6	4 33	7 32	10 2	7 1	4 39	7 36	6 45	4 54	7 50	9 17
338	3	Th	22 13 36	7 12	4 28	8 32	2 9	7 7	4 33	8 36	10 50	7 2	4 38	8 40	6 46	4 54	8 53	10 9
339	4	Fr	22 21 32	7 13	4 28	9 41	3 0	7 8	4 33	9 44	11 45	7 2	4 38	9 48	6 47	4 54	9 58	11 0
340	5	Sa	22 29 1	7 14	4 28	10 49	3 55	7 9	4 32	10 51	ev. 41	7 3	4 38	10 53	6 48	4 54	11 0	11 55
341	6	**49**	22 36 5	7 15	4 28	11 57	4 53	7 10	4 32	11 58	1 40	7 4	4 38	11 59	6 49	4 54	morn.	ev. 53
342	7	M	22 42 41	7 16	4 28	morn	5 53	7 11	4 32	morn.	2 39	7 5	4 38	morn.	6 49	4 54	0 4	1 53
343	8	Tu	22 48 51	7 17	4 28	1 7	6 57	7 12	4 32	1 7	3 41	7 6	4 38	1 7	6 50	4 54	1 8	2 57
344	9	W	22 54 35	7 17	4 28	2 13	7 54	7 13	4 32	2 12	4 39	7 7	4 38	2 11	6 51	4 54	2 9	3 54
345	10	Th	22 59 51	7 18	4 28	3 21	8 51	7 14	4 32	3 19	5 36	7 8	4 38	3 17	6 52	4 54	3 12	4 51
346	11	Fr	23 4 39	7 19	4 28	4 27	9 44	7 15	4 32	4 24	6 30	7 9	4 38	4 21	6 53	4 55	4 13	5 44
347	12	Sa	23 9 1	7 20	4 28	5 32	10 33	7 15	4 32	5 29	7 18	7 9	4 39	5 25	6 54	4 55	5 15	6 33
348	13	**50**	23 12 51	7 21	4 28	sets.	11 20	7 16	4 33	sets.	8 2	7 10	4 39	sets	6 54	4 55	sets.	7 20
349	14	M	23 16 20	7 22	4 28	5 16	11 55	7 16	4 33	5 20	8 38	7 11	4 39	5 25	6 55	4 55	5 39	7 55
350	15	Tu	23 19 18	7 22	4 29	6 18	morn.	7 17	4 33	6 22	9 32	7 12	4 39	6 27	6 56	4 56	6 41	8 46
351	16	W	23 21 48	7 23	4 29	7 12	0 46	7 18	4 33	7 16	10 15	7 12	4 40	7 20	6 56	4 56	7 33	9 29
352	17	Th	23 23 50	7 24	4 29	8 8	1 29	7 18	4 33	8 12	10 54	7 13	4 40	8 15	6 57	4 56	8 27	10 12
353	18	Fr	23 25 24	7 24	4 29	9 5	2 12	7 19	4 34	9 8	11 37	7 14	4 40	9 11	6 58	4 57	9 21	10 53
354	19	Sa	23 26 29	7 25	4 30	10 2	2 53	7 20	4 34	10 5	morn.	7 14	4 41	10 7	6 58	4 57	10 14	11 35
355	20	**51**	23 27 6	7 26	4 30	10 59	3 35	7 20	4 35	11 0	0 21	7 15	4 41	11 2	6 59	4 58	11 7	morn.
356	21	M	23 27 15	7 26	4 31	11 58	4 20	7 21	4 35	11 58	1 7	7 15	4 42	11 59	6 59	4 58	morn.	0 20
357	22	Tu	23 26 55	7 26	4 31	morn	5 8	7 21	4 36	morn.	1 53	7 16	4 42	morn.	7 0	4 59	0 1	1 8
358	23	W	23 26 7	7 27	4 32	0 55	5 57	7 22	4 37	0 55	2 43	7 16	4 43	0 54	7 0	4 59	0 54	1 57
359	24	Th	23 24 51	7 27	4 32	1 54	6 52	7 22	4 37	1 53	3 37	7 17	4 43	1 52	7 1	5 0	1 48	2 52
360	25	Fr	23 23 7	7 28	4 33	2 55	7 44	7 23	4 38	2 53	4 29	7 17	4 44	2 51	7 1	5 0	2 44	3 44
361	26	Sa	23 20 54	7 28	4 33	3 59	8 42	7 23	4 39	3 56	5 27	7 17	4 44	3 53	7 1	5 1	3 44	4 42
362	27	**52**	23 18 13	7 28	4 34	5 3	9 35	7 23	4 39	4 59	6 21	7 18	4 45	4 56	7 2	5 2	4 44	5 35
363	28	M	23 15 4	7 29	4 35	rises.	10 29	7 23	4 40	rises	7 14	7 18	4 46	rises	7 2	5 2	rises.	6 29
364	29	Tu	23 11 28	7 29	4 36	5 10	11 20	7 24	4 40	5 15	8 4	7 18	4 47	5 19	7 2	5 3	5 31	7 20
355	30	W	23 7 23	7 29	4 37	6 16	ev. 11	7 24	4 41	6 20	8 57	7 19	4 47	6 24	7 2	5 4	6 37	8 11
366	31	Th	23 2 50	7 30	4 37	7 26	1 3	7 24	4 42	7 29	9 49	7 19	4 48	7 33	7 3	5 4	7 46	9 3

ECLIPSES FOR THE YEAR 1868.

There will be only two Eclipses this year, both of the Sun, and neither of them visible in the United States.

I. An Annular Eclipse of the Sun, February 23. Visible in South America, Africa and Southern Europe.

II. A Total Eclipse of the Sun. August 18. Visible in Eastern Africa, Southern Asia, and in Australia.

A Transit of Mercury over the Sun's disc, will occur November 5. Invisible in the United States.

MORNING STARS.

Venus (♀) after July 16.

Mars (♂) from January 2 to November 13.

Jupiter (♃) from March 10 to July 4.

Saturn (♄) until Feb. 24, and after Nov. 29.

EVENING STARS.

Venus until July 16.

Mars until January 2, and after November 13.

Jupiter until March 10, and after July 4.

Saturn from February 24 to November 29.

THE FOUR SEASONS.

			D.	H.	M.		D.	H.	M.
Winter	begins, 1867,	December	22,	1	31	mo., and lasts . .	89	0	56
Spring	" 1868,	March	20,	2	27	mo., "	92	20	27
Summer	" 1868,	June	20,	10	54	eve., " ...	93	14	31
Autumn	" 1868,	Sept.	22,	1	25	eve. "	89	17	55
Winter	" 1868,	December	21,	7	20	mo., Trop. year,	365	5	49

CYCLES OF TIME AND CHURCH DAYS.

Dominical Letters	E D	Septuagesima Sund... Feb.	9	Easter Sunday......	April	12
Epact	6	Sexagesima " "	16	Low Sunday	April	19
Golden Number............	7	Quinquagesima " "	23	Rogation Sunday....	May	17
Solar Cycle...............	1	Ash Wednesday....... "	26	Ascension Day	"	21
Roman Indiction	11	Quadragesima Sund., Mar.	1	Pentecost Sunday ...	"	31
Jewish Lunar Cycle......	4	Mid-Lent Sunday. .. "	22	Trinity Sunday......	June	7
Dionysian Period..........	197	Palm Sunday. ......April	5	Middle of the Year..	July	1
Julian Period............	6581	Good Friday......... "	10	Advent Sunday	Nov.	29

On the 12th of May, 1866, a star of the second magnitude suddenly appeared in the constellation of the Northern Crown, but quickly began to lose its brillance. Its light being examined by the spectroscope, showed two distinct spectra, one like that of the other stars and of the sun, the other consisting of four bright lines, indicating the combustion of gas, especially hydrogen. The great brightness of the lines showed that the luminous gas was hotter than the star itself. These indications, together with the suddennes of the outburst of light, and its rapid decline from the second magnitude to the eigtht in twelve days, suggest the startling conception that the star had suddenly become enwrapped in the flames of burning hydrogen which also intensified the heat and light of the star itself, till the caase of the combustion was exhausted, and the star relapsed to its former insignificance. All this, though so recently visible to us, must have occurred many years ago.

The Meteoric Shower of November. 1866, which was so brilliant in Europe and so insignificant or invisible in America, has led two eminent astronomers in Paris and Milan to form the same conclusions — each from his own observations and calculations. They agree in ascribing these meteors to one or more vast nebulous masses, moving in very elliptical orbits, which bring them at long regular intervals within the earth's attraction and the oxidizing and igniting influence of the atmosphere. Le Verrier judges that their orbit extends as far at least as to the orbit of Uranus; and both astronomers fix their period of revolution at 33¼ years. The orbit of the November meteors nearly coincides with that of Tempel's comet, the first of 1866; while the August meteors have an orbit almost identical with that of the great comet of 1862.

Entered acording to Act of Congress, in the year 1867, by Frdr. Gerhard, in the Clerk's Office of the District Court of the United States for the Southern District of New-York.

THE GREAT REMEDY,

WHICH HAS

Been favorably known and Extensively Used in New York City and vicinity for upwards of

TWENTY-FIVE YEARS.

MADAME ZADOC PORTER'S

CURATIVE COUGH BALSAM,

Price, 25, 50 & 75 Cents per Bottle.

The Best, Cheapest, and most effectual Remedy for Coughs, Colds, &c., the World has ever produced. Purely Vegetable, contains no Minerals or other Deleterious Drugs.

THE CURATIVE BALSAM is Warranted, if used according to Directions, to cure or relieve in all cases, COUGHS, COLDS, CROUP, WHOOPING COUGH, ASTHMA and all affections of the THROAT and LUNGS.

Madame Zadoc PORTER'S BALSAM is a purely Vegetable Expectorant, prepared with great care and scientific skill, from a combination of the best remedies the vegetable kingdom affords.

Its remedial qualities are based on its power to assist the healthy and vigorous circulation of the Blood through the Lungs.

It enlivens the muscles and assists the skin to perform the duties of regulating the heat of the system, and in gently throwing off the waste substance from the surface of the body.

It loosens the phlegm, induces free spitting, and will be found VERY AGREEABLE TO THE TASTE. It is not a violent remedy, but emollient, warming searching and effective; and can be taken by the oldest person or youngest child.

If you have a Cold, if ever so slight, do not fail to give the Balsam a trial, as the very low price at which it is sold brings it within the reach of every one, that they may always keep it convenient for use. The timely use of a 25 cent bottle will often prove it to be worth a hundred times its cost.

The 75 cents bottle is more profitable to the consumer as it contains four times the quantity contained in the small bottle. Sold by all Druggists.

RUCKEL & HENDEL, Proprietors,

58 BARCLAY ST. N. Y.

THE CHRISTIAN CHURCH IN 1867.

The "American Ecclesiastical Almanac" intends to give a brief account of the most important events in the religious history of the year, together with the latest and completest statistical intelligence on the several religious denominations of this and other countries It is to be a brief compendium of important facts and figures, which, it is supposed, will interest alike members of all religious denominations. It has been our endeavor to avoid all partizanship, and to be, in all our statements, impartial and accurate; and, so far as the brief space of the Almanac allows, we have aimed at completeness.

Although the Almanac briefly notices religious movements of every kind, it is chiefly a chronicle of the history of the Christian Church. Commonly, the Christian Church is divided into three large groups. The first of these is the Roman Catholic Church; the second is formed by the Greek and the other Eastern Churches; while all the others have frequently been comprised under the collective name of Protestants or of Bible Christians, although neither name has been generally accepted.

One of the largest denominations of Christians the Anglican Church, is in a state of transition. One party in it claims to be one of the Protestant group of churches; another wishes to be regarded as substantially one with the Greek and Eastern Churches, and endeavors to bring about a closer union with these churches. The conflict of these parties gives a special importance to the "Pan-Anglican Synod," or the first general meeting of Bishops of all the branches of the Anglican communion, which was held in 1867.

A majority of the Protestant churches, although differing in some points of their creed, agree in believing in the divinity of Christ, in the inspiration of the Bible, and in the Bible as the only rule of faith. They are commonly designated by the collective name of "Evangelical Denominations." They have endeavored to effect a permanent union by the establishment of the "Evangelical Alliance," which last year held its fifth œcumenical council. They have also in common many religious Societies, such as Bible and Tract Societies and Young Men's Christian Associations.

Among the denominations not represented in the "Evangelical Alliance," are the Unitarians, Universalists, and the "Christian Connection," which have of late begun to unite in the establishment of "Liberal Christian Unions." They differ from the denominations comprised under the name of "Evangelical" in many doctrines, regarded by the latter as essential, but agree with them in accepting the Bible as the rule of their faith

There are a number of smaller communions, also accepting the Bible as the rule of faith, but keeping outside of the above-mentioned organizations.

There are, finally, organizations which profess a belief in the religion founded by Christ, but refuse to accept the Bible as the unchanging standard of faith. This opinion is held by men and parties in a number of the European State Churches, where it is commonly designated as Rationalism or Liberalism. A new organization, intended to embrace men of these views, was established last year in the United States, under the name of "Free Religious Association."

All the more important facts in the history of these churches and organizations will be noticed in this Almanac; and though it is impossible to obtain absolute completeness, we feel confident that no other publication in the English or any other language presents a fuller amount of information.

———o———

THE EVANGELICAL ALLIANCE.

I.—History of the Evangelical Alliance.

It is about twenty-two years since the idea of the Evangelical Alliance was elaborated by a conference held at Liverpool. This conference was preparatory in its character, and after a long discussion of the points common to "evangelical denominations," it made membership of the alliance dependent upon nine tenets, among which were the inspiration of the Scriptures, the Trinity the utter depravity of human nature, the Divinity of Jesus Christ and the Atonement, justification by faith alone, and the Divine institution of the sacraments of Baptism and the Lord's Supper. The first attempt to fix a common creed of evangelical Protestantism did not meet general approval, as it excluded denominations like the Friends and the Plymouth brethren. The *first General Assembly* of the members and friends of the Alliance was held in 1846, in London, under the Presidency of Sir Culling Eardley Smith, one of the originators and active promoters of the alliance. England, the United States, and Germany, were represented. Belief in immortality, the judgment of the world through Christ, the everlasting bliss of heaven, and the everlasting damnation of the wicked, were added to the principles previously adopted. The alliance spread in France, Switzerland, and Belgium, without agreement with its definition of the evangelical creed being insisted on. It met with much opposition in Germany from the Lutherans, who did not find the creed sufficiently explicit on certain points, and from the disciples of Schleiermacher, who disapproved of some of the articles. A *second assembly* was held in Paris in 1855, on the occasion of the World's Exhibition. The *third meeting* was held in Berlin, in 1857. The ("Confessional") Lutherans became more determined in their opposition, while the Evangelical party of Germany, though approving of the general scope of the alliance, deemed it inexpedient to insist on acceptance of the nine principles as a condition of membership. This meeting was largely attended, delegates from Macao, Africa, and Australia being present, and brought the alliance more prominently before the churches of Continental Europe. The *fourth meeting* was held at Geneva in 1860. It was successful, notwithstanding the declension of the Genevan National Church to sympathize with its objects. Dr. Guthrie, of Scotland; Dr. Baird, of the United States; Monod, Presensé, and Gasparin, of France; Krummacher and Dosner, of Germany; Groen van Prinsterer, of Holland; and Merle d'Aubigne, of Switzerland, were among the most prominent and active members. The fifth meeting was to have been held at Amsterdam in 1866, but was postponed, on account of the prevalence of the cholera at the appointed time, till 1867.

2.—Conference of 1867.

The *fifth General Conference* actually took place at Amsterdam on the 18th of August, 1867. The citizens of the place extended a hearty welcome to all the members. The meeting was largely attended. There were delegates from France, Germany, Switzerland, Holland, Great Britain, the United States, the British American Provinces, Italy, Spain, Sweden, and Eastern countries. Baron Van Wassenaar Catwijk presided. Among the more prominent delegates were Dr. Krummacher, Prof. Herzog, Dr. Tholuck, and Prof. Lange, of Germany; Pasteur Bersier, Dr. de Pressensé, and Prof. St. Hilaire, of France; Dr. Guthrie, of Scotland; John Pye Smith, Archdeacon Philpot, and S. Gurney, M. P., of England; Merle d'Aubigne, of Switzerland; the Rev. Dr. Prime, of the United States, and many others. The opening sermon was preached by Prof. Van Oosterzee. Among the subjects discussed were the religious condition of the Church of England, the Scottish churches, the connection of Missions with Civilization, Christianity, and Literature, and Art and Science; the methods of operating missions: the religious condition of Germany, France, Holland, Belgium, and Italy; Evangelical Nonconformity; Christianity and the Nationalities; and various subjects of theology and philosophy. Interesting reports were received of the progress of religious liberty in Turkey, and of the thraldom of opinion in Spain. The observance of the Sabbath received especial consideration, resulting in the adoption of a resolution calling upon the members of the Alliance to use, in their several places of abode and spheres of influence, earnest endeavors to secure from States, Municipalities, and masters of establishments, from every one, the weekly day of rest from labor, in order that all may freely and fully participate in the temporal and spiritual benefits of the Lord's day."

A letter of affection and sympathy was adopted to Christians scattered abroad, particularly to those who are laboring against the hostile influences of heathenism or of superstition, and whose rights of public worship are restrained or abridged. An address of protest against war was adopted. Statistics were given of Young Men's Christian Associations, showing that there are in the Christian world upwards of eight hundred such associations, numbering upwards of 55,000 members. Special meetings were held on Sunday Schools and systematic benevolence. A series of meetings for the poor were held in one of the mission rooms of the city, with wholesome effect, and two temperance meetings.

An invitation was presented and urged by the representatives of the American branch to hold the next General Conference at New York, which was referred to the different branches of the Alliance for consideration.

The assembly adjourned on Tuesday, the 27th of August, but on the following day an open-air missionary meeting was held at Vogelgesang, at which ten thousand persons were addressed in French, Dutch, and German.

The Evangelical Alliance of the United States was organized in New York city on the 30th of January, 1867. Eminent divines and laymen of the Episcopal, Methodist, Presbyterian, German Reformed, Reformed Dutch, and Baptist churches, and from various parts of the country, signified their approval of the movement, either by attendance in person or by letter. A letter of coöperation was read from the Secretary of the British branch of the Alliance. Hon. Wm. E. Dodge is President of the American branch.

The central idea of the Evangelical Alliance is to represent to the world the spiritual unity of the Evangelical denominations, and to establish between them a bond of union. The British branch, only, of the National branches, has been in the practice of holding annual meetings.

3.—Report of the American Branch.

The report on the state of religion in the United States of America, which was presented by Dr. Henry B. Smith, Chairman of the Executive Committee of the American branch of the Alliance, after a brief reference to the ties of sympathy, particularly in a religious aspect, between the United States and Holland, dwelt at length upon the character and results of the American civil war; its causes, the nature of the questions, moral and political, which were involved in it, and what has been obtained by it, particularly the national unity and the extinction of slavery. It referred to the workings of the Freedmen's Bureau, and the bright prospects which are presented for the moral and intellectual development of the colored population.

The doctrine of the separation of Church and State was incidentally referred to as sustained by the events of the war. This separation, it was shown, does not imply indifference, still less opposition, of the Government to Christianity, for the Government, in numerous acts of its highest officers, shows a tacit recognition of Christianity; an effort is being made, moreover, to have an express recognition inserted in the National Constitution. American churches, under the voluntary system, show a larger growth than any other. The operations of the churches have not been impeded, but invigorated and accelerated, by the war. Its direct fruits were an impulse of benevolence shown in the organization and liberal support of the Sanitary and Christian Commissions, and other enterprises for the benefit of the soldiers, statistics of the operations of which were given. The rapid advances of other benevolent enterprises, and of education, were described.

The report then gave a summary of the educational statistics of the country, the operations of the missionary, religious, and charitable societies, of Young Men's Christian Associations and Sunday Schools; and finally, a review of the strength, enterprise, and condition of all the churches severally, of the United States.

In conclusion, it is said, referring to the diversity of denominations in America: "But in all this diversity of tongues, there is still one language. We have one Lord, one faith, and one baptism. Our differences are chiefly external and superficial; our union is eternal and vital."

—o—

THE PAN-ANGLICAN SYNOD.

The so-called "Pan-Anglican Synod" was called in pursuance of a resolution passed by the Convocation of Cantorbury in February last, requesting the Archbishop to give an invitation to all bishops in communion with the Church of England to assemble for the purpose of united deliberation on matters of common interest at home and abroad. The 24th of September was appointed as the time of meeting.

The following is a summary of the churches called Anglican, whose Bishops were included in this invitation:

1.—The Anglican Churches.

I. *The Established Church of England.*—This has two Archbishops, of Canterbury and York, with twenty-six Bishops, of whom twenty are attached to the Convocation of Canterbury, and six to that of York. It is estimated that one-half, or 10,000,000, of the population of England, are under the control of this church.

II. *Church of Ireland.*—It has two Archbishops, of Dublin and Armagh, with ten Bishops, equally divided between the Provinces. The population connected with it is estimated at 657,661.

III. *The Scotch Episcopal Church.*—This has seven Bishops. The membership is small.

IV. *The Episcopal Colonial Churches.*—These have fifty Bishops, all except those of Jerusalem, the Sandwich Islands, Melanesia, and Central Africa, within British dominions. Ecclesiastical Provinces with Metropolitan heads, have been formed in Canada, India, South Africa, Australia, and New Zealand.

V. *The "Protestant Episcopal Church of the United States."*—This has forty-four Bishops. The Senior Bishop (Hopkins, of Vermont,) presides over the House of Bishops at the triennial General Convention, and is styled the Presiding Bishop. Number of communicants (1866), 161,224.

2.—Meeting of the Synod.

The Synod was formally opened in the Archiepiscopal Palace at Lambeth on the 24th of September, with religious services, which were followed by a discourse by Bishop Whitehouse, of Illinois, who had been present at the meeting of the Convocation, at which the calling of the Synod was projected, and was chosen to this office for that reason, and as a compliment to the American church. Seventy-six Bishops were in attendance.

The sessions were not open to the public, but the Archbishop was commissioned to furnish an official report of the proceedings. The more important portions of them were communicated to the public immediately after the adjournment of the Synod, in a semi-official manner. They are covered by a series of resolutions, which were preceded by a preamble expressing the conviction of the Bishops that the unity of the church "will be most effectually promoted by maintaining the faith in its purity and integrity—as taught in the Holy Scriptures, held by the Primitive Church, summed up in the Creeds, and affirmed by the undisputed General Councils—and by drawing each of us closer to our common Lord, by giving ourselves to much prayer and intercession, by the cultivation of a spirit of charity, and a love of the Lord's appearing." The Resolutions were as follows:

1—That it appears to us expedient, for the purpose of maintaining brotherly intercommunication, that all cases of establishment of new sees and appointment of new Bishops be notified to all Archbishops and Metropolitans, and all presiding Bishops of the Anglican Communion.

2—That, having regard to the conditions under which intercommunion between members of the Church passing from one distant diocese to another may be duly maintained, we hereby declare it desirable: 1. That forms of letters commendatory on behalf of clergymen visiting other dioceses be drawn up and agreed upon. 2. That forms of letters commendatory for lay members of the Church be in like manner prepared. 3. That his Grace the Lord Archbishop of Canterbury be pleased to undertake the preparation of such forms.

3—That a committee be appointed to draw up a pastoral address to all members of the Church of Christ in communion with the Anglican branch of the Church Catholic, to be agreed upon by the assembled Bishops, and to be published as soon as possible after the last sitting of the Conference.

4—That, in the opinion of this Conference, unity of faith and discipline will be best maintained among the several branches of the Anglican Community by due and canonical subordination of the Synods of the several branches to the higher authority of a Synod or Synods above them.

5—That a committee of seven members (with power to add to their number, and to obtain the assistance of men learned in ecclesiastics and canon law) be appointed to inquire into and report upon the relations and functions of such Synods, and that such report be forwarded to his Grace the Lord Archbishop of Canterbury, with a request that, if possible, it may be communicated to any adjourned meeting of this Conference.

6—That, in the judgment of the Bishops now assembled, the whole Anglican Communion is deeply injured by the present condition of the Church in Natal; and that a committee be now appointed at this general meeting to report on the best mode by which the Church may be delivered from the continuance of this scandal, and the true faith maintained. That such report be forwarded to his Grace the Lord Archbishop of Canterbury, with the request that he will be pleased to transmit the same to all the Bishops of the Anglican communion, and to ask for their judgment thereupon.

7—That we who are here present do acquiesce in the resolution of the Convocation of Canterbury, passed on June 26, 1866, relating to the Diocese of Natal, to wit:

If it be decided that a new Bishop should be consecrated—as to the proper steps to be taken by the members of the Church in the Province of Natal for obtaining a new Bishop, it is the opinion of this House—first, that a formal instrument, declaratory of the doctrine and discipline of the Church of South Africa, should be prepared, which every Bishop, priest and deacon should be required to subscribe; secondly, that a godly and well-learned man should be chosen by the clergy, with the assent of the lay communicants of the Church; and thirdly, that he should be presented for consecration, either to the Archbishop of Canterbury—if the aforesaid instrument should declare the doctrine and discipline of Christ as received by the United Church of England and Ireland—or to the Bishops of the Church of South Africa, according as hereafter may be judged to be most advisable and convenient.

8—That, in order to the binding of the churches of our Colonial Empire and the missionary churches beyond them in the closest union with the Mother Church, it is necessary that they receive and maintain without alteration the standards of faith and doctrine as now in use in that Church. That, nevertheless, each province should have the right to make such adaptations and additions to the services of the Church as its peculiar circumstances may require, provided that no change or addition be made inconsistent with the spirit and principles of the Book of Common Prayer, and that all such changes be liable to any revision by any Synod of the Anglican communion in which the said province shall be represented.

9—That the committee appointed by resolution 5, with the addition of the names of the Bishops of London, St. David's, and Oxford, and all the Colonial Bishops, be instructed to consider the constitution of a voluntary spiritual tribunal, to which questions of doctrine may be carried by appeal from the tribunals for the exercise of discipline in each province of the Colonial Church, and that their report be forwarded to his Grace the Lord Archbishop of Canterbury, who is requested to communicate it to an adjourned meeting of this Conference.

10—That the resolutions submitted to this Conference relative to the discipline to be exercised by Metropolitans, the Court of Metropolitans, the scheme for conducting the election of Bishops, when not otherwise provided for, the declaration of submission to the regulation of the Synods, and the question of what legislation should be proposed for the Colonial churches, be referred to the committee specified in the preceding resolution.

11—That a special committee be appointed to consider the resolutions relative to the notification of proposed Missionary Bishops, and the subordinates of Missionaries.

12—That the question of the bounds of the jurisdiction of different Bishops, when any question may have arisen in regard to them, the question as to the obedience of Chaplains of the United Church of England and Ireland on the Continent, and the resolution submitted to the Conference relative to their return and admission into home Dioceses, be referred to the committee specified in the preceding resolution.

13—That we desire to render our hearty thanks to Almighty God for His blessings vouchsafed to us in and by this Conference; and we desire to express our hope that this our meeting may hereafter be followed by other meetings, to be conducted in the same spirit of brotherly love.

The resolution in relation to Bishop Colenso was adopted almost unanimously, there being but three hands raised against it.

A Pastoral Address was adopted, and signed individually by the Bishops, addressed "to the faithful in Christ Jesus, the priests and deacons, and the lay members" of the Church, exhorting them to keep whole and undefiled the faith, to strive heartily against the frauds and subtleties wherewith it has been and is assailed; to hold fast as the sure Word of God all the canonical Scriptures of the Old and New Testament, and, by diligent study of these oracles of God praying in the Holy Ghost, to seek to know more of the Lord Jesus Christ our Savior, whom they reveal, and of the will of God which they declare; to guard "against the growing superstitions and additions with which, in these latter days, the truth of God hath been overlaid," particularly the sovereignty of the Pope and the exaltation of the Virgin Mary; to grow in graee and show a godly walk and example; to "hold fast the creeds, and the pure worship and order, which of God's grace has been inherited from the primitive church; to beware of causing divisions contrary to the doctrine ye have received," and to pray and seek for unity among themselves and amongst all the faithful in Christ Jesus.

A memorial was presented, signed by Dr. Pusey, Dr. F. G. Lee, the Rev. A. H. Maconochie, and other clergymen, expressing sorrow at the long-continued divisions of christendom, and praying that steps might be taken to promote intercommunion between the Church of England and the orthodox Church of the East.

The Synod made no expression on the subject of ritualism.

Saturday the 28th of September, was given to the closing ceremonies of the Synod, which were celebrated with a choral service and communion in the parish church of St. Mary, Lambeth, and a sermon by the Rev. Dr. Fulford, Bishop of Montreal and Metropolitan of Canada.

The Synod was a mere voluntary and informal gathering of such Bishops as chose to respond to the invitation, and is without legal force or effect. Its significance, in the opinion of the Archbishop of Canterbury and the Bishops who were instrumental in its convocation, must be looked for in its moral results, which may be great and permanent. They will be found in the better understanding which will be promoted among the Bishops, increased harmony of action, particularly between those of different jurisdiction who occupy contiguous territory, and in the stronger tendency to preserve uniformity of doctrine and practice. Though an informal one, it may be regarded as a first step towards uniting all the Anglican churches into a common body.

BIBLE SOCIETIES.

1.—American Bible Society,

One hundred and fifty-five auxiliary societies have been recognized during the year ending May 1st, 1867, of which sixty-four were in the Southern and border States. The whole number of auxiliaries in the field is 1609, and of branch societies 3,805. The Society employs forty-five agents, of whom there are in foreign lands sixteen assistant agents, and sixty-one colporteurs, besides whom there are 135 agents employed by County societies, and 20,373 voluntary local agents, or Bible visitors. Its agencies are established in every State o the Union, except those that are occupied by State Bible Societies that employ their own agents.

The total receipts of the year ending May 1st, 1867, were $734,659 14, coming from thirty-nine States and Territories and twelve foreign countries. Of these, $431,654.66 were from sales of books. $174,835.46 from donations and collections, $105,971.96 from legacies, and 21 006.94 from rents. These are $31,403.94 larger than the receipts of the Jubilee year, $56,237.76 larger than those of any previous year of largest receipts

The issues from the Depository were 406,351 volumes, worth $52..835.73, of which 843,177 volumes, worth $443,387.08, were sold, and 173.177 volumes, worth $61.924.07, were given away. This is the largest number of issues ever given out, except during the war.

There were printed at the Bible House during the year, 635.7 8 volumes of editions of the Bible, Testaments and parts of the Bible, and 313.550 volumes abroad, making a total of 1,249,-318. The entire number of Bibles published by the Society, during the fifty-one years of its existence, is 22,940,404.

In accordance with a resolution passed at the Jubilee of May, 1866. a third general supply of the United States with the Holy Scriptures has been begun. The books given away in pursuance of it, numbered, at the date of the last annual report, 173,177 volumes, and they were valued at $61.921.07. Of these. 141,571 volumes were for the South, and 31,606 for other sections of the Union. But these really include but a small portion of the gratuitous work which has been accomplished by the Society. Those volumes which have been purchased, and distributed by auxiliaries, must be added. The extent of the resupply will be more truly seen in the facts reported by agents, that 496.248 families have been visited by Bible distributers; that 35.533 families have been supplied with the Scriptures, besides 10,554 to children, and other individuals; that 709 Sabbath and other schools have been furnished, in addition to all those supplied by the American Sunday School Union and similar societies, to which grants have been made for this purpose. During the year previous 307,695 families were visited; 14,846 destitute supplied; making a total in two years of 8 4.186 families visited, and 51,379 destitute families supplies.

Especial attention has been paid to the Southern States. Including those purchased, 270.312 Bibles were sent to the South during the year, making about half a million since the close of the war. The most interesting part of this work is among the freedmen, whose anxiety to possess and read the Bible is pronounced remarkable, and has nothing comparable to it among the whites or foreigners. Bible societies composed of colored people have been formed at Nashville and Knoxville, Tenn., Columbia, S. C., and other places, and several societies employ colored colporteurs. The army agency has been continued in connection with the agency to the freedmen, and also that to the naval and mercantile marine.

The Gospels of Matthew and John and the Epistle to the Ephesians have been published in Micronesian. and the Arabic Bible has been printed. Plates have been prepared for a Hawaiian Family Bible.and a Slavic and Bulgarian Testament. This society publishes 262 editions of the Bible and parts, in upwards of forty different languages and dialects, of America, Asia, Europe, Africa, and the Islands of the ocean.

The foreign work of the American Bible Society is prosecuted in all quarters of the earth. The total distribution is 241,666 volumes, as follows, so far as has been reported:

Brazil 659; Argentine Confederation 3,742; Italy 8,130; Russia (Esthonia) 11,441; Germany and Switzerland 16,920; Africa 1,361; Turkey upwards of 16,641; China 166,117; India about 2 ,000: Sandwich Islands 1,426; Canada (French) 166. Smaller grants have been made to Guiana, Venezuela, Liberia, Cuba. India, &c.. which cannot be reported in detail, but amount to about 11,000 in the aggregate. The Scriptures are printed abroad in forty different languages and dialects, and at home in thirty-two.

The stated meetings of the Society, which have been held monthly since the anniversary in May, exhibit continued enterprise and prosperity on the part of the Society, its branches and auxiliaries, showing new accessions, and disclosing new fields of distribution.

2.—British and Foreign Bible Society.

The field of operations of this Society extends into nearly all the accessible quarters of the world. It has its headquarters at London, and has branch and auxiliary societies throughout the British Isles, in all the British colonies in America, Asia, Africa, and Australasia, and at Carlsruhe, Florence. Hamburgh, Constantinople. Frankfort. Stuttgar and Cronstadt, Gibraltar, Corfu, Dresden, on the continent of Europe, and Smyrna, and depositories at Paris, Brussels, Amsterdam, Frankfort. Cologne, Berlin, Vienna, Stockholm, various points in Norway, Copenhagen, St. Petersburg. Leghorn, Lisbon, Mexico and Buenos Ayes, and several other places in Europe and other countries The number of auxiliaries and branches in England and Wales given in the repo t of May 1st, 1867, is 4,031, to which should be added 508 connected with the Hibernian Bible Society, and 1,275 in the colonies, other dependencies, &c. Besides these, 63 foreign Bible societies (including three in the United States), have been assisted by it. The Society has printed the Bible, Testament, or portions of the Bible, in 134 languages and dialects, and assisted in the circulation in 44 others, making a total of 178 languages and dialects in which it has assisted the circulation of the Scriptures, and 218 versions.

The receipts during the year ending May 1st. 1867, from ordinary sources, were £171,923, 12s., 6d., £10,093, 18s., 5d. in advance of last year, in addition to which the special funds (China, India, for new building, and for the Paris Exposition), swell the grand total to £187,508, 17s., 7d, the largest year's receipts ever enjoyed by the Society. The receipts are thus classified: From sale of Scriptures, £84,-102, 16s., 6d; Donations, £12,063, 4s., 4d.; Legacies, £15,159, 16s., 7d.—all showing an increase over the previous year. The number of copies of the Scriptures circulated (exclusive of the Indian vernacular Scriptures) is 2,383,380, an increase of 87,250 over the circulation of the previous year. The total issues of the Society now amount to fifty-two millions, six hundred and sixty nine thousand and eighty-nine copies. The increase in issues is in those from the foreign depots, which have increased 164,318 copies, while those from the home depots have fallen off 77,068 copies. The foundation of a new Bible House was laid June 11th, 1866. It is to cost about £46,068. Happy results have generally attended the operations of the society, the only serious embarrassment being met in some Catholic countries, like Portugal, where, however, 8,778 copies have been circulated; and Spain, where, to circulate the Bible, is still made a crime.

3.—American and Foreign Bible Society (Baptist).

The thirtieth annual meeting was held May 25th, 1867, in Chicaco, Illinois. The receipts of the treasury from all sources, including a balance on hand at the commencement of the year, amount to $51,467.45. The appropriations to India were as follows: Burmese and Karen Scriptures, $3,000; Assamese, $500; Teloogoo, $500; Chinese at Tie Chien, $500; Ningpo, $500; also $300 to China by other channels. Issued from the depository during the year, 21,568 copies of Scriptures, of which number 5,663 were sold at full or reduced prices.

4.—American Bible Union.

The anniversary of this Society was held in New York in October. Speaking of the fruits of the Union, the report states that the Bible Union has issued 603,164 copies of sacred Scripture; number of pages, 108,604,418; tracts and quarterlies, 1,716,269; number of pages, 28,-385,140. These make an aggregate of 2,319,453 publications, and 136,989 558 pages. The financial progress which the Union has made, may be judged by the following statistics: Receipts, 1863, $16,599.01; 1864, $21,189 22; 1865, $29,-231.36; 1866, $41,799.96; 1867, $55,127.79.

5.—Other Bible Societies.

The following are the statistics of some other Bible Societies in Europe:

BIBLE SOCIE IES.	Expenditures.	Issues.
Bible Translation Society....	8 891.08	——
Trinitarian Bible Society....	——	4,000
National Bible Society of Scotland.................64.885.04		204.432
Upper Canada Bible Society.	24.727.56	49,591
Bible Society of France.....	2,901.44	6,334
Protestant Bible Society of Paris........................	7,744.00	10,540
Basle Bible Society	1,030.92	13,269
Netherlands Bible Society...	18.592 00	35,634
Central Prussian Bible Soc...	7,744.00	89 293
Bavarian Bible Society......	——	7,058
Leipsic Bible Society........	566.28	——
Würtemberg Bible Institution	——	21,685
Danish Bible Society........	——	8,009

—o—

YOUNG MEN'S CHRISTIAN ASSOCIATION.

1.—The American Convention.

The Executive Committee of the National Convention *of Young Men's Christian Associations* reported at the Convention which was held at Montreal in June 1867, that they had corresponded with 2.115 Associations, of which 141 reported an aggregate of 32.347 members, 94 reported an expenditure during the year in the aggregate of $164,013,211, 63 reported a total of 52,378 volumes in their libraries, 25 had courses of free lectures, 59 courses of sermons for young men, and 108 maintained more than one weekly prayer-meeting. Eleven years ago the whole number of associations was sixty-seven. The convention of 1867 was attended by about 600 delegates, from 106 different associations. Among the more important topics discussed were the best means of reaching young men apparently outside of religious influences, and German young men and French Canadian residents of the United States and British Provinces, the giving aid to the formation of colored associations in the South, and the introduction of worldly amusements into the association rooms. An adverse expression was arrived at concerning the last.

2.—Foreign Associations.

The following statistics of the associations throughout the world were given by Mr. W. E. Shipton at the Amsterdam meeting of the Evangelical Alliance: In England there were 51 associations reported, with 7.390 members; in Scotland 23, with 2,031; in Ireland 6, with 662; in the colonies 12, with 223; Holland had 100 associations, with 2,009 members; Belgium 11, with 167; North Germany 107, with 3,026; Westphalia 112, with 5,033; Wurtemberg 44, with 560; France 54, with 867; French Switzerland 59, with 587; German Switzerland 45, with 400; Italy 5, with 100; Mediterranean 5, with 100; North America 143, with 33,374. Altogether there are perhaps at present upward of eight hundred associations, numbering upward of fifty-five thousand members.

To this must be added over 100 American associations, which have not been reported definitely.

THE ROMAN CATHOLIC COUNCIL AT ROME.

1.—The Eighteenth Centenary of the Martyrdom of St. Peter and St. Paul.

The eighteenth centenary anniversary of the martyrdom of St. Peter and St. Paul was the occasion of calling together at Rome a grand council of the bishops and clergy. The ostensible object was to celebrate the ceremonies in honor of the Holy Apostles, and to assist in the canonization of several saints. Five hundred and eighty-seven Cardinals and Bishops, as follows: Cardinal Bishops 5, Cardinal Priests 32, Cardinal Deacons 9, Patriarchs 6, Archbishops 95, Bishops 420, and about 300 clergymen and members of the religious orders, were in attendance.

On Tuesday, the 25th of June, the Pope received the American clergy. The archbishops of Baltimore, St. Louis, New Orleans, Cincinnati, and the bishop of Philadelphia, twenty-two other American bishops and many clergymen were present at this interview, during which the Pope took occasion to speak very warmly and kindly of the American Minister, General King, and to especially compliment the American prelates upon the result of their recent convention at Baltimore.

An offering of $200,000 in gold was presented, of which $60,000 was offered by Archbishop Purcell, of Cincinnati, on behalf of the Province of Cincinnati, and a part of this in a gold model of a yacht. A noteworthy fact in the composition of the convention was that America sent more prelates than even Catholic Austria.

On Thursday, June 27th, the Pope delivered an allocution to the assembled prelates, in the course of which he praised their great zeal in coming to Rome from such distances, and thus evincing their attachment and devotional obedience to the Holy See. He said that the example shown to the world by the union of the church at large in its celebration of the canonization of several new saints and the eighteenth centenary anniversary of St. Peter's martyrdom, would show forth to the enemies of the chair of Peter the immense power which the Church wields on earth.

The Pope confirmed the condemnation of the errors of the act of December 8th, 1864. He also expressed his desire to convoke at an early day an œcumenical council, with a view to deliberate on the best means of repairing the evils which oppress the Church.

The observances of the celebration proper commenced on the evening of the 28th, with a general illumination of the city of Rome. At seven o'clock the next morning there was a grand procession of prelates, priests, monks, and soldiers from the Vatican, to St. Peter's. The Pope was carried on his throne. There was an immense crowd assembled in the interior of the church before his arrival. St. Peter's was most magnificently decorated with cloths of gold, silver tapestries, paintings, and two hundred thousand yards of crimson silk. The building was lighted with many millions of wax candles. There were one hundred thousand people inside its walls, including the ex-King of Naples, the foreign Ministry, five hundred cardinals, archbishops, and bishops, and many thousands of clergymen, priests, friars, and monks. There were even nuns and soldiers from almost every country in the world present, and the assembled multitude made up a most brilliant congregation. Pope Pius the Ninth celebrated the Gregorian mass in Latin and Greek. There were two interruptions to the ceremony. The curtains of one of the windows of the church caught fire at one moment, but they were speedily torn down by the guard, and no damage occurred. After this, a man who had become crazy from excitement, produced by the pomp, and glitter, and lights, cut his throat, and died just under the bronze statue of St. Peter. There was no confusion in consequence. His body was quickly removed outside. The Pope at once proceeded to reconsecrate the church stained by the blood of the suicide, and then proceeded with the service of the altar. Liszt composed extra music for the Grand Mass, and a chord placed on the dome of St. Peter's made the angelical responses, the cannon of the Castle San Angelo thundering forth the accompaniment.

The following saints were canonized: Blessed Johosaphat Kuncevich, Archbishop; Blessed Peter De Arbues, and Nicholas Vich, with 18 companions, martyrs; Blessed Paul of the Cross, passionist; Blessed Leonard of Port Maurice, Franciscan confessors; Blessed Mary Francis of the Wounds of our Lord; and Blessed Germana Cousin, a poor shepherdess virgin.

The place of honor at the Pope's right hand, on occasion of the canonization, was occupied by Archbishop Purcell, of Cincinnati.

The Bishops presented an address to the Pope in reply to his allocution, acknowledging the courtesies received in 1862, lauding the virtues of Pius IX. and his fidelity and zeal in defending the faith against error, and promising implicit obedience to him and his decrees. It also expresses joy at the Proclamation of the speedy assembling of the Œcumenical Council, from which the bishops expect abundant fruit.

This address, it is stated, had five hundred and thirty-seven signatures. The bishops of each nation held a special meeting for appointing the members of the committee charged with drawing up the Address. In this committee, France was represented by four bishops; Austria, Spain, Italy, North America, and the East by three each; England, Ireland, Prussia, by two each; and Belgium, Holland, Bavaria, Switzerland, Portugal, Brazil, and Mexico, by one each. The Eastern bishops in the committee were the Patriarch of Jerusalem, the Archbishop Primate of the Catholic Armenians, and a Vicar Apostolic of China.

2.—The Coming General Council.

The Pope has named a congregation of seven Cardinals, to whom he has entrusted the duty of arranging the preliminaries for the meeting of the Council which he has expressed his intention of calling.

3.—Councils that have been held.

The Catholic Church recognizes nineteen General Councils, the first of which was that of the Apostles, at Jerusalem, A.D. 50. The others were held as follows:

1st of Nice, in Bythinia, A.D. 325.
1st of Constantinople,.. " 381.
1st of Ephesus......... " 431.

Chalcedon	A.D.	451.
2d of Constantinople	"	553.
3d of Constantinople	"	680.
2d of Nice	"	787.
4th of Constantinople	"	869,
4 councils of Lateran—Rome	"	1123,1139,1179,1215
1st and 2d of Lyons	"	1245, 1274.
Vienne, in Dauphiny	"	1311.
Constance	A.D.	1414.
Basle	A.D	1431.
Trent	"	1545.

The councils of Pisa in 14 9, of Florence in 1439, and the fifth of the Lateran, in 1512, are regarded by some a œcumenical. The conference of 1854, when the dogma of the immaculate conception was proclaimed, was not an œcumenical council.

—o—

UNION MOVEMENTS IN THE CHRISTIAN CHURCH.

The present year will be conspicuous in the history of the Christian Church for the number and earnestness of the efforts made in all parts of the Christian world for promoting the union of denominations heretofore separated. This movement has been going on for many years, and is annually increasing in magnitude and importance. In no previous year have an equal number of important meetings been held, having for their especial object the promotion of union.

The most important of these meetings in the Protestant group of churches was the fifth œcumenical assembly of the Evangelical Alliance at Amsterdam. The interest of the Protestant churches in the object, the permanent organization and the periodical meetings of the Alliance have been growing slowly, but steadily. The meeting of Amsterdam has undoubtedly attracted the attention of the churches, and of the world generally, to a larger extent than any of the four preceding ones, and gives a new impulse to the question how to secure a definite and permanent organization. The alliance does not aim at abolishing the landmarks which separate the Christian denominations from each other, but at bringing to the consciousness of the churches commonly designated by the collective name of evangelical, the fact of their union in the matter regarded by all of them as essential. The Alliance has enlisted the cordial sympathy of the Methodists, Baptists, Congregationalists, Presbyterians, and the "evangelical" or "low church" parties in the Anglican, Lutheran, Reformed and the German United Evangelical churches, beside a number of smaller denominations; and the meeting at Amsterdam has made it more probable than ever that this attempt to consolidate the confederation of all these bodies on one common platform, so as to represent them as a unit against the Roman Catholic and Eastern churches and the "High Church" and "Rationalistic" schools of the Protestant Church, will be, in course of time, entirely successful. If carried through, the organization is likely to embrace the majority of the aggregate membership of the Protestant churches of the world, though this result will be somewhat contingent upon the issue of the dissentions in the Anglican and the Lutheran denominations, two of the largest divisions of the Protestant world.

The movement for reducing the number of Methodist and Presbyterian denominations in this country and England has been earnestly continued. Definite results have not been obtained during the year; on the contrary, the attempted fusion of the Methodist Protestant Church and the American Wesleyans and that of the Old and New School Presbyterians, has for the present failed. The movement, however, is actively continued. In Scotland a union of the Presbyterian churches, except the Established Church seems to be sure of speedy consummation. In the United States the convocation of a general Presbyterian Convention, embracing all the Presbyterian denominations, at Philadelphia, in November, is an important union movement. Numerous movements of the same kind have been made in other religious denominations.

Among the Protestant denominations, not included under the head of Evangelical, a movement has been started for the organization of "Liberal Christian Unions." Thus far it is chiefly the Unitarians, the Universalists, and the Christian Connection in this country and in England, which have taken part in the movement, but it is expected that ere long a coöperation with the "Liberal" (Rationalistic) parties of the European State churches can be secured.

The first effort to establish an organic union among all the branches of the Anglican Communion was made this year by the convocation of the Pan-Anglican Synod. This movement had the approval of nearly every bishop of the Anglican churches; and the resolutions which were adopted by the Synod, provide for the periodical repetition of these Synods. Among the bishops of the Anglican churches, the opinion on the desirability of these gatherings seems to be so general that a further progress toward the permanent establishment of "Pan-Anglican Synods" can hardly be doubted. With the success of this movement, the efforts for establishing a closer intercommunion with the Greek and Eastern churches, which has already received the approbation of the English convocations and of the General Convention of the United States, will naturally assume an increased importance.

The "Radical" party in the Unitarian and Universalist churches of the United States, endeavor to establish a regular and permanent coöperation with the Spiritualists, Reformed Jews, Hicksites, and Progressive Friends. The first convention of this kind was held in 1867.

Many of the Christian churches continue to be greatly agitated by the strife of parties widely differing in their religious views. In the Lutheran Church of the United States, a number of Synods which urge a strict adhesion to the unaltered Confession of Augsburg, withdrew from the "General Synod" of the United States, and resolved to establish a new "General Council," with which also some of the heretofore independent Synods will unite.

In the Church of England the appointment of a new bishop for the diocese of Nata , in the place of Dr. Colenso, completes the separation which has already existed for some time between the Anglican Church as represented by its bishops, and the followers of Colenso. There is, however, no prospect of a long duration of this schism, which, if not sooner, will come to an end by the death of Colenso.

Germs of disruption exist in a number of other churches in this country and in Europe, but we have to report no other accomplished facts.

—o—

THE RELIGIOUS SOCIETIES OF THE UNITED STATES AND GREAT BRITAIN.

The following is a summary of the Receipts of the chief Religious Societies of the United States and Great Britain during the year 1866-67:

I.—American.

1. *National Societies.*

The following are the receipts for the year ending May, 1867, of the American Benevolent Societies whose headquarters are in New York:

American Bible Society—Sales and rents	$453.165	
Do.—Donations and legacies	280,843	
		734,069
American Tract Society—Sales	384,359	
Do.—Donations and legacies	159,860	
		544,151
American Tract Society (of Boston)—Sales	91,273	
Do.—Donations and legacies	44,192	
		135,466
American Seamen's Friend Society		98,230
American Guardian Society		87,768
American Missionary Association		253.000
American Board Com. Foreign Missions		448 090
Methodist Episcopal Missionary Society		660,000
American Church Missionary Society		50,000
American Home Missionary Society		212.567
American Sunday School Union		77,753
Protestant Episcopal Board Domestic Missions		123,273
Protestant Episcopal Board Foreign Missions		72,613
American and Foreign Christian Union		110,000
American and Foreign Bible Society		30.719
American Baptist Missionary Union		190,994
American Baptist Home Missionary Soc.		137.810
American Baptist Free Missionary Soc.		30,009
Presbyterian Board For. Missions (O. S.)		207,526
Presbyterian Board Dom. Missions (O. S.)		168,241
Presbyterian Board Church Extensions (O. S.)		35,670
Presbyterian Committee Home Missions (N. S.)		128.603
Presbyterian Committee Education (N.S)		20,455
Presbyterian Com. Publication (N. S.)		13,325
Board For. Missions Ref. Dutch Church		68 685
Board Dom Missions Ref. Dutch Church		24 569
National Temperance Society		26,592
American Freedmen's Union Commission		50,000
Total		$4,766,698

2. *Local Societies in New York City.*

New York Association for the Poor	$51,643
New York Sunday School Union	30,000
New York and Brooklyn Foreign Missionary Society	43.802
New York Children's Aid Society	93,577
New York Juvenile Asylum	87.439
New York City Mission	29,064
New York Five Points House of Industry	67.186
New York Ladies' Five Points Mission	16,682
New York Howard Mission	26,000
New York Female Assistance Society	24.751
New York Ladies' Union Aid Society	5,079
New York Ladies' Christian Union	12.817
Wilson Industrial Mission	10,6[illegible]8
New York Bible Society	23.915
New York Port Society	30,000
Union Home and School	20,259
Female Benevolent Society	8.869
New York Prot. Episcopal City Mission	26.899
Methodist Episcopal City Mission	31.853
New York Prison Association	13.250
New York Soc. for Ruptured & Crippled	19.942
New York Widows' Society	13.165
New York Nursery and Child's Hospital	29,394
New York Half Orphan Asylum	15.776
Total	$732,059

II.—British.

1. *Principal Foreign Missionary Societies.*

Church Missionary Society	£150,356
Wesleyan Missionary Society	148,140
Society for the Propagation of the Gospel in foreign parts	91,180
London Missionary Society	78 958
Baptist Missionary Society	30,105
South American Missionary Society	7.431
Moravian Missions	6.848
English Presbyterian Missions	6,[illegible]10
Turkish Missions-Aid Society	2,638
Total	£522,482

2. *Colonial, Jewish, and other Missions.*

London Society for Promoting Cristianity among the Jews	£33,327
Colonial Continental Society	31,679
United Methodist Churches, (Home, Colonial, and Foreign)	9 664
Primitive Methodist (Home and Colonial) Missions	9,557
British Society for the Propagation of the Gospel among the Jews	7,140
Colonial Missionary Society	3,042
Evangelical Continental Society	2,455
Foreign Aid Society	2,424
Total	£98,668

3. *Home Missions.*

Church Pastoral Aid Society	£47,829
Bishop of London's Fund	41,090
London City Mission	30,495

Additional Curates' Society	29,800
Wesleyan Home Missions	24,459
Irish Church Missions to the Roman Catholics	22,507
Church of England Scripture Readers' Association	12,354
Army Scripture Readers' Society	8,176
Incorporated Church Building Society	7,720
Missions to Seamen	7,681
Home Missionary Society (Congregational)	7,541
Protestant Reformation Society	4,727
Baptist and Home Missions	4,512
Baptist and Foreign Sailors' Society	3,934
Irish Evangelical Society	2,633
Midnight Mission	1,223
Baptist Building Fund	1,140
Royal Navy Scripture Readers' Society	683
Church Home Mission	683
Ragged Church and Chapel Union	477
Total	£264,633

4. *Religious Educational Societies.*

National Education Society	£14,152
Irish Society for Education of Roman Catholics	10,055
Christian Vernacular Education Society for India	6,345
Wesleyan Education Committee	5,670
Ragged School Union	4,714
British and Foreign School Society	3,669
Congregational Board of Education	3,017
London Society for Teaching the Blind	2,531
Sunday School Union	2,432
Home and Colonial School Society	2,261
Church of England Sunday School Institute	806
Total	£55,652

5. *Miscellaneous.*

Society for Promoting Christian Knowledge	£28,54/
Religious Tract Society	14,170
Protestant Alliance	1,821
Naval and Military Bible Society	1,783
Bible Translation Society	1,552
Lord's Day Observance Society	1,417
Prayer Book and Homily Society	1,163
Workingmen's Lord's Day Rest Assoc'n.	916
Book Society	459
Total	£51,619

6. *Other Societies.*

Operative Jewish Converts	£ 1,151
Baptist and Foreign School Society	13,583
Church of England Sunday School Institute	2,719
National Temperance League	3,252
Church of England Temperance Society	268
Trinitarian Bible Society	1,153
British Home for Incurables	6,007
Total	£28,733

British and Foreign Bible Society	£103,346

THE PRESBYTERIAN NATIONAL UNION CONVENTION.

The ministers and elders from the various presbyteries and kindred bodies met in Convention at the First Reformed Presbyterian Church, Philadelphia, on November 6th. The Convention was called for the purpose of adopting measures looking to a consolidation of the different branches of Presbyterians into one family. The first impulse to this assembly proceeded from the General Synod of the Reformed Presbyterian Church, which, at its late meeting in Philadelphia, passed a resolution to invite the several Presbyterian bodies to take part in such a meeting, and appointed a committee to effect arrangements for the calling of the Convention. The attendance was very large, there being delegates from all parts of the Union present. The Convention was organized by the election of George H. Stuart, Esq., as Chairman, and Rev. Dr. Archibald, of New Jersey, as Secretary. Mr. Stuart addressed the members of the Convention, welcomed them to the city, and hailed their coming as the harbinger of better days for Zion. This, as far as known, was the first Convention of the kind ever held. He believed that all had been praying for the union of the great Presbyterian family in America, and that measure would soon be effected. Mr. Stuart read a lengthy letter from a number of Scottish Presbyterian clergymen, favoring the union of the churches.

On November 7th, addresses were delivered by Robert Carter, of New York, Rev. Mr. Park, and Rev. Mr. Pratt, favoring the union of the Presbyterian churches, and advocating a grand coöperation in the great work of the gospel. Rev. Dr. Cyrus Dixon, of Baltimore, said that there were 5,000 Presbyterian churches, 6,300 ministers, and 700,000 communicants; and in Reformed Dutch Church, 444 churches, 461 ministers, and 68,000 members. There are embraced in these churches four millions of children. He advocated in strong language the union desired by the Convention. Troubles, he feared, were soon to be felt in the Church, and it therefore became necessary that the whole body should unite their forces against the evils with which the Church is threatened.

The Committee on Credentials reported that there were 180 Old School, 75 New School, 26 United, 20 Reformed Presbyterian, 5 Cumberland, and 4 Reformed Dutch churches represented. Total, 313.

Rev. Dr. Eagleson, chairman of the committee to prepare and report a bond of union, to be submitted for consideration, by the various branches of the Presbyterian Church represented in the Convention, submitted the following:

1. An acknowledgment of the Scriptures of the Old and New Testament to be the Word of God.

2. That in the United Church the Westminster Confession of Faith shall be received and adopted, as containing the system of doctrines taught in the Holy Scriptures.

While the committee recommend the foregoing basis of doctrine, they do not wish to be understood as impugning the orthodoxy of the

Heidelberg Catechism, and the candor of the Synod of Dort.

3. That the united Church shall receive and adopt the Presbyterian form of church government.

4. The Book of Psalms, which is a divine inspiration, is well adapted to the state of the church in all ages and circumstances, and should be used in social worship; but, as various collections of psalmody are used in the different churches, a change in this respect shall not be required.

5. That the sessions of each church shall have the right to determine who shall join in communion in the particular church committed to their care.

The committee recommended the adoption of the following resolutions:

1. That we unite in requesting our respective churches in their supreme judicatures to appoint a committee of five each, which shall constitute a joint committee, whose duty it shall be to meet, at a time and place to be agreed on, and proceed with all convenient despatch in an attempt to form a basis of union, according to the principles of this report, which basis they shall submit to the churches for their consideration and adoption. It being understood that this is not designed to interfere with the existing arrangements for reunion between two of the larger bodies represented in this Convention.

2. As there is so much agreement among all the churches here represented in all essential matters of faith, discipline, and order, it is recommended that friendly and fraternal intercourse be cultivated by interchange of pulpits, by fellowship with one another in social religious meetings, and by communion with each other at the Lord's table, subject to the regulations of each branch of the church.

3. In case the above paper should be adopted, that a committee be appointed to lay this action of the Convention before the highest judicatures of the various branches of the church here represented.

4. That the members of this Convention who may vote for the foregoing plan of union to be laid before the churches, shall not thereby be regarded as being committed to advocate its adoption when laid before the branches of the church respectively, but shall be free to act according to the indications of Providence at the time.

The *first* article was put, and carried.

On the *second* article, Rev. H. B. Smith, of New York, moved to amend by adding the words, "it being understood that this Confession is received in the historical, that is, the Calvinistic or reformed sense." The amendment was agreed to, and the section as amended passed, by a vote of four in favor, to one against, as follows: For the amendment, New School, Old School, United Presbyterian, and Dutch Reformed. Against it, Reformed Presbyterian. Rev. W. W. Barr moved to further add to the section the words, "with the larger or shorter catechism," which was lost, two churches voting in its favor—namely, New School Presbyterian and Reformed Dutch; and three against—namely, Old School, United, and Reformed Presbyterian. Upon a reconsideration, the amendment was agreed to. The delegation of the Cumberland Presbyterian Church declined to vote; but when their right to sit in the Convention, unless they took part in the vote, was questioned, recorded their vote *against* the amendment to the second section, which made the final vote four churches in favor to two against.

Section *three* was adopted without amendment.

To section *four* Dr. Engleason moved the following as a substitute: "The Book of Psalms, which is of divine inspiration, is well adapted to the state of the church in all ages and circumstances, and should be used in the worship of God. Therefore, we recommend that a new and faithful version of the Book of Psalms be provided as soon as practicable. But inasmuch as various collections of psalmody are used in the different churches, a change in this respect shall not be required."

The *fifth* article was laid on the table.

Of the resolutions, the first, third, and fourth were adopted.

The *second* was amended so as to read: "As there is so much agreement among all the churches here represented in all essential matters of faith, discipline, and order, it is recommended that friendly and fraternal intercourse be cultivated, by interchange of pulpits, by fellowship with one another in social religious meetings, and in every practicable way."

An address to all the Presbyterian churches, defining the importance of the action of the Convention, and requesting all interested in the subject to stand by the union, was read. It met with the approbation of the members.

The Convention voted by *Churches*, and on the adoption of the Basis as a whole, the final vote stood:

Old School, unanimous.
New School, unanimous.
United Presbyterian, 10 for, and 1 against.
Reformed Presbyterian, 5 for and 4 against.
Reformed Dutch, unanimous.
Cumberland Presbyterian, declined voting.

The Report was declared adopted by the Churches voting *unanimously*.

The only delegate from the South, in the Convention, was Professor A. D. Hepburn. He appeared with credentials of his appointment from the Presbytery of Orange, Synod of North Carolina.

TEMPERANCE.

1.—National Temperance Society and Publication House.

The Principal Temperance Society in the United States is the National Temperance Society and Publication House, which was organized in 1865. State societies are working in co-operation with it in New York, Connecticut, New Hampshire, Vermont, New Jersey, Pennsylvania, Indiana, Ohio, and auxiliary societies have also been organized in the cities of New-

York, Brooklyn, Philadelphia, Detroit, Dayton, Newark, Chicago, etc.

It is in friendly communication with the Sons of Temperance and the Good Templars, which together number some four hundred thousand members and six thousand Lodges and Divisions. A society auxiliary to this society has been formed among the members of Congress; from which salutary results are hoped. The society, with its auxiliaries, has worked earnestly, since its organization, to revive the cause of temperance and cultivate the sentiment in favor of it, and for legislation to more effectually repress the traffic in intoxicating drinks. "During the past year," also says the report, "the cause of temperance for the children has been pressed upon the attention of ministers, Sabbath-school teachers, parents, and others, with more than usual earnestness and persistency, and with the most gratifying results. Large numbers of children and youth have been gathered into the several Bands of Hope and juvenile temperance organizations, now rapidly multiplying throughout the country."

The receipts of the society for the year ending April 30, 1867, were $17,959.96, and from all sources, $32,489.55. It publishes two papers, one a children's paper, the joint circulation of which is 41,000 copies monthly, and the aggregate circulation 549,000 copies since the organization of the society. It circulated also during the year, 2,656,000 pages of tracts, and 2,856,000 since its organization. The total number of pages—books, papers, and tracts—published since the formation of the society, is 10,802,700. Eighteen thousand dollars have been raised towards a $100,000 endowment fund.

2.—Sons of Temperance.

The twenty-fifth anniversary of this Order was celebrated this year on the 30th of September, with appropriate ceremonies throughout the United States and the Dominion of Canada. The Order was instituted September 29th, 1842, by sixteen men in the city of New York, and has extended into every State and Territory in the Union, and the British provinces.

During the twenty-five years, it has numbered over a million and a half of men in its ranks, and though its numbers are not as great now as at some former periods, it has been so well organized and disciplined that its power for good to the cause of temperance never was greater than at present.

Ladies now are admitted to full membership in nearly all the States. Youths of both sexes of fourteen years and upward are permitted to join.

3.—United Kingdom Alliance.

The anniversary of this society was held at Manchester on the 22d of October. The report stated that the work of the Alliance in Scotland was never in a more promising condition than at the present moment. In Ireland there had been an unusually active and healthy agitation. In London there had been a series of demonstrations to bring the principles of the Alliance before public notice. At no former stage of the agitation had the press showed greater willingness to receive information. At the meeting of the British Association at Dundee, and at the Social Science Congress at Belfast, the principles of the Alliance had been ably supported; and the questions of temperance and the liquor traffic had arrested the attention of church congresses and annual conferences of religious denominations. Among collateral efforts had been a conference of influential friends of teetotalism at Exeter Hall. The licensing system had again forced itself on the attention of Parliament. Good results were hoped from the future consideration in Parliament of bills to regulate public houses, &c. The committee had nothing to do with the Sunday-sales bill. The public-house closing acts of 1864-5 had worked in a beneficial and satisfactory manner. Efforts had been made in contested elections to secure the return of members favorable to the cause. The committee had received several suggestions of compromise, but refused to be influenced by them. Of the £5,000 five years' agitation fund, £1,500 have been collected. The total receipts for the year were £14,510. The present condition and prospects of the Alliance are regarded as very promising. Resolutions were adopted to work in behalf of temperance with the new voters enfranchised by the Reform bill, in favor of medical treatment of patients on the non-alcoholic system, calling upon all patriotic, moral, and religious men to aid the Alliance in its efforts to banish intemperance from the land, and calling upon the government to deal with the question.

The principal speech was by Archbishop Manning, mover of the third resolution, in favor of it. Neal Dow and William L. Garrison, of the United States, were present and spoke.

4.—The Temperance Cause on the Continent of Europe.

The following is a summary of a report presented by the Rev. L. Nippert before the last session of the German and Swiss Methodist Mission Conference:

In Prussia, temperance societies have existed since 1837, and a journal (the *Mancherlei gegen den Branntwein*) is issued by two of them. The Königsberg Society, which is the central point of all the temperance operations in Eastern and Western Prussia, has published for twenty-seven years the organ for all the societies of those parts of Prussia, the Rhine provinces, and Westphalia. The provinces of Posen, Pomerania, and Saxony, are influenced by the Berlin Society. In Hanover there is a society which publishes its paper, and throughout the kingdom (now become Prussian) great success has crowned the efforts of the advocates of temperance. In Holland, the cause has been rapidly progressing for twenty-five years, and the most distinguished and prominent men in the country are identified with it. In England and Scotland there are over one hundred societies, while Father Matthew's labors are still bearing good fruit in Ireland. In Sweden, King Oscar abolished all the distilleries in the crown lands, and thereby, within the space of twenty years, the one hundred and seventy thousand distilleries have been reduced to only two hundred, and the manufacture of fifty million quarts of brandy has been reduced to from ten to fourteen millions. In Denmark, the principal preacher, Visly, of Storchedniz, Zealand has been carrying on the battle against brandy for twenty-five years; yet he gets but little sympathy, since the so-called "believers" stand up against him, and the ruling ecclesiastical party (which is the

High-Lutheran) are unanimous in their opposition to the clergy taking part in the affair, and such clergymen as show any favor toward temperance are persecuted, calumniated, and charged with being apostates from Christ. In Russia, where drunkenness abounds to an alarming extent, there have been at least some successful efforts for its decrease. In Switzerland, where whole cantons are now in danger of being morally and physically ruined by drinking brandy and other strong liquors, temperance societies have already been organized.

All these societies proclaim war against distilled liquors alone, and do not touch the question of beer and wine.

——o——

NEW YORK SABBATH COMMITTEE.

The New York Sabbath Committee was organized in 1857. Its object is, by personal influence, by the aid of the pulpit and the press, and in all judicious, prudent, and practicable methods, to promote the proper observance of the Sabbath. It seeks the enforcement of the Sunday laws, and the enactment of new ones, where they appear to be necessary. In its prominent movements it has had the aid of nearly all the religious and many of the secular journals of New York. The result of its labors are thus summed up: "Information gathered in regard to the Sunday Laws of New York, and the alarming extent of Sabbath desecration; the suppression of Sunday desecration in the Central Park: of Sunday public parades and pageants; of Sunday theatres and other Sunday nuisances; protection of the Sabbath interest in the Army and Navy during the war, culminating in the issue of President Lincoln's famous Sabbath Order to the Army and Navy, in 1862 (this order was prepared by the Sabbath Committee, and adopted by the President as his own); the National Sabbath Convention at Saratoga in 1863; nearly 100 sermons on Sunday observance preached by the Secretary during 1861 and 1866, in German and English churches in New York and the surrounding cities; seven German mass meetings in New York and vicinity, in favor of Sabbath observance; help to Sabbath movements in other States and in Europe, rendered in various ways; and in the suppression of the Sunday liquor traffic through the Metropolitan Excise law of 1856, and by obtaining decisions of the Supreme Court and the Court of Appeals against Sunday theatres and in favor of the Excise law. The Excise law is the crowning triumph of the cause of Sunday Observance. It has been well enforced, and with perceptible results in the comfort of citizens, public order, and the diminution of crime and arrests on Sunday. The evidence of official reports on this subject is decisive." Efforts similar to those of this Committee have been made in other cities with different degrees of success, and in Europe, where, particularly in Prussia and other portions of Germany, considerable progress has been made towards the adoption of the American idea of the Sabbath. The Committee, during the ten years of its existence, has published and circulated 34 original Sabbath documents and other works.

——o——

RELIGIOUS TRACT SOCIETIES.

1.—American Tract Society, New York.

During the year 126 new publications have been stereotyped or electrotyped, in English, German, Danish, Swedish, Italian, Spanish, Portuguese, Hawaiian, and the Gilbert Islands language, of which 37 are volumes, making the whole number of publications on the Society's list 3,784, of which 765 are volumes of larger or smaller size. Forty-one publications have been approved to be issued at foreign stations, making the whole number approved for publication abroad, 3,798, of which 523 are volumes. The three periodicals of the Society—the *American Messenger*, the *Botschafter* (German), and the *Child's Paper*—have an aggregate monthly circulation of 502,000 copies, and the total circulation of the three for the year has been 6,097,500 copies.

The total receipts for the year have been $515,131.13, of which $159,800.47 have been from donations and legacies, and $384,350.96. The expenditures were $544,343 24.

The Society have realized $57,000 of a sum of $100,000 which they are trying to raise from voluntary contributions. Two hundred and nineteen colporteurs have been employed, in twenty-one States of the Union and the British Provinces. They have sold and given away 10,876,672 volumes, addressed public meetings and held prayer-meetings to the number of 228,846, conversed or prayed with 5,834,990 families, and paid 9,595,657 family visits.

The total amount of publications circulated since the formation of the Society is 21,028,680 volumes, 280,911,656 publications.

The Society has branches or agencies at Boston, Philadelphia, Rochester, Richmond, Va., Cincinnati, Chicago, and St. Louis. In connection with the Rochester agency six colporteurs have been employed in Canada West, who have visited about 7,000 families, held 189 religious meetings, and circulated, by sale and grant, $3,642.36 worth of publications. The Society has expended in Canada, during nineteen years, $42,303.78, employed 187 colporteurs, who have made 223,617 family visits, and distributed 291,360 volumes.

A beginning of work has been made in Mexico and South America.

Ten thousand dollars have been granted to foreign lands for the year. The total of cash grants to foreign lands, since the organization of the Society, is $553,895.78. Publications have also been granted to foreign lands to the value of $3.500.

The foreign work of the Society is carried on in France (coöperating with the Paris Religious Tract Society). Italy, Hamburg, Denmark, Sweden, Turkey, Syria, Egypt, West and Central Africa, India, China, Micronesia, &c., where it coöperates with the Missionary and other evangelical societies.

2.—American Tract Society, Boston.

The cash receipts of this Society, from all sources, were $160,569.78. Of this, $58,050.10 were from donations, $10,553.46 from legacies. The donations were greater, and the legacies less, than last year. The publications of the Society were: Tracts, in the 12mo series, 1,160,-500 copies; envelope, pocket, and children's tracts, 156,000; leaflets, etc, 234,000. Total, 1.526,500 copies, embracing 6,235,000 pages. Volumes, 359,250, comprising 42,076,500 pages, and papers, 3,103,000 copies. The Society's catalogue now numbers 851 publications in the English, German, Spanish, and Dakota languages. The whole number of publications since the institution of the Society, in 1859, is 16,091,276 copies of books and tracts, with 329,-844,200 pages, and 24.541,700 copies of periodicals. The value of publications granted during the year was $43,500, $4,000 for foreign fields.

The work of the Society among the freedmen is particularly worthy of notice. It has been diligently prosecuted, with most encouraging success. The general work is carried on throughout the United States, in the army and navy, and at foreign mission stations. The work in this country is under the charge of ten district secretaries. Two labor in the New England States, one in New York New Jersey, and Pennsylvania, one is located at Cleveland, Ohio, three in Illinois, Michigan, and Wisconsin, one in Iowa and Minnesota, and one among the freedmen. The secretaryship at Memphis, Tennessee, was vacant at the time of the last annual meeting.

The subject of the union of this with the Society at New York, is under consideration.

3.—Religious Tract Society, London.

Receipts for the year ending March 31st, 1867, £110.774, 19s. 3d. Total grants £13,012, 4s. 11d. Publications during the year, at home and abroad, 46.720,101; total since the foundation of the Society, 1,193,000,000. The foreign work of the Society is prosecuted on the continent of Europe, in the British colonies, and at nearly all points where there are Missionary stations.

4.—Religious Tract Society, Paris.

Receipts (to April, 1866) 69,000 francs, or $19,000 in gold. Publications, 347, in Spanish, German, Italian, and Breton. Sales, 40,000 copies. Total issues since foundation (14 years), 25,006,000.

5.—Other Tract Societies.

[For the operations of the Tract Society of the Methodist Episcopal Church in the United States, see Statistics of Methodist Episcopal Church.

For an account of Baptist tracts published in the United States, see Statistics of Baptists.]

Societies.	Expenditures.	Issues.
English Monthly Tract Soc....	£2[illegible],551	713.515
Weekly " "	873	663,295
Baptist " " ..	--	359,325
Rel. Tract and Book Society of Scotland	—	851,617
Tract Soc. of Methodist Episcopal Church (German Branch, Bremen)............	2,721	587,236
Upper Canada Religious Tract Society......	—	210,641
Religious Tract Soc. of Paris...	1,781	400,000
Basle Christian Book Society..	160	—
Prussian Tract Society........	1,502	137,390
Danish Tract Society	—	137,000

6.—City Mission and Tract Societies.

New York City Mission and Tract Society.

Receipts, $60,000; stations, 14; missionaries 45. who made 118.277 visits; voluntary visitors, 539; tracts distributed, 1,076,779; children led to Sunday schools, 3,722; persons induced to attend church, 10,029.

Brooklyn City Mission and Tract Society.

Receipts, 21,621.60. Twenty missionaries are employed. who have distributed 1,323,032 pages of tracts, made 36,474 visits, and induced 1,148 children to attend Sunday and public schools, and 1,179 to attend church

Boston City Mission.

Missionaries, 21; receipts, $3 994.45; visits 44,247.

Other Societies are the New Jersey, Philadelphia, New Brunswick, Albany, Troy, Utica, Syracuse, Milwaukie, San Francisco, &c.

—o—

SUNDAY SCHOOLS.

1.—American Sunday School Union.

The object of the American Sunday School Union, which is now in the forty-fourth year of its existence, is to establish and carry on Sunday Schools of an undenominational character. It has agents in all the States, whose zeal and success are well represented by the summary of the work for the year previous to the last Anniversary, in May, which is as follows:

Schools organized	1,671
Teachers in the same................	10,559

Scholars	67,204
Schools visited and addressed	6,090
Teachers in the same	45,175
Scholars	351,485
Whole number of schools organized and aided	7,761
Teachers in service	55,734
Scholars	418,689
Families visited	35,924
Bibles and Testaments distributed	9,621
Miles traveled	314,410
Grants made to needy Sunday-schools	$15,331.98
Addresses delivered	8,602

The receipts of the Society during the year, were $108,833.25. The whole number of the Society's publications exceeds fifteen hundred.

The following is an exhibit of the mission work of the Society for the last eleven years:

New schools organized	18,983
Teachers enlisted	121,378
Children gathered in	775,981
Other schools visited and aided	33,441
Children in attendance	1,545,438
Whole number of children	2,531,820
Amount granted to poor schools	$102,992.54

The usefulness of the Society is indicated by the statement in its last report, that an examination of the statistical returns of the several States, where a Sunday-school canvass has been made, shows that in no State are one-half of the children and youth regular attendants of the Sabbath-school, and in some of our Western and Southern States the large majority are beyond the reach of any organized church.

2.—Sunday School Union of England.

The total number of schools, teachers, and scholars now connected with the Union, are as follows:

	Schools.	Teachers.	Scholars.
9 Metropolitan auxiliaries	670	14,920	166,036
162 Country Unions	2,679	67,970	500,683
Total	3,869	82,890	660,719
Increase from last year	26	1,175	12,924

The income of the benevolent fund (exclusive of the Continental fund, was £2,432. 11s. 2d. The subscriptions to the Continental fund were £122, 0s., 11d. The sales at the Depository amounted to £22,339 13s., 4d., being an increase of over £700 from last year. 472 lending libraries were granted to schools containing 111 876 scholars, of whom 75,253 were Scripture readers.

The Society supports agencies in Germany, Holland, Switzerland, and other points on the continent, and assists the Paris Society in supporting a missionary agent.

3.—The Continent of Europe.

The first Sunday School in France was formed at Bordeaux in 1815. Now there are 874 schools, with about 3,500 children.

The Sunday School movement makes progress in Germany. There are now 10 schools in Berlin, with 3,490 children and 284 teachers, and 31 in other parts of Germany, with 2,746 children and 260 teachers.

CENTENARY OF AMERICAN METHODISM.

The year 1866, being the centenary, or hundredth anniversary of the establishment of Methodism in the United States, was celebrated by the several denominations of Methodists, and particularly by the Methodist Episcopal Church, by extraordinary exertions to raise funds for various church purposes, and for the endowment of Biblical schools, colleges, and academics, and for local objects. Meetings were held in all the churches, and subscriptions taken. The success of the movement was truly wonderful, and exceeded all anticipations.

The General Conference of the Methodist Episcopal Church, at its session of 1864, decided that the thank-offerings of the Church during the centenary year should be divided into two general classes—Connectional and Local. The connectional objects designated are as follows:

1. The Centenary Educational Fund.
2. The Garrett Biblical School at Evanston.
3. The Methodist General Biblical Institute at Concord, to be removed to the vicinity of Boston.
4. A Biblical Institute in the Eastern Middle States.
5. A Biblical Institute in Cincinnati or vicinity.
6. A Biblical Institute on the Pacific coast.
7. The erection of Centenary Missionary Buildings for the Mission House at New York.
8. The Irish Connectional Fund.
9. The Biblical School at Bremen, Germany.
10. The Chartered Fund. (Such sums as contributors may desire to appropriate in that way to the support of worn-out preachers, their widows and orphans).
11. The Sunday School Children's Fund. (A fund to be raised by the Sunday-school children of the Church, the interest of which should be devoted to aiding meritorious Sunday-school scholars in obtaining a more advanced education.)

It was decided that the Local Funds should be appropriated to the cause of education and church extension under the direction of a committee, consisting of an equal number of ministers and laymen, appointed by the several Annual Conferences within the bounds of which they are raised.

The following gentlemen were appointed as a "Central Centenary Committee": J M'Clintock, D D., D. Curry, D.D., G. R. Crooks D D., Oliver Hoyt, Esq., James Bishop, Esq., C. C. North, Esq. Rev. W. C. Hoyt, Secretary.

The reports of the amounts of contributions

have not yet (November, 1867,) been completed and classified. Enough has been returned, however, to give an approximate idea of the amounts that have been realized, and the proportions in which they will be applied to the various designated objects.

The fullest estimate yet given appeared in the *Methodist* of November 23d. The returns from which the aggregates were computed were all incomplete. Hence the aggregates cannot be made to agree. The sums given will in all cases be exceeded by the complete returns when they are made. The aggregates as given are as follows:

Grand totals from 45 Conferences.	$6,931,255.96
Totals for connectional objects, from 22 Conferences....	767,011.04
Totals for local objects, from 23 Conferences....................	4,092,572.99
SPECIFIC OBJECTS:	
Centenary Education fund, 18 Conferences..........	9.195.36
Garrett Biblical Institute, 9 Conf.	11,426.22
[To this $100.000 of the contributions of the New England Conference should be added.]	
Drew Theological Institute, 2 Conf.	500.016.00
General Biblical Institute (at Boston)	11,426 22
New York Mission House, 15 Conf.	68.9"6 40
Irish Connectional fund, 14 Conf..	29,768.53
Biblical School in Germany, 12 Conferences.....................	1,675.00
Chartered fund, 15 Conferences..	12,639.35
Sunday-school Children's fund, 12 Conferences...........	27,846.79
Not designated, 10 Conferences...	27,538.63
Church Extension, 14 Conferences.	9,445,298.95
Payment of Church and Parsonage debts, 7 Conferences............	212,575.27
Colleges and Schools, and local education, 17 Conferences.........	750.082.23
Preachers' Aid Societies, 5 Conf..	15,704 20
Other objects	42,533.25

---o---

CHURCH AND STATE.--PROGRESS OF RELIGIOUS LIBERTY.

Upon the establishment of independence, the United States made the absolute separation of Church and State, and the legal equality of all forms of religion, one of their fundamental institutions. Thus, a new principle was formally established in the Protestant world, and the history of this principle since that time constitutes one of the most interesting portions of modern Church history. Great political events, such as the revolutionary movements of 1789, 1830, and 1848, gave powerful impulses to this movement which is now being vigorously carried on throughout Europe. Progres has been made in every country, though the final goal has not yet been attained.

In the *United States* all political and ecclesiastical parties agree that the right of every citizen to worship God according to the dictates of his own conscience shall not be curtailed, and that the voluntary principle in church affairs shall be maintained.

Full religious freedom also exists in *British America*, although the separation between church and state is not yet fully carried out.

In *Latin America*, the Roman Catholic Church is almost every where the only form of religion acknowledged by the state. But full religious liberty has been proclaimed in the United States of *Colombia* and in the Republic of *Mexico*, and will undoubtedly be reinforced in the latter country. In *Chili*, in 1866, and in *Peru*, in 1867, the enlargement of religious toleration was the subject of a very animated discussion, which materially advanced the cause of religious freedom. In *Brazil* and the *Argentine Republic*, religious toleration is practically established, and the number of Protestants is rapidly increasing in consequence of a steady influx of emigrants from Northern America and from Europe.

In *England*, the personal right of religious freedom is as firmly established and as generally acknowledged as in the United States. The State Church still enjoys enormous privileges; but no year passes in which Parliament does not reduce, or at least assail, these privileges, and in which not some progress is made towards the final separation of Church and State.

Holland and *Belgium* enjoy full liberty of religion, and the separation between Church and State is nearly accomplished.

In *France* the right of religious opinion is secured to the individual; but religious meeting suffer from a restrictive legislation, as well as political meetings, and the State vigorously maintains its control of the state churches, denying, in particular, to the Reformed Church the right of reorganizing the General Synod.

In *Germany*, the absorption of the minor States by the North German Confederation, has put an end to the persecution to which many Christian sects were exposed in some of the minor States. Religious toleration is making steady progress; public opinion strongly expresses itself in favor of universal religious liberty; and the prospective consolidation of the Protestant State Churches into one, will bring, if not the full separation between Church and State, at least a larger degree of ecclesiastical self-government. In *Austria*, the "Reichsrath" (Parliament) was, in 1867, almost a unit in demanding the abolition of the Concordat of 1855, which secured to the Roman Catholic Church many privileges, and in asking equality of civil rights for the professors of every kind of religious belief. The Hungarian Diet expresses views equally liberal.

Denmark is in possession of full religious liberty, and the separation between Church and State makes progress. *Sweden* has repealed part of her intolerant legislation against Catholics and Baptists; and *Switzerland* is becoming liberal toward the Jews.

Italy firmly adheres to the independence of the secular government in the regulation of church affairs, and to the principle of religious freedom; and some of her leading statesmen have declared for the absolute separation between Church and State, as it exists in the United States.

In *Portugal*, public opinion expresses itself

in favor of religious toleration, but *Spain* continues to forbid every public form of worship except that of the Roman Catholic Church.

Russia still disgraces herself by bloody edicts of persecution against Catholics; although her legislation with regard to Protestants has become somewhat more tolerant.

The Christian tribes of *Turkey* are preparing to shake off the yoke of the Mohammedans, but they deny the liberty which they claim for themselves to the Jews, who, in several of the Christian provinces of Turkey, have suffered a terrible persecution. In *Egypt*, the Coptic Patriarch instituted a furious persecution against the Protestant American Missionaries and their adherents among the Copts. For a long time the Egyptian government encouraged this persecution, until at length the Consul-General of the United States caused it to be stopped.

In *Japan* the government severely persecuted the descendants of the former Christians, who, in consequence of the friendly relations now existing between Japan and the Christian countries, had thought it safe to show their religious faith. It was hoped that the influence of France would put an end to this persecution. In all other missionary fields, the toleration of the native Christians was not disturbed.

On the whole, therefore, it may be said that the cause of religious toleration and liberty is making steady progress, and that the time seems to draw near when religious persecution will belong among the things of the past.

——o——

THE CHURCH, THE SLAVERY QUESTION, AND THE FREEDMEN.

1—American Churches North and South.

In consequence of the different views entertained with regard to slavery, and the right of church and state to pass ordinances for its abolition, a split gradually arose between the churches in the Northern and Southern sections of the United States. In 1844 the great division in the Methodist Episcopal Church occurred, and the Methodist Episcopal Church South was established. In 1845, the Southern Baptist Convention was organized, and in 1847 the Southern Baptist Publication Society. In 1857, the Southern Presbyteries of the New School Presbyterian Church organized the United Synod of the Presbyterian Church. After the beginning of the war, the Southern Presbyteries of the Old School Presbyterian Church, the Southern Dioceses of the Protestant Episcopal Church, and some of the Southern Synods of the Lutherans, effected independent Southern organizations. Where no formal division occurred in a church, there was, of course, an interruption of communication between the Northern and Southern branches. After the war, a movement began in many quarters for reuniting the separated churches. There are quite a number of churches who are now fully united; such are the Protestant Episcopal Church, the Cumberland Presbyterians, the German Reformed Church, the Friends, the Swedenborgians, and the Roman Catholics.

There is another class of religious denominations which before the war had hardly any representation in the former slave States, and which since then have begun to extend southward, and to prepare for the establishment of congregations in every State of the Union. The aggregate of the new congregations of these denominations in the former slave States already represents a considerable aggregate of members. Thus the Congregationalists, who, beside an isolated church in Charleston, had, in 1860, only two or three churches in Missouri, have now, in the latter State alone, upward of forty churches, and have established themselves in all the large cities of the South. The United Brethren in Christ have established new conferences in Kentucky and Tennessee. The United Presbyterians have organized a new Southern Presbytery, and the Free Will Baptists and others now support missions in several States which were formerly not occupied by them.

As regards, finally, those churches which have long been separated by difference of views on the slavery question, they have all begun, more or less, to outgrow their sectional organization, and to assume national dimensions. It is mostly the churches of the Northern section which grow southward; though also, on the other hand, the Southern churches begin, in some instances, to expand northward. In this respect, the greatest progress has been made by the Methodist Episcopal Church. In 1860, the Southern congregations of the Methodist Episcopal Church were mostly scattered at a short distance from the boundary line between North and South, in Missouri, Kentucky, and Maryland, now the Church has a firm organization in almost every Southern State, with a number of new Annual Conferences (Virginia and North Carolina, South Carolina, Alabama, Georgia, Tennessee, Mississippi) and a membership of more than one hundred thousand, mostly white members.

The New School Presbyterian Church has reörganized the Synod of Tennessee with three Presbyteries; while the Old-School Church has Presbyteries fully organized in North Carolina, South Carolina, and Tennessee, with a prospect of additions in other States.

The Southern Methodist Church, on the other hand, has absorbed a part of the Baltimore Conference of the Methodist Episcopal Church. It has, moreover, organized, in 1867, an Annual Conference in Oregon ("Columbia Conference"), and another in Illinois, the latter from congregations formerly belonging to the "Christian Union," a new religious denomination established since the beginning of the war, and sympathizing with the views held by the Southern churches on the subject of slavery. In a like manner the Southern Presbyterian churches, in 1867, received additions from Presbyteries in Maryland, Kentucky, and Missouri, and may annex others even more northward, among those who prefer the position of the Southern Presbyterian Church to that of the Northern.

A large portion of the colored population of the Southern churches has, since the end of the war, either connected itself with Northern churches or joined independent African churches. The African Methodist Episcopal Church, which, in 1860, reported a membership of about 20,000, now claims upwards of 200,000 members, the additions being almost exclusively in the Southern States. The African Methodist Episcopal Zion Church had, in 1860, only 6,000 members, which have now increased to upwards of 50,000. The Baptist colored churches have in many States been organized into independent Associations, and annually hold a General Convention. In Georgia, some colored Presbyterian churches have organized themselves into an independent Presbytery, and the organization of a colored Protestant Episcopal Church has been discussed. In Tennessee, a colored Conference is to be organized in connection with the Methodist Episcopal Church South.

Thus, while a part of colored church members remain in connection with the Southern churches, another part prefer incorporation with the churches of the North; and still another part—as far as we can judge, by far the largest—deems it best to join independent colored church organizations.

2.—Education of Freedmen.

After the abolition of slavery in the Southern States, nearly all the American churches, both North and South, paid a particular care to the religious instruction of the Freedmen, and many of them have organized special committees on Freedmen.

The fourth Annual Report on Schools for Freedmen was made on July 1, by J. M. Alvord, General Superintendent of Schools, in the Bureau of Refugees, Freedmen, and Abandoned Lands. We learn from this report that there are officially reported 1839 day and night schools; 2087 teachers, and 111,442 pupils; showing an increase since the last report of 632 schools, 657 teachers, and 33,444 pupils.

By adding industrial schools, and those "within the knowledge of the superintendent," the number will be 2207 schools, 2442 teachers, and 130,735 pupils; making a total increase of 908 schools, 784 teachers, and 40,222 pupils.

Sabbath-schools also show much larger numbers during the past six months, the figures being 1126 schools, and 80,647 pupils; and if we add those "not regularly reported," the whole number of Sabbath-schools will be 1468, with 105,786 pupils; thus giving an increase since last report of 686 schools, and 35,176 pupils.

TOTALS.

Schools of all kinds, as reported.......	3,695
Pupils..................................	238,345

TOTAL INCREASE FOR THE LAST SIX MONTHS.

Schools.................................	1,503
Pupils..................................	76,638

Of the above schools, 1055 are sustained wholly or in part by the freedmen, and 391 of the buildings in which these schools are held are owned by themselves. 699 of the teachers in the day and night schools are colored, and 1388 white—a small proportionate increase of the former during the six months.

28,068 colored pupils have paid tuition. The average amount per month being $14.555, or a fraction over 51 cents per scholar. Only 6911 of the pupils were free before the war.

This Bureau has supplied four hundred and twenty-eight of the school buildings, and furnished nine hundred and seventy teachers with transportation. The total expenditure for all educational purposes by the Bureau has been $220,833.01.

The following is an incomplete list of papers published, in 1867, by and for colored people:

The *Elevator*, at San Francisco, circulates 2,300 copies; *The Pacific Appeal*; *The New Orleans Tribune*, daily and weekly, circulates about 10,000 of each issue; *The True Communicator*, at Baltimore; *Zion's Standard and Weekly Review*, published at New York, edited by William Howard Day (colored), circulates 4,000 copies; *The Christian Recorder*, Philadelphia, published by the African Methodist Episcopal Church, and edited by Rev. James Lynch, a man of color, circulates 5,000; *The People's Journal*, Brooklyn, edited and printed by a colored man, circulates 2,000, and the *Freedman's Torchlight*, are both published by the African Colonization Society; *The Colored Citizen*, issued at Cincinnati, Ohio, circulates 2,400 copies, and is under the entire control of colored men.

3.—The Paris Anti-Slavery Conference.

The Anti-Slavery Conference convened by the Comité Francais d' Emancipation, the Spanish Abolitionist Society, and the British and Foreign Anti-Slavery Society, met at Paris on the 26th and 27th of August, 1867. M. Laboulaye, President of the French society, presided. Delegates were present from the United States, Porto Rico, Brazil, Hayti, Liberia, Sierra Leone, Spain, Great Britain, France, the South American Republics, Russia, Italy, Jamaica, &c. Letters of adhesion were also read from several members of the British Parliament and other well-known friends of the Anti-Slavery movement, at home and abroad. A resolution, embodying several arguments based on what is proven by experience, was read by Prof. Horn, of the Ecole de Commerce, urging the abolition of the slave-trade and slavery, which are still practiced by Spain, Portugal, Brazil, Turkey, Egypt, and the Transvaal Republic, South Africa, besides uncivilized countries. It also proposed an address to the Pope, urging him to follow the example of his predecessors, and raise his voice in favor of the unhappy slaves held in Catholic countries. M. Elisé Reclus, of the *Revue des Deux Mondes*, proposed also a series of resolutions denouncing all institutions, laws, customs, and prejudices growing out of slavery. Among those who spoke on the resolutions was Senor Beraza, one of the Spanish delegates, who asserted that the Cubans and Porto Ricans were favorable to emancipation, but the government would not accede to the demand for it; and Senor Olozaga, another Spanish delegate, who said that heretofore the Spanish government had been pressed from without for emancipation, but that now the pressure came from within, from the colonies themselves, a fact which he regarded as unprecedented and highly encouraging. Bishop Payne, of the African M. E. Church of the United States, spoke of the results of emancipation so far as the negroes belonging to his denomination were concerned. An address was delivered also by William Lloyd Garrison, of the United States, and by J. G.

Palfrey. M. le Général Dubois gave an outline of the history of Hayti, and vindicated the people calumniated by the allegation that they are incompetent of self-government. A second resolution was adopted of thanks to the Almighty for emancipation in the United States and Russia; also acknowledging the merits of statesmen and philanthropists who have contributed to emancipation, to the travelers and missionaries who are exploring and evangelizing Africa, and to the organs of the press of all countries who have aided anti-slavery principles.

——o——

THE CHURCHES AND SECRET SOCIETIES.--STATISTICS OF FREE-MASONRY.

A considerable number of Christian churches forbid their members to join secret societies, and this question continues to be discussed in the church assemblies with considerable animation. This prohibition is especially directed against the Free-Masons.

Among the churches which vigorously enforce the prohibition to join secret societies are the American Wesleyans and the United Brethren in Christ. When the former, in 1866, endeavored to form a union with the Methodist Protestants, the non-concurrence of the latter body in prohibitory measures against Freemasonry was one of the reasons why the union movement proved a failure. The quadrennial General Conference of the Wesleyan Connection, in 1867, by an overwhelming majority, reaffirmed its old position on this question. The question is also agitated in other denominations; and some Presbyteries, Congregational Conferences and Lutheran Synods have, in 1867, taken decided ground against Freemasonry.

An "Anti-Secret Society Convention" met at Aurora, Ill., on Oct. 31. The Convention consisted of eighty members, from five different States, representing ten evangelical denominations (Wesleyans, United Brethren in Christ, Free Methodists, Baptists, Congregationalists, etc.) Resolutions were adopted declaring the secret orders hostile, in their nature, to the Christian religion, and a National Convention of Christians was resolved on, to meet some time next May.

In the Roman Catholic Church Free-Masons are excommunicated; and the present Pope, in 1865, issued a very severe encyclical against the society, and called the attention of the church members to the ecclesiastical censures incurred by all Free-Masons. But numerous lodges have, nevertheless, been established in all the Roman Catholic countries. Only Austria and Spain continued to conform their legislation to that of the Roman Catholic Church. But in Austria the prohibition was repealed in 1867. The Spanish government, on the other hand, tried to enforce its legislation by prosecuting the members of the lodges in Cuba, in which island there are about twenty lodges.

The following is a list of Grand Lodges of Freemasons in 1866, together with the number of affiliated lodges, as far as the same was known:

LIST OF GRAND LODGES, WITH NUMBER OF AFFILIATED LODGES, IN 1866.

1. *United States.*

Grand Lodges.	Affiliated Lodges.
Alabama	325
Arkansas	—
California	163
Colorado	7
Colombia	13
Connecticut	70
Delaware	13
" colored	9
Florida	—
Georgia	—
Illinois	395
Indiana	285
Iowa	152
Kansas	37
Kentucky	324
Louisiana	128
Maine	112
Maryland	41
" colored	6
Massachusetts	143
" col'd.	—
Michigan	169
Minnesota	—
Mississippi	—
Missouri	229
Nebraska	—
Nevada	8
New Brunswick	—
New Hampshire	52
New Jersey	67
" colored	—
New York	523
" city col'd.	6
North Carolina	—
Ohio	318
" colored	—
Oregon	28
Pennsylvania	174
" col'd.	21
Rhode Island	16
South Carolina	—
Tennessee	—
Texas	109
Vermont	63
Virginia	—
Washington	10
West Virginia	9
Wisconsin	127
	4152

2. *In Other Countries.*

Grand Lodge	Affiliated
G. L. Toronto, Canada	170
G. L. Halifax, Nova Scotia	10
G. O. Lima, Peru	8
G. O. Valparaiso, Chili	4
G. O. Rio Janeiro, Brazil	84
G. O. Caracas, Venezuela	15
G. L. Montevideo, Uruguay	97
G. L. Buenos Ayres, Argentine Republic	—
G. L. Santiago de Cuba	—
G. L. Port-au-Prince, Hayti	—
G. L. to the 3 Globes, Berlin, Prussia	103
N. L. Berlin, Prussia	70
Royal York, Berlin, Prussia	29
G. L. Hamburg	25
G. L. Bayreuth, Bavaria	13
G. L. Dresden, Saxony	17
G. L. Frankfort on the Main, Prussia	10
G. L. Hanover, Prussia	22
G. L. Darmstadt, Hesse-Darmstadt	2
G. L. Berne, Switzerland	28
G. L. London, England	1058
G. L. Edinburgh, Scotland	386
G. L. Dublin, Ireland	319
G. L. the Hague, Holland	58
S. C. Luxemburg, Luxemburg	2
G. L. Stockholm, Sweden	19
G. L. Copenhagen, Denmark	5
G. L. Brussels, Belgium	—
S. C. " "	14
G. O. Florence, Italy	87
G. L. Lisbon, Portugal	1
G. O. Paris, France	248
S. C. " "	10

[G. L. stands for Grand Lodge; G. O. for Grand Orient; S. C. for Supreme Council, and N. L. for National Lodge.]

FOREIGN MISSIONS.

I. The Protestant Missionary Societies of the World.

We give below a list of Protestant missionary societies with the year of their foundation and the mission fields occupied by each. More information on most of the American Societies, may be found under the head of denominational statistics; on some of the more important European Societies we subjoin a statement of their operations to the list of the Societies.

1.—*American Missionary Societies.*

1. The American Board of Commissioners for Foreign Missions. 1810. East Indies, South Africa, Turkey, China, Polynesia, North America.

2. The Baptist Missionary Union. 1814. Burmah, Farther India, Siam, China.

3. The Methodist Episcopal Miss. Soc. 1819. West Africa, India, China, North and South America, Polynesia.

4. The Episcopal Board of Missions. 1820. North America. West Africa, China, Japan.

5. The Free-Will Baptist For. Miss. Soc. 1843. India.

6 The Board of For. Miss. of the Presbyterian Church. 1837. West Africa, India, Siam, China, Japan, North and South America.

7. Foreign Mission of the Reformed Presbyterian Synod. Syria.

8. Lutheran Missionary Society. 1837. India, West Africa.

9. Seventh-Day-Baptist Miss. Soc. 1842. China.

10. American Indian Miss. Association. 1842. North America.

11. The Baptist Free Miss. Soc. 1843. West Indies.

12. The United Presbyterian Board of Missions. 1844. India, Turkey, Polynesia.

13. Mission of the German Lutheran Synod of Iowa (?) North America

14. The Southern Baptist Convention Board of Miss. 1845. West Africa, China.

15. The Southern Methodist For. Miss. 1846. North America, China.

16. The American Miss. Association. 1846. North America. West Indies. Egypt, Siam, Polynesia.

17. The Reformed Protestant Dutch Church's For. Miss. 1857. India, China, Japan.

18. Foreign Mission of United Brethren in Christ. Africa.

19. American Church Missionary Society, 1859. U. S. of Columbia.

20. The Board of Foreign Missions of the Presbyterian Church of Nova Scotia. 1848. New Hebrides.

21. The Micmac Missionary Society. Nova Scotia.

2.—*British Missionary Societies.*

22. Society for the Propagation of the Gospel in Foreign Parts. 1701. East and West Indies, South Africa, Australia, New Zealand, North America.

23. The Baptist Miss. Soc. 1792. East and West Indies, West Africa, China.

24 The London Miss. Soc. 1795. South Sea East and West Indies, South Africa, Madagascar.

25. The Church Miss. Soc. 1800. East and West Indies, Turkey, China, New Zealand, West Africa, Mauritius, Madagascar, North America.

26. The General Baptist Miss. Soc. 1816. East Indies, China.

27. The Wesleyan (Methodist) Miss. Soc. 1817. East and West Indies, West and South Africa, China, Australia, Polynesia. North America.

28. Established Church of Scotland's Foreign Miss. 1824. East Indies. (£55 5, 13 missionaries, 116 native agents, 5 stations, 250 communicants.)

29. Society for promoting Female Education in the East. 1834.

30. Welsh Foreign Miss. Soc. 1840. East Indies (Silbet).

31. The Irish Presbyterian Church's For. Miss. 1840. East Indies. (Gugjerat). Syria. (7 missionaries, 6 stations, 300 communicants.)

32. The Edinburgh Medical Miss. Soc. 1841.

33. The Reformed Presbyterian Church's For. Miss. 1842. New Hebrides.

34. The Free Church of Scotland's For. Miss. 1843. East Indies, South Africa. (£15,751. 22 missionaries, 70 stations, 144 native agents).

35. The English Presbyterian For. Miss. 1844, China, East Indies. (£3907. 107 missionaries.)

36. The South American (Patagonian) Miss. Soc. 1844. South America. (£7132. 10 stations.)

37. The United Presbyterian Church's For. Miss. 1847. East and West Indies. West and South Africa. (£21,296. 28 missionaries, 121 native agents, 740 communicants).

38. The Chinese Evangelization Soc. 1850. China.

39. The Primitive Methodist Miss. Soc. 1858.

39. The Free United Methodist Miss. Soc. 1860. East and West Africa.

40. The Moslem Miss. Soc. 1860. Syria, Egypt. (£2623. 120 native agents.)

41 The Universities Miss. Soc. 1861. East Africa.

42. The Foreign Evangelist Soc. 1864. (£1890).

44. Methodist New Connexion Missionary Society.

45. Foreign Aid Society. (£2002. 3s 8d.)

46. Evangelical Continental Society (£2466 2s 8d.)

3.—*German Missionary Societies.*

47. Mission of the Evangelical Moravian Brotherhood. 1732. Greenland, Labrador, North America, West Indies, South Africa, Australia. Thibet.

48. Evang. Miss. at Bale. 1815. West Africa, India, China.

49. Society for the Advancement of Evangelical Missions at Berlin. 1823. South Africa. (£7421).

50. Rhenish Miss. Soc. at Barmen. 1828. South Africa, Holland, East Indies, China.

51. North Ger. Miss. Soc. of Bremen. 1835. West Africa, New Zealand. (£3707. 29 agents, 28 stations.)

52. Evangelical Lutheran Missionary Society, of Leipsic. 1836. India. (£1477).

53. Gossner's Evangelical Missionary Union of Berlin. 1842. Farther India, Holland, India, Australia. (£4175. 4 Missionaries.)

54. Berlin Woman's Missions for China. 1852 China. (£857 4 Missionaries.)

55. Berlin Man's Union for China. 1852. China (£771. 1 agent.)

56. Hermannsburg Missionary Society. 1854, South Africa, India. (31 missionaries)

57. Pilgrim's Mission of St. Krischona near Bale—Palestine, Abyssinia.

58. Kaiserswerth Deaconesses Institute. Asia Minor, Syria, Egypt.

59. Jerusalem Union at Berlin. Asia Minor Syria, Egypt. (£953.)

4.—Dutch Missionary Societies.

60. Netherland Missionary Society at Rotterdam. 1797. Ambon. Minahassa, South Celebes, Java. (£6926. 24 missionaries.)

61. The Java Society at Amsterdam. 1854. Java, Sumatra. (£835. 7 missionaries.)

62. The Ermeloer Missionary Society. 1854. Talaut Islands.

63. Mission of the Separatist Reformed Church at Kampen. 1857. Surinam, Orange Republic.

64. The Netherland Missionary Society. Rotterdam. 1859. Sava. (£1930. 5 Missionaries.)

65. The Utrecht Missionary Society, 1859. New Guinea, Bali. (£2666. 12 missionaries.)

66. The Netherland Reformed Missionary Society. Amsterdam. 1859. Java. (16 missionaries.)

67. Mennonite Association for the Diffusion of the Gospel in the Dutch Maritime Possessions at Amsterdam.

68. Java. The China Society.

69. Netherland Auxiliary Miss. Soc. at Batavia. (£835. 7 missionaries.)

70. Netherland Society for Israel.

5.—Scandinavian Missionary Societies.

71. Swedish Missionary Society of Stockholm. 1857. Eastern Africa.

72. Missionary Society of Lund for China, 1852.

73. Missionary Institute of the Evangelical Fatherland's Foundation of Stockholm. 1860.

74. Missionary Society of Göteborg.

75. The Norse Missionary Society of Stavanger. 1842. South Africa.

76. The Danish Missionary Society of Copenhagen. 1821. India. (£860.)

77. Finnish Missionary Society of Helsingfors. 1861.

6.—French Missionary Societies.

78. Society of Evangelical Missions. Paris. 1824. South Africa, Senegambia, Polynesia. (£8239)

7.—Colonial Missionary Societies.

79. The Reformed Church Mission to the Cape. Capstadt. 1861. South Africa.

80. Society of Internal and External Missions. Batavia, 1851. Holland, India.

81. Presbyterian Missionary Society. Melbourne. (?) Australia.

82. Melanesian Miss. Soc. (?) at Aukland, 1861. Melanesia.

83. Hawaiian Missionary Society at Honolulu. Micronesia, Marquesas Islands.

84. Jamaica Baptist Miss. Soc. (?).

85. West Indian Missionary Board. West Africa.

86. Palestine Christian Union Mission to Arabs. (1 agent).

The following is a fuller statement of the operations of some of the larger societies.

American Board of Commissioners of Foreign Missions.

The income for the year has been as follows: From donations, $350,172 08; from legacies, $74,428 44; from other sources, $12,763 25—making a total of $437 864 77. There was a balance in favor of the treasury September 1st, 1866, of $6,201 07. Now there is a balance against it of $4,432 34.

The number of foreign missions established, including stations and out-stations, are 604; the whole number of laborers employed, including natives, physicians, and ordained missionaries, 1264. The Secretary reports as the number of foreign churches under the Board's control, 205; the number of church members, as far as reported, 25,502; added during the year, 1447.

The Prudential Committee, in their report, ask for eighteen new missionaries, three missionary physicians to reenforce the stations already occupied, and for forty new missionaries to be forwarded to a new field, making sixty-one, which they request to be sent without delay.

The appropriations for the coming year have been fixed at $525,000. The Prudential Committee in their report lay especial stress upon the importance of the Chinese mission.

(English) Baptist Missionary Society.

The receipts of the Baptist Missionary Society were £30,104 8s 1d. somewhat in advance of those of last year. They have been exceeded by the expenditures, which have been increased chiefly because of the advance of the prices of living in India. The society publishes three periodicals, two monthly, and one quarterly.

The mission stations, etc., are as follows: India, 4 stations, 9 English missionaries and assistants, 8 natives; Bengal, 67 stations, 18 English, 98 natives; Northern India, 14 stations, 11 English 64 natives; Southern India, 2 stations; China, 3 stations, 2 English, 6 natives; Ceylon, 57 stations. and sub-stations, 3 English, 17 assistants; West Indies, 6 missions, 2 missionaries, 6 assistants; Bahamas, 42 stations, 2 missionaries, 71 assistants; Haiti, 26 stations, 2 missionaries, 7 assistants and Bible readers; Jamaica, 1 mission, 2 missionaries; Western Africa, 9 stations, 5 missionaries; 6 assistants; France, 9 stations, 3 missionaries, 6 assistants and teachers; Norway, 1 station and 1 missionary.

The returns from the stations were so imperfect that no statistics were given. The report of the previous year gave 17,177 as the number of nominal christians connected with the missions.

London Missionary Society.

The London Missionary Society is principally sustained by the Independents, or Congregationalists. The receipts of the Society for the year were £105,090 10s 4d. The total income of the Society since its institution in 1695, has been £3,255,193. Several of the mission churches under the care of the Society have contributed liberally to the spread of the Gospel. Collections have been made on a large scale in the West Indies. South Africa, and South Seas. The total foreign contributions for several years have amounted to £15,000 a year. Of total contributions from abroad during the last year about £9000 were offerings of native churches to directly religious objects. Among other specific items of their year's work, the Society calls attention to the fact that in China they have held 7000 religious services, instructed 170 theological students, and 40,000 children, and exercised pastoral care of congregations with 26,000 members and 150,000 people. Two of the missionaries starting from Tientsin, undertook a journey of 1700 miles into the interior of North China.

The following are the statistics of the Society's missions.

Missions.	Missionaries.	Communic'ts.	Scholars in Vernacular Schools.
China	19	1,248	214
North India	19	295	754
South India	24	841	1,746
Travancore	8	1,876	5,783
Madagascar and Mauritius	13	4,54.	850
South Africa	35	4,642	2,161
West Indies	16	4,798	2,285
Polynesia	27	9,321	10,541
Total	161	27,562	24,334

There are also connected with the missions 120 native ordained pastors and missionaries, 590 Evangelists, Colporteurs, and readers, (and mostly in the Indian missions), 134 boys in boarding schools, 3327 boys in the Anglo Vernacular schools, 2823 girls in the day schools, 445 girls in the boarding-schools, and 70 women (in the North Indian mission). The South Sea missions have contributed £2650 to the mission funds, the China missions, £1,615, North India, £2521, South India, £3269, South Africa, £797, Demarara, £1689, Berbice, £1944, and Jamaica, £2069. The total number of native local assistants, if they could be ascertained, is supposed to be about 1400. The Society publishes a monthly Chronicle of its work. It has 10 theological institutions, in the Eastern and South Sea missions, and classes have been formed in Savage Island and the Loyalty Group. The total number of students is 170, of whom 60 are in India, and 108 in the South Seas.

Church Missionary Society.

The receipts of the Church Missionary Society for its 68th year, 1866—'67, were £150,365 5s 10d, a decided advance over the receipts of the previous year, as those were over those of the year before. Of the receipts, £4000 came in the form of an anonymous donation for a mission to Japan, which being deducted, leaves the ordinary general income £145,386 5s 10d. The expenditures were £5477 18s 4d above this, and swallowed up more than the surplus from the previous year. The publications of the Society consisting of Bibles and numerous works suitable to its objects, are issued in the English, Arabic, Armenian, Greek, Italian, Maltese, Persian, Turkish, Armeno-Turkish, Chinese, and New Zealand languages, nineteen languages of Africa, ten of India, and two of North-West America. The Society publishes four monthly and two quarterly periodicals. It sustains a missionary institution, in which the number of students is reported to be diminishing, and a Missionaries' Childrens Home.

The following are the statistics of the missions.

Missions.	Stations.	Missionaries and lay teachers.	Native Communic'ts.
West Africa	8	32	1,228
Yoruba	8	60	839
Niger	4	19	77
Mediterranean	4	16	59
Western India	9	67	167
South India	29	941	8,502
North India	31	647	1,635
Ceylon	12	218	742
Mauritius	2	13	72
Madagascar	1	2	—
East Africa	1	1	—
China	6	41	160
New Zealand	18	31	—
Rupert's Land	16	39	1,001
Fort Simpson	1	5	—
Total	154	2,132	14,762

The number of native Scholars in the schools, so far as reported, is as follows: West Africa, 532; Yoruba, 1068; Niger, 136; Mediterranean, 401; Western India, 1555; South India, 13,123; North India, 11,452; Ceylon, 3802; Mauritius, 368; China, 70; Rupert's Land 758; Fort Simpson, 170.

Society for the Propagation of the Gospel.

The object of the Society for the propagation of the gospel in foreign parts is to receive, manage and dispose of funds contributed for the religious instruction of "the Queen's subjects beyond the seas, to maintain clergymen in the plantations, colonies, and factories of Great Britain, and to propagate the gospel in those parts". Its President is the Archbishop of Canterbury, and its Vice-Presidents are the Bishops of the Anglican Churches in Great Britain and the Colonies, noblemen, gentlemen, and clergymen. Thirty local Associations, in England, Ireland, and Scotland, co-operate with the Society. Its total receipts last year were £91,186 8s 7d. Its Indian appropriations prove insufficient for the work in that region, and it calls for £12,500 additional, to enable it to discharge its obligations there. Its missionaries in all the colonial dioceses, number 517. An auxiliary society was formed last year, called the "Ladies Association for Promoting Female Education among the Heathen." The Society issues a number of gratuitous publications and two monthly magazines.

Wesleyan Missionary Society.

The report of the Wesleyan Missionary Society gives £109,288 16s 6d as the total of home receipts, and the total, including the foreign receipts at £148,140 14s 9d, being an increase of over £3268 in the Home receipts, and of nearly £3000 in the Foreign receipts. The income is in excess of the Expenditure. Twenty-seven missionaries and 12 wives of missionaries have been sent out during the year. The missions include 668 principal stations. 3227 preaching places, 1011 ministers and assistants, 1630 paid and 20,340 unpaid agents, 148,900 members, and 17,029 probationers, 161,402 scholars, and 8 printing establishments. An exhibit by stations is given under the head of the Wesleyan Connection.

Methodist New Connexion Missionary Society.

The total income of this society was £6504 8s 8d. £1661 12s 10d were contributed for home missions. Other particulars are given under the head of the Methodist New Connexion Church.

Primitive Methodist Missionary Society.

The receipts of this Society were £12,525 6d. The expenditure has been increased, and an increased income is called for. Other statistics are given under the Primitive Methodis head.

Missions of the United Methodist Free Churches.

Income, £7626 14s 5d. Foreign local income, £2425 13s 11d; total, £10,052 8s 4d. Fourteen persons have been engaged in the home missions, have held hundreds of meetings, made nearly 20,000 visits, and report between one and two hundred hopeful cases of conversion. Other particulars and foreign mission statistics are given under the head of this denomination.

Society for the Propagation of the Gospel among the Jews.

The British Society for the Propagation of the Gospel among the Jews is regarded as its mere immediate field of operations London and the larger towns of the United Kingdom, and co-operates with the church of Scotland's mission to the Jews. Its objects are explained by its title. It employs 24 missionaries at home and abroad. Those abroad labor at Paris, Nancy, Pressburg, Vienna, Bromberg, Wurtemberg, Nuremberg, Breslau, Konigsberg, Wallachia, Adrianople, Algiers Oran, and in Italy. Its total income for the year was £6776 8s 1½d. It issues a monthly periodical, called the *Jewish Herald*.

Colonial and Continental Church Society.

The object of this Society is to supply clergymen, Catechists, and Teachers to British residents and sojourners in the colonies, on the continent, and other parts of the world. It employs 253 agents; viz. 103 Clergymen, 89 Catechists and schoolmasters, and 61 female teachers. Its receipts last year were £33,640 16s 6d.

Christian Vernacular Education Society for India.

The object of the Christian Vernacular Education Society for India is to establish in the great towns of that country, Christian Vernacular training Institutions, male and female, and to supply school-books and other works prepared on Christian principles, in the native languages of India. It has in Bengal, the North West Provinces, Punjab, Bombay, Madras, and Ceylon, 4 Institutions, with 136 scholars, and 98 institutions with 4423 scholars. It has printed 307,350 volumes, and has circulated 231,361. Its receipts were £6231 19s 9d.

The Kaiserswerth Deaconesses.

The Kaiserswerth Deaconesses Institution in Prussia had 139 stations during 1866. There were 401 sisters, 311 deaconesses, and 180 on trial. The hospital numbered 820 patients in the course of the year. Fifteen new stations were occupied during the year, but many requests had to be denied for lack of sisters. Thirty-six sisters devoted themselves to cholera patients, and two died; 56 were also engaged during the war in various hospitals. The total number of persons, old and young, who came under the hands of the deaconesses was 37,991.

Basle Missionary Society.

The income of this Society for the past year is stated to have been as follows:

From auxiliaries	Fr. 230,185
" individuals	220,424
" half batz and kreutzer collections	236,749
" other sources	100,968
	Fr. 788,316

The expenditures were 832,547 francs. The expenses in the different missions were as follows:

The mission of Africa	223,438
The mission in India	400,503
The mission in China	50,058
Efforts elsewhere	5,940

The following are the statistics of the missions

India, 15 stations, 1558 communicants, 112 non-communicants, 1557 children, total, 3227.

West Africa, 7 stations, 528 communicants, 71 non-communicants, 419 children, total, 1048.

China, 3 stations, 235 communicants, 9 non-communicants, 97 children, totol, 341.

The whole number of male laborers is reported as 91, (of whom four are "at home,") 53 having received ordination, and 38 being "unordained." The proportion of the latter is unusual, in consequence of the peculiar policy adopted in India and West Africa, there being a large number of mechanics in both these fields.

Fifty of these are married, and there are 2 unmarried woman in the foreign service.

These returns are from the latest formal report of the Society, which is given in the *Christian Work* of July 1867, as the fifty-first. From the reports of the last anniversary, it appears that the income of the society for the last year has fallen off 30,000 francs, being this year 757,000 francs, and that the expenditure has been 858,870 francs, the expense of the African mission having been increased 25,000 francs. The expenses of the Indian and China missions are reduced. The Southwestern Indian mission flourishes very encouragingly, the number of native Christians having risen in ten years from 2500 to 3810.

Leipzic Missionary Society.

From the report presented at the last anniversary of this Society it appears that the mission seminary has at present 10 students. In India there are 6 missionaries, and 1 is at present on a visit to Germany. During the last year 741 heathen were baptized by the missionaries, and there are now 6303 converts, in 373 places. The receipts have increased, notwithstanding the war. The Director of the Seminary, Pastor Hardeland, is about to undertake a tour of inspection to the stations, taking with him one new missionary.

Moravian Missionary Society.

The total income for the year, including special contributions for individual stations, and what the stations themselves raised, was about 350,000 thalers, or £52,500. The number of stations was 88; of laborers 318, and of converts, 70,311. The home contributions alone were 100,280 thalers.

French Missionary Society.

The Evangelical Missionary Society of Paris commenced a mission in South Africa in 1822. The attendants on religious services number 5000; there are 2000 communicants, and 1500 pupils in the Sabbath-school. The society has recently commenced a new station at Senegambia, in West Africa. The number of missionaries connected with the Society is 16.

2.—Protestant Mission Houses.

The Basle Institute.

This Institute was foundedin 1815. The first young men who finished their studies left the institute in 1818. Since then over 400 others have left its walls. The first object of the institution was to educate missionaries. To send them abroad on its own account was the thought of several years afterwards. The Professors are mostly of the Lutheran and Reformed churches, but the management of the institute has always been exceedingly liberal. For instance, it has trained 88 young men for the Church Missionary Society.

Church Missionary College.

The Church Missionary College at Islington, London, was established in January, 1825. It has educated about 350 missionaries.

St. Augustine's, Canterbury.

This institute was established about 15 years ago, by the society for the propagation of the Gospel. It has educated about 100 missionaries, and has now about 40 students.

St. Aidare's, Birkenhead.

This is a new institution, under the charge of the Rev. Dr. Baylee, of the established Church of England. It had at the last accounts, about 15 students.

Wesleyan Training School.

The committee of the Wesleyan Missionary Society have established a Missionary Training School at Richmond, near London, to which part of the revenues received during the jubilee year (1864), are to be devoted.

London Missionary Society Institution.

The London Missionary Society have established a training school at Highgate, near London.

Free Church of Scotland.

The general assembly of the Free Church of Scotland have resolved, in accordance with a recommendation of the Rev Dr Duff, to establish a training school, and to institute a chair of "Evangelistic Theology" in connection with their Theological Seminary.

Mission House in Philadelphia.

A mission school under the care of the Episcopalians was opened at Gambier, Ohio, in 1864, with the Rev. J. G. Auer as principal. It was removed, a year afterwards, to West Philadelphia and connected with the Divinity-school there.

NEW THEOLOGICAL PUBLICATIONS.

HARPER & BROS., N. Y.

Cyclopedia of Biblical, Theological and Ecclesiastical Literature. Prepared by the Rev. John McClintock, D. D. and James Strong, S. T. D.

This work is to be in six volumes, of which the first, containing the letters A and B, has been issued, and the second is soon to follow. It is the fullest and most complete work of the kind in the English language, giving not only the substance of all that is to be found in other similar ones, but much that is new, and has never before been embodied in a Cyclopedia. In the preparation of the matter all the standard works of the United States, England, Germany, and France have been consulted, and no book of importance has been overlooked. Many of the most prominent men of the different denominations of this country are among its contributors, the matters relating to each denominations particularly having generally been prepared by some one connected with it. The excellence of the work has been already generally acknowledged by the best religious and secular papers of the country. It is a book indispensable in every theological library.

College Life. Its Theory and Practice. By Rev. Stephan Olin, L. L. D., late President of the Wesleyan University.

A selection of the later baccalaunate discourses and lectures of this distinguished divine and instructor, embodying his mature views of mental and moral culture, as developed in the experience of nearly a quarter of a century of college life.

Lectures on the Evidences of Christianity in the Nineteenth Century. By Albert Barnes, author of "Notes of the New Testament" etc.

This work is the substance of ten Lectures delivered in January and February in 1867 in New York on the Ely foundation of the Union Theological Seminary. The lecturer reviews the subject in the light thrown upon it by modern discoveries and doctrines, and meets the arguments of modern skepticism with great clearness and boldness.

The Huguenots; their Settlements, Churches, and Industries in England and Ireland. By Samuel Smiles, author of "Self Help", "Lives of the Engineers", etc

A very interesting work, on one of the most striking episodes of religious history. The appendix contains, some detailed statements, lists of refugees etc., which could not be formally incorporated in the body of the work. An excellent article is added by the American publishers on the Huguenots in America. It is written by G. P. Disosway, Esq., who has given much attention to the subject, and writes with a love of his work.

D. APPLETON & CO., N. Y.

Origin, Rise, and Progress of Mormonism Biography of its Founders and History of its Ch rch. Personal Remembrances and Historical Collections hitherto unwritten. By Pomeroy Tucker. Palmyra, N. Y.

Mr. Tucker was a townsman of Joseph Smith in the days when the Mormon faith originated. He was a witness of the proceedings of the discovery of the "tables" in the hill, and of the publication of the Book of Mormon, having been a proof-reader in the office in which it was published. His acquaintance with the subject was intimate and personal. His book is the most complete and reliable history of the sort that has been published, and is written in a style that makes it generally acceptable.

A comprehensive Dictionary of the Bible, mainly abridged from D. Wm. Smith's Dictionary of the Bible, but containing important additions and improvements from the works of Robinson, Gesenius etc., and many other eminent scholars, commentators, travellers, and authors in various departments. Edited by Rev. Samuel W. Barnum.

This is an abridgement for more general circulation than the larger work of Dr. Smith can command. The aim of the editor has been to make everything intelligible to those who understand only English, to condense the greatest possible amount of valuable information into a single volume; and to guard against all influences hostile to Christian faith and love. The words of the vocabulary are pronounced, and syllabized. Maps have been added and pictoral illustrations, intended for instruction and utility, rather than for mere ornament. It is published in semi-monthly numbers of 48royal octavo pages each, to be completed in abou 22 numbers. The editor, the Rev. Samuel W. Barnum was a colaborer of the late Prof. Goodrich, in 1845—'47, in the revision of Webster's Dictionary.

Ezekiel and Daniel; with Notes, critical, explanatory and practical designed for both pastors and people. By Rev. Henry Cowles, D. D.

This work is a continuation of the series on all the prophets which was commenced last year by the publication of "The Minor Prophets". The design is to be concise and lucid, to bring out the true sense of the original without prejudice. The former volumes were well received and met with high commendations from the more judicious secular and religious papers, and from such well known ministers as Drs. Bacon and J. P. Thompson. The series will be completed by the publication of volumes on Isaiah and Jeremiah.

The Human Element in the Inspiration of the Sacred Scriptures. By T. F. Curtis, D. D., late Professor of Theology in the University at Lewisburgh, Pa.

The author perceived his views on the subject of this work assuming a different character from those entertained by his denomination, and felt it his duty to resign his professorship, and devote himself to the examination of the subject. This work embodies his conclusions. He gives the human element a more prominent place in, and agrees for a more liberal construction of the Scriptures, with a less implicit reliance on their entire infallibility, than are admitted by Evangelical Christians generally. The tone of his work is temperate.

Christianity and its Conflicts, ancient and modern. By E. E. Marcy, A. M.

A vindication of the doctrines and History of the Roman Catholic Church. It reviews the doctrines taught by Jesus Christ, assuming that they are identical with those of the Catholic Church, reviews the history, decrees, and doctrines of that church and criticises Protestantism, its origin, development, and fruits, in Europe and America.

Bible Teachings in Nature. By the Rev. Hugh McMillan, Author of "First Forms of Vegetation."

Sixteen essays on subjects consonant with the title, the design of which is to show "that the teaching of nature and the teaching of the Bible are directed to the same great end; that the Bible contains the spiritual truths which are necessary to make us wise unto salvation, and the objects and scenes are the pictures by which these truths are illustrated." In a portion of the essays "the objects of nature are described for the sake of their own beauty and wonder, and for the evidences of Divine wisdom, power and love which they display. In the second section, they are viewed entirely in their typical aspect." Dr. McMillan is a pleasing and instructive writer and endowed with bright imaginative faculties

ROBERT CARTER & BROS., N. Y

Sermons of the late Alexander McClelland, D. D., edited by Richard W. Dickinson, D. D.

Dr. McClelland was from 1815 till 1822 pastor of the Rutgers St. Presbyterian Church, New York City, from then till 1839 Professor of Rhetoric, Logic, and Metaphysis in Dickinson College, and afterwards Professor of Languages in Rutgers College, and of Oriental Literatûre and Biblical Criticism in the Theological Seminary of the Reformed Dutch Church. His sermons were characterized by clearness, strength variety, and aptness of illustration with a vein of sarcastic humor, and by turns argumentative, expositing, descriptive, inferential and experimental.

The Word. The House of Israel. By the author of the "Wide, Wide World."

The second volume of a series of works, in conversational style on subjects from Bible History, relating the stories, and describing the customs of the times. The articles in this are nineteen in number, leading the story from the time of Isaac through the sojourn in Egypt.

"Out of Harness." Sketches narrative and descriptive. By Thomas Guthrie, D. D., Editor of the Sunday Magazine.

Our Father's Business. The same author.

The first of these consists of sketches of the authors missionary labors in and about Edinburgh, with three papers relating to Paris, and articles which are real recreations. They are narrative, descriptive, reflective and didactic, by turns.

The second contains eleven essays, or short sermons conveying practical admonitions in Christian duty. Dr. Guthrie is one of the most pleasing religious writers of Scotland.

JOS. M. WILSON, Philadelphia.

The Presbyterian Historical Almanac and annual Remembrancer of the Church. Philadelphia: Joseph M. Wilson. The best and completest Denominational Almanac in the United States.

CARLTON & PORTER, N. Y.

History of the Methodist Episcopal Church. By Abel Stevens, LL. D.

A Compendious History of American Methodism. The same author.

The fourth volume of Dr. Stevens' History of the Methodist Episcopal Church in the United States was published in October, completing the work so far as the author considers it best to be completed at present. The history begins with the first planting of Methodism in the country, with the founding of the first class and preaching of the first sermon, and traces the growth of the denomination and every phase of its developement in all parts of the country, until 1820, when the denomination was firmly established, and had all its agencies organized and successfully at work. It is characterized by the spirited personal sketches of the early ministers of which it in great part consists, and by vivid pictures, and is one of the most attractive, as well as faithful and accurate works of the kind in English literature.

The compendium is an abridged edition of this work and is in one large octavo volume, for more popular use.

Scribner & Co., N. Y.

A Commentary, Critical, Doctrinal, and Homiletical, with special reference to Ministers and Students. By John Peter Lange, D. D., in connection with a number of European Divines. Translated from the German, and edited, with additions original and selected, by Philip Schaff, D. D., in connection with American Divines of various evangelical denominations.

Dr. Lange's Commentary, so far as it has been finished, is accepted as a standard by German Evangelical Christians, and has acquired a reputation second to that of no work, in every country in which it has been made known. The author, Dr. Lange, is one of the most prominent theologicans of Germany. His theology, as Dr. Schaff says, is essentially biblical and evangelical Catholic, and inspired by a fresh and refreshing enthusiasm for truth under all its types and aspects, more positive and decided than that of Neander and Tholuck, yet more liberal and conciliating than the orthodoxy of Hengstenberg. His commentary is critical, doctrinal, and homiletical, the three departments being kept separate. The translation and revision of the American edition is superintended by Dr. Schaff, who does a share of the work personally and is responsible for the whole, and is aided by a number of scholars of known reputation, whose names are sufficient testimony of their capacity and conscientiousness, and the accuracy of their work. Dr. Lange's work is given entire, exactly translated into idiomatic English, except the scripture text, which instead of being translated from his translation, is taken from the English authorized version. The additions, comments, and corrections of the editors, swelling the work to the comprehension of nearly one third more matter than the original German, are given separately, and with distinctive marks, to avoid the danger of confounding them with Dr. Lange's own. The work has been received with unexampled favor by clergymen and religious journals of all the evangelical denominations which generally pronounce it the best that has appeared. Four volumes, averaging from 480 to 550 pages 8vo, have been published, comprising the Gospels of Matthew, Mark, and Luke, the Acts of the Apostles, and the Epistles of James, Peter, John and Jude. The first volume contains also a general theological and homiletical introduction to the New Testament. The work will embrace the whole of the Old and New Testaments. No clergyman who has ever examined one of the volumes will want to remain without the whole work.

History of the Christian Church. By Philip Schaff, D. D. Author of the History of the Apostolic Church.

Dr. Schaff's reputation is established as one of the best biblical scholars and greatest church historians. His works have all been recognized as authoritative here as well as in Europe. The present work, which is a continuation of the former one, on the Apostolic Church, completes the author's History of Ancient Christianity, bringing it down to the close of the sixth century. It embodies the results of the latest German and English research, to a higher degree than any other work of the kind published either in the English and German languages. For the period over which it extends we regard it as the best work extant.

Homiletics and Pastoral Theology. By Wm. G. T. Shedd, D. D.

Dr. Shedd is well known as an able preacher and a thorough biblical scholar. The substance of this work was delivered as lectures in the Auburn Theological Seminary in 1852 and 1853. The volume is an excellent practical as well as theoretical aid to ministers in their efforts to cultivate the highest degree of efficiency.

Prayers from Plymouth Pulpit. By Rev. Henry Ward Beecher.

These Prayers were selected from reports of Mr. Beecher's Prayers which were taken phonographically without his knowledge, but Mr. Beecher afterwards consented to the publication. They are distinguished for the same features of excellence which have made Dr. Beecher's sermons so famous.

The Methodist, N. Y.

The *N. Y. Methodist*, a christian family paper now in its eighth year has already obtained a weekly circulation of over 15,000. The increase of circulation during the past year has been greater than during any previous period of its history, and from all appearances the increase during the coming year, will exceed that of the past. We call special attention to the fuller statement of the plan as set forth by the publisher of the paper on another page. Some of its features, as the regular publication of sermons from the most eminent pulpit orators of the Methodist and other Protestant Churches, and the completeness of its department of religious intelligence, which aims at giving a complete history of all the religious denominations of the world during the current year, recommend it to the attention of clergymen and members of all religious denominations.

DENOMINATIONAL RECORD.

——0——

In this department we give, under the head of the several denominations, a collection of interesting events and incidents in the religious history of the year 1867. It is not intended to give a history of the several denominations, but merely to select a few of the most memorable facts of their history,

Baptists.

New Mission to Farther India.

A new mission has been established among the Laos. A church has been formed of three persons, one of whom is preparing for the ministry.

Baptist Colony in Turkey.

Cataloi, in Turkey, is declared entirely a Baptist colony. The church has forty-nine members, and the congregations average 70 persons. There are now 78 members in Turkey, and more awaiting baptism. Thirty have been baptized during the year.

Southern Baptist Convention.

The Southern Baptist Convention met at Memphis on May 9th. Two hundred delegates were present from thirteen States, including the District of Columbia. The Foreign Mission Board reported the expenditures, amounting to $22,100 during the past year. They have six missions in China and Africa. The Domestic Board, located in Marion, Ala., has collected and distributed $41,000. It employs 124 home missionaries and 10 Indian missionaries among the Chicopee and Cherokee tribes.

The Board of Indian Missions reported but little progress during the past year, owing to a meagreness of funds. Six missions only had been kept in the field. The receipts during the year amounted to $6,740; the disbursements to $6,629.

It was resolved to pray for the conversion of the Jews, and to hold future conventions annually. The convention also adopted a report in favor of contributing to the moral and religious improvement of the colored people, by the establishment of Sunday schools, missions, and day schools, and to accept the coöperation of the Northern Baptist Home Missionary Society. They also invited the colored Baptist churches to coöperate with them in sustaining missionaries and colonists fitted to missionary work in Africa.

Colored Baptists in East Tennessee.

This year's session (the fourth) of this association, developed the interesting fact that in four years it has grown from eight churches to thirty-two.

Louisiana Colored Baptist Association.

This has been recently organized. It has 19 churches, all but four formed since 1861.

Deputation from the North to the Southern Baptist Convention.

During the meeting of the American Baptist Home Missionary Society at Chicago, says a correspondent, "an exciting scene occurred on a motion to appoint a delegation to the Southern Baptist Convention, to meet in Baltimore next May. As might have been expected, a strong diversity of sentiment was manifest, and some sharp words were uttered in opposition to the motion, as well as in its favor. For a time the confusion was marked, hissings mingling with applause in a manner more suited to a political caucus than to the house of God. But, finally, the motion prevailed by a large majority, and the delegation was appointed."

Free Will Baptist Mission in the South.

Ten thousand dollars have been offered the Free-Will Baptists towards the establishment of an educational institution at the South. The offer came from a gentleman in Maine, of another denomination, and is conditioned on the raising an equal amount by them before the first day of January next; the whole to be a permanent fund, which shall itself be increased to $40,000 by January, 1873; or otherwise the entire income shall be used only to bring the fund up to this latter amount; after which the corporation will take charge of it for educational purposes. A provisional act of incorporation has been secured, the work of raising the ten thousand dollars has been vigorously entered on, and ample grounds purchased at Harper's Ferry, the site selected for the purpose. A normal school will be opened here next September.

Theological Institutions.

A new Baptist Theological Institution has been founded in Pennsylvania. The family of the late John P. Crozer have given land and buildings worth $85,000, and $170,000 as an endowment fund, to which $25,000 have been added by Mr. Wm. Bucknell. The institution will not be opened before the fall of 1868.

An effort is being made to endow the Chicago Theological Seminary.

Home Mission Society in the South.

Among the colored people the Society has had fifty ordained ministers under commission, or about one-sixth of the whole number employed during the year. Ninety-seven colored Baptist churches have been aided. The work of educating ministers for this people has been prosecuted. Schools have been sustained at Washington, Alexandria, Culpepper, Fredericksburg, Williamsburg, Richmond, Portsmouth, Raleigh, New Orleans, Murfreesboro, Nashville, Albany, and Ashland. Instruction has been given to more than three hundred colored preachers, and persons having the ministry in view. Among the colored youth, fifty-nine teachers have been employed as teachers of day-schools, who have had under their tuition 6,136 pupils. The appropriations in the education of freedmen for the year amount to $39,925.11.

Bibles for the Freedmen.

The American and Foreign Bible Society have printed an edition of the Testament, especially for the freedmen, in large, clear type.

Six-Principle Baptists.

The one hundred and ninety-seventh anniversary of the Massachusetts and Rhode Island Six-Principle Baptist Association met this year at North Kingston, R. I., in a church which dates its history from 1665. The six principles comprising the faith of this denomination are: repentance, faith, baptism, laying on of hands, the resurrection, and a general judgment. The fourth principle has the same place as the third, wherein this differs from other Baptist churches. The sect is decreasing, and is little known out of the above-mentioned States.

Mr. Spurgeons' Boys' Home.

The Rev. Mr. Spurgeon, on the 9th of September, laid the corner-stones of three homes for fatherless boys, to be erected at Stockwell, England, the fruits of a donation of £20,000 from Mrs. Ann Hillyard. The homes are each to accommodate from eighteen to twenty boys, who are to receive a godly education, in hope that they may become ministers and missionaries.

Mr. Spurgeon's Church.

The church edifice is known as the Metropolitan Tabernacle, and will seat five thousand persons. It cost, with ground, about $750,000. The church has a membership of 3,800. A Bible-class of 200 young men is conducted by one of the elders. Mrs. Bartlett commenced a lady's Bible-class with three scholars—it has now an average attendance of 700. Over 600 young men are engaged every Lord's day in preaching in halls, stations, &c. Sixty churches are now supplied with pastors from thi church. The College under its care has 93 students, and 263 night pupils. The students are sent out to preach as soon as they are deemed qualified The College costs about $24,000 per annum—the church contributing weekly of this sum $250 by voluntary subscriptions.

The Anglican Church.

Ritualism.

The ritualistic controversy has continued in both England and the United States to be prosecuted with much vigor on both sides, and has received considerable attention from the church authorities, and been made the subject of several official declarations.

On the 10th of January, 1867, a declaration against ritualism was issued at Buffalo, signed by 28 of the American Bishops. This declaration declares that by the 24th article of religion, each particular or National church has authority to ordain, change, or abolish the ceremonies or rites of the church of merely human authority; that they need not be alike in all times and places, but may be changed and adapted to circumstances, if always accordant with God's word; that the American church is "a particular and National church, and has equal authority with the English to establish ceremonies and rites, and that those directed in the prayer-book in use in America are the law of the church. "which," the declaration continues, "every bishop, presbyter, and deacon of the same has bound himself by subscription to the Promise of Conformity in Article VII. of the Constitution, to obey, observe, and follow; and that no strange or foreign usages should be introduced or sanctioned by the private judgment of any member or members of this church, clerical or lay. * * * * That no Prayer-book of the Church of England, in the reign of whatever sovereign set forth, and no laws of the Church of England have any force of law in this church such as can be justly cited in defence of any departure from the express law of this church, its liturgy, its discipline, rites, and usages.

"And we, therefore, consider that in this particular National Church, *any attempt to introduce into the public worship of Almighty God usages that have never been known, such as the use of incense, and the burning of lights in the order for the Holy Communion; reverences to the Holy Table or to the elements thereon*, such as indicate or imply that the sacrifice of our Divine Lord and Savior, '*once* offered,' was not a 'full, perfect, and sufficient sacrifice, oblation, and satisfaction, for the sins of the whole world;' the adoption of clerical habits hitherto unknown, or material alterations of those which have been in use since the establishment of our Episcopate, *is an innovation which violates the discipline of the Church, offendeth against its common order, and hurteth the authority of the magistrate, and woundeth the consciences of the weak brethren.*'

"Furthermore, that we be not misunderstood, let it be noted that we include in these censures all departures from the laws, rubrics, and settled order of this church, as well by defect as by excess of observance, designing to maintain in its integrity the sound scriptural and primitive, and therefore the catholic and apostolic spirit of the Book of Common Prayer."

This declaration was signed by the following bishops:

Bishop Smith, of Kentucky; Bishop McIlvaine, of Ohio; Bishop Kemper, of Wisconsin, Bishop McCoskry, of Michigan; Bishop Lee, of Delaware; Bishop Johns, of Virginia; Bishop Eastburn, of Massachusetts; Bishop Chase, of New Hampshire; Bishop Upfold, of Indiana; Bishop Payne, African Mission; Bishop Williams, of Connecticut; Bishop Davis, of South Carolina; Bishop Kip, of California; Bishop Lee of Iowa; Bishop Clark, of Rhode Island; Bishop Gregg, of Texas; Assistant Bishop Bedell, of Ohio; Bishop Whipple, of Minnesota; Assistant Bishop Talbot, of Indiana; Bishop Wilmer, of Alabama; Bishop Vail, of Kansas; Bishop Coxe, of Western New York; Bishop Clarkson, of Nebraska; Bishop Randall, of Colorado; Bishop Kerfoot, of Pittsburg; Bishop Williams, China Mission; Assistant Bishop Cummins, Kentucky; Assistant Bishop Armitage, of Wisconsin.

In the Convocation of York, on the 20th of March, the following resolution was adopted unanimously by the President and Bishops, and in the Lower House by 23 to 7:

"*Whereas*, certain vestments and Ritual observances have recently been introduced into the Services of the Church of England, this House desires to place on record its deliberate opinion that these innovations are to be deprecated, as tending to favor errors rejected by that Church, and as being repugnant to the feelings of a large number both of the laity and clergy. And this House is further of opinion that it is desirable that the minister in public prayer and the ministration of the sacraments and other rites of the Church, should continue to use the surplice, academical hood, or tippet for non-graduate, and the scarf or stole; these having received the sanction of long-continued usage."

The Upper House of the Convocation of Canterbury on the thirteenth of February unanimously declared that, "having regard to the dangers, first, of favoring errors deliberately rejected by the Church of England, and fostering a tendency to desert her communion; second, of offending even in things indifferent devout worshipers in our Churches who have been long used to other modes of service, and thus of estranging many of the faithful laity; third, of unnecessarily, departing from uniformity: fourth, of increasing the difficulties which prevent the return of separatists to our communion—we convey to the Lower House our unanimous decision that, having respect to the considerations here recorded, and to the rubric concerning the service of the Church in our Book of Common Prayer, our judgment is that no alterations from long-sanctioned and usual ritual ought to be made in our Churches until the sanction of the bishop of the diocese has been obtained thereto". This resolution being sent down to the Lower House, that House, after some discussion, agreed to concur in the judgment of the Upper House, leaving the reasons given by the bishops out of the question.

The bishops of the Irish Church have unanimously signed a reply to an address from a committee of laymen in favor of adherence to the established usages of the church, and against "excesses of ritual."

Early in June the Queen of England appointed a commission to inquire what were the practices, orders and rubrics of the Church, and the true interpretation of the same, to suggest such orders and amendments to them, additions to the service and alterations in the lessons as they might deem fit and proper. The Commission consisted of the following persons: The Archbishops of *Canterbury* and Armagh; Earls Stanhope, Harrowby, and *Beauchamp*; the Bishops of London, S. Davids, *Oxford*, and *Gloucester*; Barons Portman and Ebury, *Spencer H. Walpole*, Edward Cardwell, Sir Joseph Napier, Sir *William Page Wood*. Sir *Robert Joseph Phillimore*, *Travers Twiss*, *John Duke Coleridge*, John Abel Smith, *Alexander James Beresford Beresford-Hope*, *John Gellibrand Hubbard*, Arthur Penrhyn Stanley, *Harvey Goodwin*, *James Amerauх Jeremie*, Robert Payne Smith, Henry Venn, *William Gilson Humphrey*, *Robert Gregory*, and *Thomas Walter Perry*. (The names given in *Italics* are supposed to be High Church men). On the 19. of August they rendered their first report, in regard to the use of vestments, to the effect that they considered it expedient to restrain in the public services of the United Church all variations in respect of vesture from that which has long been the established usage of the Church, and that this may be best secured by providing aggrieved parishioners with an easy and effectual process for complaint and redress.

Incumbents and Curates in England.

The London Times gives statistics showing that the number of incumbents in the Church of England has increased in 30 or 40 years, from 5000 to about 13 000, while the number of curates has remained stationary, at about 5000. These statistics prove the growing activity of the Church, and the large amount of work done by private voluntary effort, in founding new encumbencies and providing livings. No corresponding increase has been made in the number of Bishops which is now nearly the same as three hundred years ago.

Clerical Retreats.

There was last year a "retreat" for laymen at St. Barnabas, Pimlico, conducted by the Rev. E. D. Cleaver, of Christ Church, Oxford. The work of the day began with the Holy Communion at a quarter to nine, and devotional exercises of various kinds were continued without intermission until about a quarter to eight in the evening, allowing three quarters of an hour for breakfast and two hours for dinner anb recreation.

Father Ignatius.

The *Church News*, states that "St. Bartholomew's, Moorfields, which in some respects has efficiently helped on the Catholic revival, is so well attended since the Rev. L. Lyne (Father Ignatius) became assistant clergyman, that the galleries, unused for some years, have been lighted with gas, and are now open and crowded every Sunday."

Episcopal Independence in Australia.

The synod of the diocese of Adelaide, South Australia has taken a practical step towards the assertion of its independence of the Established Church of England, and towards its self-government as an Episcopalian Church. At a special meeting it formally resolved, "That it is not desirable that all bishops in the British colonies should receive their mission from the see of Canterbury, and take the oath of canonical obedience to the archbishop." This resolution was carried by 24 to 7. By another resolution it was decided, by 18 to 7, that it was desirable that future bishops of the diocese should be elected by the diocese.

Church Congress at Wolverhampton.

The seventh annual session of the Church Congress was opened at Wolverhampton on the 15. of October. A large number of prominent men attended, among whom were several American Bishops. The Bishop of Illinois spoke of the necessity of supplementing secular education in the United States by religious teachings. The Bishop of Tennessee deprecated sectarianism, or individualism in the church, and expressed his belief that the church was the only power that could elevate the Freedmen in America. During the Congress a meeting was held of those who favored ritualism.

Division of Dioceses.

Wisconsin is divided into four Convocations with Deans, and with express reference to a future division into *four Sees* as speedily as possible, the Bishop of the Diocese having given his consent. In Indiana, a resolution was carried in favor of the See Episcopate, small Dioceses, and the Provincial System; and the Assistant Bishop declared himself strongly in favor of dividing Indiana into *three* Dioceses.

The Maryland Diocesan Convention have adopted a resolution providing for the division of the diocese, and the erection of the Eastern Shore into a separate Episcopal See. A committee was appointed to determine the boundaries of the new dioce e.

In Ohio the Convocation of Cleveland unanimously sent in a petition to be set off as a separate See. The Bishop expressed himself rather unfavorable on the movement, but the Diocesan Convention referred the subject to a committee of fifteen to report next year.

The Diocesan Convention of Western New York adopted a report in favor of division. The dividing line is to follow the eastern boundaries of Wayne, Ontario, Yates, Schuyler, and Steuben counties. New dioceses are also talked of at Brooklyn and Albany, New York, and at Reading, Pa.

The Bishop of Nebraska reports three churches now being erected in Dakota—*the only places of public worship in the whole Territory*—which shows the *use* of giving destitute regions a Bishop of their own.

The Bishop of Capetown is taking measures for a subdivision of his South African diocese.

Bishop of London's Fund.

Within less than four years a sum of £202,000 has been directly subscribed to the fund, and a further sum of about £90,000 has been promised: while at the same time, independently of the fund, £853,000 has been subscribed by private donors toward the same objects; and a further sum of £530,000 has been voted by the Ecclesiastical Commissioners toward the endowment of small livings in the diocese. By means of the money directly subscribed to the fund, one hundred and fifteen clergy and sixty-four lay assistants have been added to the staff of the diocese. Grants have been made for fifty-seven permanent churches, and for seventy-one sites for churches, parsonages, etc., while a sum of £28,668 has been voted for educational purposes. This statement does not include two large donations of £1500 and £5000 appropriated to churches and schools in two parishes specified by the donors. Dr. Tait remarks, however, that notwithstanding the exertions already made, there remains a vast population as yet not reached. In order to secure one clergyman for every two thousand of the population, there will be needed twice as many additional clergy as have been already secured, with a proportionate number of churches and schools.

Board of Missions.

It appears from the last report of this board, made at New York in October, that at home the sum of $130,386.24 was paid out for domestic missionary labors, and $142,136.44 received. For Foreign Missions the committee show the following statement: receipts, etc., $82,604 68; expenditure, $81,694 39; while the report of the Freedmen's Commission shows an expenditure of $30,319.42, against a fund of 29,223.54. Over $26,859 has been received in legacies alone for the general fund of the mission.

Deaconesses.

At a conference of those interested in the extension of the female deaconate, under the Presiding of the Bishop of Ely, the Bishop spoke favorably of the project, in which he had early interested himself and hoped that by means of wise measures the ministration of women might be restored to the Church. The Rev. T. Pelham Dale gave an account of the effect made in the diocese of London, after which the Bishop of Gloucester and Bristol moved a resolution, to the effect that it was desirable to extend the movement to other dioceses which, with other resolutions in support of the objects of the meetings, was adopted. A committee was appointed to take practical steps to extend the movement.

Roman Catholics.

The Italian Deputation to the Pope.

On the evening on the first of July the Pope received a deputation commissioned to present to him addresses of devotion from one hundred cities, presented through Count Baschetti, the originator of the project. The Count's address was not regarded as friendly to the Italian government. The Pope replied, with much emotion, with frequent responses of applause:

—"I have always loved Italy, I have prayed for her happiness, and God knows my affection for her. Nevertheless I must condemn, and I shall ever condemn, the efforts that are made in Italy to constitute a unity without charity, without justice, a unity cursed by God. I desire that the rights of all should be respected, and especially those of the church; and I, therefore, solemnly protest against the violation which those rights have suffered. I am deeply touched by so many demonstrations of affection from the veritable children of Italy. This album, your presence here, are to me solemn assurances of the piety of the majority of Italians. Bear to your families and your cities the expression of my gratitude and my special benediction."

A Catholic Church in Morocco.

In accordance with the terms of the treaty of peace between Spain and Morocco, a Roman Catholic cathedral has been erected in a square near the centre of the town which had been known as the Plaza de Espagna during the Spanish occupation of old times. The church has recently been completed, and has attached to it a monastery for the Franciscan monks, who are charged with the mission. Immediately adjoining the religious edifice is the Consular Palace, the whole forming a very imposing pile of buildings. The 19. December, 1866, being the anniversary of Queen Isabella's birthday, was selected for the solemn opening of the church, and the ceremony was performed in the presence of the Spanish Ambassador, Don Francisco Merry, and the principal members of the Legation.

New Bishoprics in Algeria.

By decree of the French Imperial Government the see of Algiers has been raised to an archbishopric, and suffragan dioceses are created at Constantine and Oran. Algeria has now a European (mostly Roman Catholic) population of 230,000, in a total population of 3,000,000.

Progress in China.

The French Roman Catholics are erecting a cathedral in Pekin, China, the towers of which are of such height that they overlook the imperial palace.

Passaglia.

The leader of the "Liberal" priests, Signor Carlo Passaglia, who drew up the famous Liberal petition to the Pope, and succeeded in getting 10,000 priestly signatures to it, was reported to have abjured Liberalism and submitted to the Bishop of Mondovi.

Missionaries in China.

We learn that so far back as 1851, after an infinitude of defeats and anxieties, the Catholic congregation of Fo-Tehcou-Fou claimed, through the medium of the French Minister, the restitution of a beautiful church built in the interior of that province, but which had been long used as a Pagan temple. "Our rights", says the bishop, "having been recognized, and the mandarin refusing to abandon this temple, they gave us in exchange a spacious territory, situated along the borders of the river. We are at present engaged laying the foundation of a residence, and when we have collected sufficient funds, we will commence building a church." It appears that the Dominican Fathers, after being long exiled from Formosa, have been able at length to replant their feet upon that beautiful but unhappy island. They had the consolation of baptizing, in the course of the year 1863, fifty-two adults, the first fruits of the renewal of Christianity. On June 29, in the following year, they opened a little seminary in the village of Ban-Kim-Ching. Greater victories than these are still before these heroic missionaries.—*Catholic Opinion.*

Japanese Mission.

The Catholic Church has strong hopes of being permitted to reopen its missions in Japan. They rest upon the number of Christian on the island, who are many, it being reported that there are 60,000 of them in one locality alone.

Persecution of Catholics in Russia.

The *Cologne Gazette* says that the Governor-General of the provinces of Podolia has just published a ukase, in virtue of which every Catholic priest wishing to preach a sermon is bound to deliver beforehand to the censorship of the police a manuscript copy of his discourse. Any priest acting in contravention of this order is to be liable to severe penalties. The Emperor Alexander has written a letter to the Pope in defence of his policy in Poland charging the priesthood with "reprehensible behavior", with being in alliance with abettors of disorder, and saying that his Holiness ought to be as anxious as he to bring it to an end regretting that circumstances had prevented his reception of a Nuncio, and expressing his readiness to accept such an envoy.

Sunday School Union in New York.

The Sunday schools of fifteen churches are now represented in the Union. The total number of children attending these schools is 10,000, of which 5,500 are boys, and 4,500 girls, under the care of 405 male and 353 female teachers. The female departments of six of the schools, however, are not included in the above. There are besides in the city the Sunday-schools of nineteen churches not yet represented.

The Jesuits.

This order, according to their lately published statistics reckoned at the close of 1866 four consistories and twenty provinces: the number of members being 8167, showing an augmentation of 215 over the year 1865. In the French province there are 2422, whereas, in 1865, there were only 2266. Notwithstanding their expulsion from Naples, Sicily, Turin, Venetia, and the Mexican empire, they are incessantly increasing in number.

Catholics in Denmark.

Catholicism is advancing in Denmark under the more liberal policy of the government. Still there are but 1500 Catholics in Copenhagen out of a population of 160,000.

Catholics in Holland.

Out of a population of 3,492,604, Holland has 1,280,062 Catholics, an increase since 1860 of 50,000, 1069 churches and chapels, and 1861 priests. Over 600 young people have entered the military service of the pope, and last year 400,000 francs were forwarded to the pope as a New Year's gift.

The Hierarchy in Scotland.

The pope proposes to re-establish the Roman Catholic hierarchy in Scotland, by giving territorial jurisdiction to the vicars apostolic, and by the appointment of other bishops. There will be an Archbishop of Glasgow, with six suffragans, who will take their respective titles from Edinburg, Aberdeen, Perth, Inverness, Stirling and Kilmarnock.

Congress at Inspruck.

The Roman Catholic Congress of Germany assembled at Inspruck, the Capital of Tyrol, on September 9th. The number present was 500. The German Catholic dignitaries expected did not attend.

Congress at Malines.

The Congress of Malines opened its third session on the 3. of September. About 2000 members were in attendance. Among them were the Bishops of Orleans, of Charleston, and of Vancouver, the Patriarch of Antioch, &c. Great devotion to the Holy Father inspired the Congress. The Unity of the Church, the means of restoring Russia to Unity, and the comparison of Catholic with Protestants propegandism, were prominent subjects of discussion. An address to the Pope was voted, which declared the object of the Congress to be the study of the wants of our times by the light of the teaching of the Church. Bishop Lynch, of Charleston, spoke of the rapid increase of Catholicism in the United States, and made an appeal in behalf of the spiritual wants of the enfranchised blacks, among whom he said were 159,000 Roman Catholics.

The "Reform Movement" in Italy.

The *Esaminatore*, a religious paper published in Florence, gives a fuller account of the "reform movement" in Italy than we have elsewhere seen. There are two schools of reformers, whose headquarters are respectively at Naples and Florence. A society called "the National Emancipation Society," pledged to open opposition to the Papacy, numbers nearly one thousand members. Their organ, *Emancipatore Cattolico* is a weekly journal, published in Naples, which combines politics and news with religion and reform. Men distinguished in civil life and ecclesiastics contribute to its pages, mostly under the evil of secresy. The association which this paper represents, announce as features of the religious reform at which they aim, the restitution to the laity of their ancient rights of electing the parochial clergy and administering the temporal affairs of the church; the independence of the bishops and metropolitans of the see of Rome, and the abolition of every oath of vassalage to the chair of St. Peter; the cessation of the enforced celibacy of the clergy; the free circulation of the Holy Scriptures among all classes: the celebration of public worship in the Italian language; the leaving the confesional optional with all ; and the administration of the communion in both kinds.

Roman Catholic Clergy in Austria.

The following are the members of clergy in Austria ; In all, 55,370. There are, 1 Patriarch 4 Primates, 11 Archbishops, 58 Bishops, 24 Assistant Bishops, 12,863 Parish Priests, 339 ordained Professors, 720 monasteries with 59 Abbots, 45 Provincials, 6,754 Priests, 654 Clercs, 240 Candidates, and 1917 Lay Brethren ; 258 nunneries, with 5198 nuns. The value of the church property is 185,672,968 florins, or £18, 567,029, and the income, 19,639,713 florins, or $1,963,571.

The Eastern Churches.

Russian Missionary Society.

The Russian Government has authorized the establishment of a society for the spread of the "orthodox" religion among heathens, Mussulmans, and Buddhists, in their territory. The operations of the society will be directed in the first instance to the conversion of the pagan tribes in the Altai and Trans-Baikal country, and the counteracting of Mussulman and Buddhist propaganda in those parts. The Caucasus, being assigned to the labors of a special society of the kind, is excluded from the sphere of the present one.

The Greeks in the West.—Establishment of a Greek Religious Paper in England.

One of the strangest of the many extraordinary projects of the day is that for setting up the Greek Religion in the West, upon the ruins of Roman and Protestant communities, which those who lead the movement profess to regard as alike beyond the pale of catholicity, and as fast approaching dissolution. The design was broached some time ago by Dr. J. J. Overbeck, in a book entitled *Catholic Orthodoxy and Anglo-Catholicism.* It has now its monthly organ, the *Orth dox Catholic Review.* Union between the Greek and English Churches is considered by Dr. Overbeck to be impossible. "There must be no illusions," he says. The Orthodox Church never will, nor can recognize the Anglican orders."

Greek Bishops on the projected Greek-Anglican Union.

It appears from a late number of the *Pall Mall Gazette*, that the party in the English Church which has been laboring for several years to bring about a union, or at least a recognized intercommunion, between that church and the Greek, still entertains sanguine hopes of success. At a meeting of the members of the Oriental Association, a society formed for the purpose of promoting the above object, encouraging communications were received from Rev. Messr. Pillow and Williams Mr Pillow reported, as one of the most important events of the past year, the elevation to the patriarchal chair of Constantinople of a prelate acceptable to all who desire to see that office independent of the intrigues of statesmen and ambassadors. The new patriarch of the Armenians, Gregory, he so showed, he said, plain indications of a disposition favorable to the reconciliation of his church with the Orthodox Eastern Church.

During the past year Mr. Williams had likewise the opportunity, during his journey through the East, to become acquainted with most distinguished personages among the Orthodox Eastern clergy. He had conversed with the patriarchs of Constantinople, Antioch and Jerusalem, and with other eminent bishops of the same communion. The patriarchs had expressed their entire approbation of the union of the churches. Mr. Williams declared, moreover, that the Metropilitan of Scio had said to him, that the time for electing commissioners from both sides to adjust the differences between them was at hand ; and that the patriarch of Antioch had assured him that he proposes to found a school, as a preparative for the union, and he desired to obtain an Englishman as a professor in it, that the members of it might learn the English language.

Russian Bible Society.

The Russian Bible Society has been recently organized at St. Petersburg, with the sanction of the Emperor Alexander. It seems, from a letter in the New York *Observer* from Rev. W. H. Bidwell, that various attempts have been made before to organize such a society in Russia, but they have been failures. This begins its career under happy auspices. The first Russian Bible Society, organized under the auspices of Alexander I., had 279 anxiliaries, and printed and circulated 861,000 copies of the Sciptures, and was still making successful progress, when it was suppressed by the emperor Nicholas.

The Greek Church in Turkey.

The Greek Church in Turkey, having secured a civil constitution from the Porte like that granted the Armenians has forced its Patriarch to resign his office. He was elected as a liberal and a patriot, but adopted another policy, and became the suppliant tool of the Turks. The Porte refused to accept his resignation till the excitement among the Greeks and perhaps a hint from St. Petersburg, left no choice. The people went further, and restored the same liberal patriarch to office whom the Porte deposed many years ago.

The Greek Catechism.

G. P. Putnam & Son, New York, publishers, have published an abridged edition of the Catechism of the Holy Greek Church under the sanction and by the request of the bishop of Jona.

Reform in the Armenian Church.

The movement for a reform in the Armenian Church gathers new interest at Constantinople, and has broken forth strongly in the interior. The publishers of the new Prayer Book in the vernacular have made so much progress in evangelical sentiment, that during the time of its passing through the press they have cancelled some of the earliest pages in order to present a better view of doctrine. The Patriarch has officially denounced the book. Some of the Armenian newspapers characterize its teachings as Protestantism, and others as yet are non-committal. The effect of the attacks upon it thus far has been only to draw attention to it and stimulate discussion of its merits. The agitation is producing a religious ferment, such as there has not been before for twenty years in Constantinople. The reformers disclaim the name of Protestant ; but they find themselves drawn towards the Protestants ; and the aid and comfort giving by the latter is having a good influence on the Protestant churches. In Karpoot the "Reform Societies" are active in preventing the attendance of adherents to the Armenian Church on Protestant meetings. The reform movement makes rapid progress especially among the young men. The Protestants, who receded from the ArmenianChurch in 1847, number 15,000, and the circulation of the Bible and religious books among those who remained in the church has led the whole body to take new views of the teachings and practices of the church. Many priests of the "enlightened" party in the old church preach evangelical doctrine, and this party has forced the Porte to deprive the Patriarch of his temporal power, and to invest it in a committee of laymen. In Smyrna and Constantinople they are especially strong and confident, while in the interior stricter lines are drawn, and reformers have to secede and join the Protestant party.

Many enter into the scheme for political reasons, as the Protestantization of the church will secure English protection for the Armenians, the only Christian sect in Turkey who have no friends abroad.

Presbyterian.

Old School Presbyterian General Assembly.

This body met on the 16. of May at Cincinnati. A report on the secessions in the synods of Kentucky and Missouri was adopted by a vo e of 207 to 6, declaring that members and churches would be received back on their application and declaration of willingness to submit to the established authority of the church, but declining followship with all who refuse to return before the meeting of the Presbytery and Synod next spring, and that they would be considered as having voluntarily withdrawn from the communion. On the subject of union, with the New School Presbyterian General Assembly the majority report, favoring reunion on the basis of the report of the joint committee, was adopted. A pastoral letter was adopted, deprecating the ordinary desecrations of the sabbath, and counselling ministers and elders to cultivate in their families, and in all over whom their influenec extends, just and scriptural views of the sacredness of the day, and recommending to pastors to preach as often as convenient, on the proper observance of the sabbath. The collections for the disabled minister's fund were reported at $27,000—$5000 mo e than last year. At the suggestion of the Presbytery of Chicago, the assembly decided to call upon the Presbyteries to report the numbers of unbaptized children whose parents are members of the communion.

New School General Assembly.

This body met at Rochester, N. Y., May 16th. The reports of committees were all favorable. The standing committee on the Erection of Churches reported one hundred churches without buildings of their own, and r commended that one hundred thousand dollars be raised to assist in providing buildings. The report on Union, of the joint committee of the two assemblies was approved. The matter of constitutional changes was referred back to the joint committee to report to the assembly of 1868. The report of the standing committee on Publication states that the publication scheme has become a fixed fact, and a success. The permanent committee on Sabbath Schools was made a distinct executive body to carry out the Sabbath School work.

The Party of the "Declaration of Testimony."

Those Old School Presbyterians in Kentucky and Missouri who have put themselves in opposition to the deliverances of the Old School Presbyterian General Assemblies on the subject of loyalty and slavery, have been known under the name of the "Declaration and Testimony" party, as in 1865 they published their views in a document called "A Declaration and Testimony." The Synods of Kentucky and Missouri were in 1867 fully dissolved, one party remaining in connection with the Old School Presbyterian General Assembly, and the other refusing to surrender the position taken by their "Declaration and Testimony." The latter were divided on the question whether it was expedient to join the Southern Presbyterian General Assembly, but it was expected that a majority would ultimately adopt that course.

Cumberland Presbyterians.

The General Assembly of the Cumberland Presbyterian Church met at Memphis on the 16th of May. The most vexed question which engaged attention was the deliverance of last year concerning slavery and rebellion, which was regarded by some members as reversing the deliverance of preceding years, and as signs of undue conversion to pro-slavery tendencies. The matter was settled by the adoption of a resolution that this deliverance did not repeal the decisions of former assemblies, and that neither this decision nor those of the former assemblies could be set up as tests of membership unless they were referred to the Presbyteries and approved by them. The assembly adopted a resolution referring the subject of the moral and religious treatment of the black men to the standing committees on Education and Missions.

United Presbyterians.

At the general assembly of the United Presbyterian Church, favorable reports were received from the foreign missions. The Board of Education reported that forty young men had been assisted during the year, eighteen of them engaged in literary and twenty-two in a theological course of study. An appropriation was voted to carry on the missions to the freedmen, and the board were instructed to inquire into the feasibility of forming a connection with the American Union Freedmen's Commission. The most exciting subject which came before the assembly was the "McCune case." Mr. McCune was condemned for holding views favorable to open communion and on the requisites of church membership which were regarded as at variance with the standards of the church.

Reformed Presbyterians.

At the last meeting of the General Synod of the Reformed Presbyterian Church, it was stated that a disintegration of the Synod had been steadily going on, and that it was falling off in members, ministers, and churches. Two churches of the Western Synod had dissolved, and two others had given notice of an intention to act similarly if not provided with ministers.

Associate Reformed Presbyterians in the South.

There are signs of a continued and vigorous existence of the Associate Reformed Church in the South. Negotiations for a union with the Southern Presbyterian church, which have been going on for years, have been dropped, and the A. R. Synod of the South has turned its attention to its own appropriate work. It has revived its paper, formerly the *Due West Telescope*, under the name of the *Associate Reformed Presbyterian*.

United Presbyterian Synod of Scotland.

The United Presbyterian Synod of Scotland, at its meeting in Edinburgh, in May, decided, after a full discussion, to adhere to its decision in 1858, against the use of organs in the churches. A motion offered by Dr. Cairns, on union, declaring satisfaction at the amount of harmony subsisting between the negotiating churches, expressing the opinion that there is no insuperable bar to union in their distinctive principles, and, in that belief, reappointing the committee to prosecute the negotiations, was adopted by a vote of 389 to 39.

The Scottish Presbyterian Churches.

The points of difference between the branches of the Presbyterian church in Scotland are thus stated in a letter from Mr. Bryant to the New York *Evening Post*: "The Presbyterians of the Established Church not only claim that public worship should be supported by the Government, but allow the Government to interfere with certain ecclesiastical matters, and permit the pastoral charge of parishes to be given by laymen to their friends. The Presbyterians of the Free Church insist that the Church ought to be supported by the Government, but deny the right of the latter to interfere in any ecclesiastical concerns. The United Presbyterians insist that the Government should have nothing to do with the Church, either with supporting its ministers or in any other manner. Presbyterians of the Reformed Church not only agree with the United Presbyterians in these respects, but insist that until the temporal sovereign of the country becomes pledged to the covenant there is no obligation on the part of the subject to obey. This sect is very small, and, notwithstanding the apparently disloyal tenet I have mentioned, is composed of persons as obedient to the laws and the civil authority, and as orderly in their conduct, as either of the others."

The Established Church does not favor the propositions for a union of the unendowed churches, fearing a weakening of its own political influence consequent upon the consummation of the union. Propositions have been offered in Presbyteries of that branch to create a diversion by encouraging in the Free Church hopes that the Established Church might offer them terms of union with itself which the Free Church could consider, but such suggestions receive no favor in the assemblies of that branch.

The General Assembly of the Free Church, at its last session, adopted a resolution directing the committee on union to continue their inquiries whether the questions of worship, government, and discipline were a sufficient bar to union between the unendowed churches. The general sentiment of the assembly evidently was that they were not, and the vote taken was in favor of union.

The United Presbyterian Synod adopted a resolution of similar effect.

The meetings of the committee of the four bodies have been resumed. A review of the proceedings of their Synods on the reports of their previous negotiations encouraged them to persevere in their work. It was agreed to consider first the subjects of finance and church property, and the titles to the latter in its bearings on the question of an incorporated union. Sub-committees were appointed to consult with legal gentlemen on various branches of the subject, and report at a meeting of the joint committee to be held towards the close of October. Notice was given of an intention to move for the appointment of a sub-committee to consider what should be done in the matter of a union between that portion of the United Presbyterian Church situated in England and the English Presbyterian Church.

Congregationalists.

American Congregational Union.

The Fourteenth Annual Business Meeting of this Society was held in Brooklyn on Thursday, May 9th. The Secretary's report stated that during the past year, through the instrumentality of the Union, the Congregational Clerical Union, consisting of Congregational ministers in New York and vicinity, has been organized, a convenient place provided at the Bible House, where ministers of the denomination may meet, and a special effort has been made to promote the work of church education. In this latter work, the receipts have been double those of any year except under the special effort of 1866. The most prominent churches in the South which have received aid have been in Baltimore, New Orleans, Memphis, Atlanta, and thirteen churches in Missouri. The seven Western States of Kansas, Missouri, Minnesota, Iowa, Wisconsin, Illinois, and Michigan, contain 816 Congregational churches. During these ten years this Union has aided in paying for the building of more than one-fourth of all these churches. The Treasurer's report stated:

Receipts of the year, total........	$32,530.22
Balance over last year.	67,119.18
Total funds for the year.........	$99,649.40

The total amount of appropriations paid feeble churches, $63 796.44. Amount voted, but yet unpaid, waiting for the erection of buildings, $23,200. Amount loaned feeble churches, $2,700.

Congregational Union of Canada.

The number of ministers connected with the Union is about 70; the number of churches 94, with a membership of about 4,000, and 147 preaching stations. They have 80 church edifices, with 20,550 sittings, and 12,407 "adherents," and 3,590 enrolled Sabbath school scholars. They have a college in Montreal for raising up ministers for their domestic missionary work. As yet, however, it numbers but four or five students, and has but one Professorship.

Congregationalism in Missouri.

There has grown up on the soil of Missouri a General Conference, with three district associations, embracing about thirty churches and more than thirty ministers. At the second annual meeting of the conference, eighteen new churches, with their pastors, were received into membership, and three new district associations were recognized.

The first church of the order was organized in 1838, near Pilot Knob, which, by the force of circumstances, was changed to a Presbyterian church in 1855; the second was organized at

St. Louis in 1852; the third at Hanniba in 1859. Two German churches were organized subsequently at Canton and Lagrange, which have become extinct. In 1864 two Welsh churches were organized at Sevier and New Cambria. Up to January, 1865, this was the extent of the effort to organize churches of this order in the State.

In October, 1865, the churches numbered eighteen, with five hundred and thirty-seven members. Since then there have been organized eleven more, making twenty-nine in all. Twenty-two of these churches are north of the Missouri river, and seven are south of it. The number of ministers is now thirty-one, against twenty a year ago.

Congregational Union in England.

At the semi-annual meeting of the Congregational Union of England, held in London, May 7, the discussion on the admission of Baptists to membership resulted in the adoption of a resolution in favor of it, by a very large majority. The resolution contained an expression of adherence to the doctrines of the churches of the Union on infant baptism. Resolutions were also adopted protesting against the growth of ritualism in the established Church.

Congregationalists and Secret Societies.

The Western Congregationalists, in conference at Ottawa, Ill., have adopted a series of strong resolutions against Free Masonry and other secret institutions, for these, among other reasons: because, while claiming a religious character, they, in their rituals, deliberataly withhold all recognition of Christ as their only Saviour, and Christianity as the only true religion; because while they are, in fact, nothing but restricted partnerships or companies for mutual insurance and protection, they ostentatiously parade this characterless engagement as a substitute for brotherly love and true benevolence; because they bring good men into confidential relations with bad men, and because, while in theory they supplant the Church of Christ, they do also, in fact, largely tend to withdraw the sympathy and active zeal of professing Christians from their respective churches. The General Association of Illinois also adapted a strong report against Secret Societies, chiefly directed against Masonry.

Congregationalism in Louisiana.

Mr. Charles Van Norden was ordained pastor of the first Congregational church of New Orleans, Louisiana, on Wednesday, December 10., 1866. This is the first Congregational Church of Louisiana.

Reformed Churches.

Liturgical Controversy in the German Reformed Church.—Meyerstown Convention.

The German Reformed Church, like the Anglicans and the Lutherans, are troubled with an agitation on ritualism. A convention of members of the Church, which was called at Meyerstown, Pa., on the 24. of September, took ground against ritualism, and condemned some of the features of the "Revised Liturgy" as at variance with the old liturgies, and with the Heidelberg Catechism and the Word of God. Upon the resolution of the Meyertown Convention being presented to the Eastern Synod at Baltimore, that body pronounced the Convention and its proceedings irregular and schismatic, and warned the members of the church against attending meetings "calculated to interfere with the peace and prosperity of the Church."

Change of Name of the Dutch Reformed Church.

The proposition to change the name of the Reformed Dutch Church in the United States by striking out the word "Dutch" has been voted on by all the classes but one. Twenty five have recorded themselves in favor of it, and six against it. Those voting in favor of the church were: Holland, Albany, Paramus, Rensselaer, Schoharie, Hudson, Saratoga, Greene, Schenectady, Long Island, (South), Montgomery, Cayuga, Kingston, Geneva, Passaic, Michigan, Monmouth, Raritan, Illinois, Poughkeepsie, South New York, Westchester, South Bergen, Philadelphia, Orange. Those voting against were: Bergen, Wisconsin, New York, New Brunswick, North Long Island, Ulster. The subject has yet to be acted on finally by the Synod. In a total of 661 votes cast the majority in favor of the amendment is 371. The vote at the General Synod had been ayes 102, noes 7.

The Reformed Churches of France.—The Orthodox and Liberal Parties.

A decree of the Consistory of Caen requiring all Protestant electors to assent to the Apostles Creed, before, excited much opposition on the part of the liberal division of the French Protestants. It was finally annulled by the minister of worship M. Baroche, who based his decision on the fact that the Central Council of the Church, a body selected *by the Government*, several years ago, declared that the certificate of admission to communion was sufficient evidence of the candidate's standing.

To get rid of this and other difficulties, the principal Consistories demand that the Government shall convoke a General Synod of the Church. This body has not met since the beginning of the French Revolution. Several eminent men have asked an audience of the Emperor, in order to secure its convocation. The elevation of Dr. Grandpierre to the Presidency of the Consistory of Paris, and of the Rev. D'Hombres to a pastorate of Paris, in spite of the claims of the Messrs. Coquerel (Liberal), is regarded by the Liberals as further separating them from the orthodox party.

The Reformed Church of Geneva.

The election of the Consistory of the National Church in Geneva this year resulted in the triumph of the orthodox party. The Consistory is chosen for four years.

Lutherans

The Split in the Lutheran Church in the United States.

Some of the Lutheran Synods have withdrawn from the General Synod, in order to take part in formation of a new organization, the "General Council". The proceedings of the first meeting of this council we report elsewhere. The old "General Synod" will endeavor to establish congregations in the territory of the seceded Synods. Thus the Lutherans will soon be divided all over the United States into an Old School and New School organization. Several particular Synods have dissolved one part siding with the General Council and the other with the General Synod.

The Millenarian Controversy.

The Confessional Lutherans, who now endeavor to effect a new organization in this country in opposition to the present "General Synod," which they repudiate on account of its Low Church platform, are divided among themselves on the subject of Millenarianism. The Lutheran Synod of Missouri has expelled the Rev. Mr. Schieferdecker, one of their oldest ministers, on the ground of his having become entangled in the web of Millenarianism, which is condemned by the seventeenth article of the Augsburg Confession, and the Smaller Catechism.

The Pennsylvania Synod on the other hand, the first which last year withdrew from the old General Synod, has tolerated and honored prominent Millenarians in its connection, the Board of its Seminary electing one of them its President.

Secret Societies.

The *Lutheran* says: "It is estimated that not less than *four-fifths* of the male members of the German Lutheran Churches in the Eastern cities belong to some secret order—such as the Odd Fellows, Red Men, Turners, and the like. The Synods which will organize the new "General Council" are generally in favor of excluding members of Secret Societies from the Church. Every one of these will have to be excommunicated, or renounce their connection with these societies, before they can become an integral part of the General Council.

The Lutherans of Germany.—The Union and Close Communion Questions.

The Religious Journals of Germany are occupied in the discussion whether, in the Protestant countries recently annexed to Prussia the Lutheran and Reformed Churches are to remain separate or to be forced into one united church, as they have been throughout the old realm. The principal opposition comes from the Lutheran church, and is strongly manifested in Hanover where, at a conference of 550 Lutheran clergymen held in July, the vast majority expressly approved a resolution declaring it wrong to admit members of the Reformed church to the Lord's Table in Lutheran churches.

Moravian.

Foreign Missions.

The *Moravian* publishes the following statistical summary of the Foreign Missions of the Moravian Church for the year ending August, 1867.

1. *Missions.*—Number of mission provinces, 15: stations, 88; preaching-places, 307.

2. *Laborers.*—Number of missionaries, 160; female assistants, 151—total of laborers sent out by the Church at home, 311; number of ordained native missionaries, 7; native assistants (as far as reported), 580; female do. do., 407; Scripture readers, 13; leaders of meetings, 45; whole number of native laborers, 1052. Whole number of laborers, native and foreign (as far as reported), 1363.

3. *Schools.*—Number of training schools, 7; station do., 80; country do., 65; Sunday do., 86: Whole number of schools, 238 Scholars in station and country schools, 12,904: in Sunday schools (children and adults), 11,852. Whole number of scholars (as far as reported), 24,746. (From Surinam there are no figures in the report on this point. In 1865 the whole number of scholars was 2338). Number of male teachers (natives) 117, female do. 75; monitors, 498; Sunday-school teachers, 1090. Whole number of teachers, 1780.

4. *Converts.*—Number of baptized members, 32,801; candidates, 7167. Whole number of adult converts, 39,968; number of "New People", 4101; number under discipline, 2336: baptized children, 23,606. Whole number of persons under instruction, 70'311.

5. *The Financial Statement.*—The total receipts from all sources during the past year were 100,280 German dollars; the total expenses 118,072; from the Continent of Europe there were received 51,425 thalers; from Great Britain, 38,687: from America, 10,164.

The missions are located in Australia (commenced 1849), 3 stations; West Himalaya (commenced 1853), 2 stations; Surinam (commenced 1735). 12 stations; West Indies (commenced 1732), 40 stations; South Africa (commenced 1736, renewed 1792), 12 stations; Greenland (commenced 1733), 6 stations; Labrador (commenced 1770). 5 stations; The Mosquito coast (commenced 1848), 6 stations, North American Indians.

The Northern Synod.

At the last session of the Northern Provincial Synod of the Moravian Church, held in Philadelphia in May last, the Committee upon Home Missions reported the success of the Moravian work among the Germans in New York, the erection of a Moravian church in Philadelphia, and conditionally appropriated a sum of money towards the erection of a Moravian church in New Haven, Conn. The Synod approved the use of the English version of the Liturgy for the Lord's Supper, directed the clergy to wear the surplice at the celebration of this sacrament, and enjoined upon the Congregations to give the "right hand of fellowship" at the beginning, and again at the close of the celebration.

United Evangelical Church of Germany.

Missions.

The Central Committee for Home Missions in Germany has directed its efforts to that vast population of Germany who go away from home at certain periods of the year to work; to the workmen in the sugar factories of Saxony, and to the miners near the Rhine. The secretary and the travelling preachers make yearly journeys to advance the object of the society, and now propose to give attention to Austria, particularly to the Protestants scattered among the Catholic populations, especially in Bohemia. The committee has its seat at Hamburg, and includes among its members some of the most eminent men of Germany. Its income is about 10,000 thalers, or £1500.

The Evangelical Church Diet of Germany.

The Evangelical Church Diet met this year at Kiel. The President, Professor Herrmann, of Göttingen, delivered a lecture on "Confession and the State Church," in which he dwelt on the historical development of the Lutheran and Reformed Churches, and showed that the territorial principle had been of scarcely less influence than their respective confessions in marking out their course through the centuries. Prof. Dorner, of Berlin, delivered a lecture on "Justification by

Faith in Christ; its importance for Christian Knowledge and Christian Life."

The Gustavus Adolphus Association.

This Society, for supporting Protestant congregations in Roman Catholic countries, is one in which most parties of the German churches unite. It met in 1867 at Worms. The reports of the coöperators revealed a state of great religious destitution. Among the subjects which received attention, were the Protestant "Diaspora" in Austria, and the wants of the Paris association for the evangelization of France. The receipts for the year 1866-7 are 177,526 thalers. The Female Unions have greatly increased their contributions, while there has been an increase of 16 new female unions and 31 auxiliarses to the parent society. The number of congregations aided is 800; 18 new churches have been built; and besides the 23 churches, 8 schools, and 6 parsonages in course of erection, it is designed to build 117 churches, 6 chapels, 169 schools, and 55 parsonages.

The German Protestant Diet ("Protestantentag.")

This is an organization of the "Liberal" party in the German churches. It held its session at Neustadt in 1867. Prof Holzmann, of Heidelberg, spoke on "the relation o. Protestant union to the present question of the historical Christ." This party has sustained a severe loss in the death of Prof. Rothe, at Heidelberg, August 20th, a remarkably learned man, gentle and amiable, highly respected, and its most influential leader.

Methodists.

Methodist Episcopal Church Lay Delegation.

The canvass for the introduction of lay delegation into the Conferences of the Methodist Episcopal Church has been very active during the year, and has been attended with results regarded as exceedingly flattering to those who have participated in it. The general results, as exhibited at this time (November, 1867.) are described by a friend of the movement as follows: It has been brought before the annual conferences and a number of them have expressed themselves absolutely in favor of it. A majority of the conferences favor it in case it can be shown that the people desire it. No Annual Conference has declared against it. Nearly all the church papers favor it. None oppose it. A majority of the delegates chosen to the General Conference are known to be in favor of it. Among the best known ministers and laymen of the church who are laboring earnestly for lay delegation, are Bishop Simpson, the Rev. Drs. McClintock, Stevens, and Crooks, Gen. Clinton B. Fisk, U. S. Senator Harlan, and others. A laymen's convention will be called to meet simultaneously with the General Conference in May next at Chicago. The action of the General Conference on the subject is looked forward to with much interest by all, and with hope by those who have been laboring to effect this great change in the economy of the church.

On the centenary collections taken up in the Church during the year 1866, we report elsewhere.

Methodist Episcopal Church, South.

The Annual Conferences of this Church took a vote on the question whether, in accordance with the proposition of the General Conference of 1866, the name of the Church should be changed from "Methodist Episcopal Church, South," to "Episcopal Methodist Church," and whether lay delegation should be introduced into the councils of the Church. The latter measure was adopted, more than three-fourths of the members of the Annual Conferences voting for it, while the former failed from want of a three-fourths' majority.

The number of Annual Conferences of this Church was increased by the establishment of one in Illinois, which, however, adopted the name of Episcopal Methodist Church.

A Union Convention, held at Montgomery, proposed a plan of union between the Methodist Episcopal Church, South, and the Southern Methodist Protestant Churches.

"The Methodist" General Conference.

The General Conference of the Methodist Church commenced its session at Cleveland, May 15. It represents mainly the late Methodist Protestant Church, whose last General Conference was held in November, 1866, when it adopted a plan of union which the non-Episcopal Methodists agreed to submit for approval to their Conferences and Churches. The Conferences of the other bodies did not adopt that plan. A few local churches (two Wesleyan and two independent) were represented. The ratio of conference representation was one minister and one layman for every thousand communicants. The roll contains over seventy names, nearly all of whom were present. The constituency represented, therefore, exceeds thirty-five thousand members.

The Conference made the following organic Disciplinary changes in their polity: The Restrictive Rule was so modified as to allow station and circuit preachers to remain in one charge for four years. The Leaders' meeting was abolished, and monthly meetings, composed of all the members of each church, together with its pastor, substituted in its stead. The old constitutional obligation of the Conference President to visit all the circuits and stations in his district. was removed, and each Annual Conference is allowed to use its own discretion as to imposing such a duty upon its President.

The next General Conference of the Church will meet at Adrian, Michigan, in 1871.

American Wesleyan General Conference.

This body met in Cleveland, O., October 2. Rev. S. Salisbury was elected president. About 50 delegates were present.

Two questions, that of the revision of the Discipline, so as to cut off churches tolerating members connected with Masonry and other secret societies, and that favoring the granting to women the right of elective franchise, gave rise to lengthy discussions. Both were decided in the affirmative, the former by a vote of 48 in favor to 5 against, and the latter by a very large majority.

The condition of the publishing house at Syracuse was reported as follows: amount of property in the hands of the Book Committee, and owned by the Publishing Association, $14,332.50; subscription list of the *American Wesleyan*, $1,800.

Canadian Wesleyan Conference.

This body, which met at Hamilton, in June, discussed the question of the division of the conference into three annual conferences, with a

General Conference to meet once in four years. A vote was taken with the following result: Yeas, 125; nays, 162; a majority of 37. So the measure fails for the present. Notice was given that the motion for division would be renewed next year.

Evangelical Association General Conference.

The General Conference of the Evangelical Association met at Pittsburg on the 10th of October. It adopted a general resolution in reply to overtures of union from the M. E. Church, in favor of the cultivation of a spirit of brotherly love and mutual coöperation in various interests of the church, but not contemplating actual union as either very probable or certainly desirable, and appointed a delegation to the General Conference of the M. E. Church. It determined to draw the attention of the Board of Missions to the importance of securing, at an early day, some town lots at important points along the Pacific railroad, for the purpose of erecting houses of worship thereon, whenever advisable, and recommended the opening of Missionary Institutes in connection with the literary institutions. The Association has missions in Germany, California, and Oregon, a board of publication, a tract and sunday-school society, and publishes two papers, one English and one German. It has two bishops.

British Wesleyan Conference.

This body met at Bristol, England, July 25. The Rev. John Bedford was elected President. For the first time in the history of the Conference, laymen were called on to offer prayer at the opening or closing of the committees. Sixty-one candidates for the ministry were ordained. Mr. William M. Punshon was deputed to attend the Canada Conference. The Rev. William Arthur was, in response to a request of the Irish Conference, appointed Principal of the new Wesleyan College at Belfast. A recommendation to seek the repeal of a law which requires the presence of a registrar at the solemnization of marriages, was discussed, and remitted to the consideration of the proper committee. The candidates for ordination were required to give pledges to abstain from the use of tobacco. The case of one candidate, who declined to give the pledge, was postponed till next year. The Conference made an informal expression against ministers wearing surplices and other vestments. A discussion took place on the number of collections taken in the churches, which some seemed to regard as burdensome to the members. The Conference agreed, in reply to a letter from the New Connexion Conference in regard to a union of Methodist bodies, that while it did not see the way to an organic union, it repeated its desire to cherish the most friendly sentiments towards kindred denominations. The increasing favor which total abstinence principles receive from the Conference is subject of remark. The Conference, by resolution, expressed its desire to maintain and extend the practice of open-air services which has existed in the denomination from its origin.

The Wesleyans have laid the corner-stone of a theological college at Leeds, the third under their control.

Irish Conference.

The 98th session of the Irish Wesleyan Conference was held at Belfast, commencing June 13th. The Rev. Dr. Robinson Scott, who recently visited the United States as a delegate, gave an interesting account of his observations, and of the condition of American Methodism. Mr. McArthur also spoke on the same subject. A congratulatory address was read from the English Conference. An entertainment was given to the members who are teetotallers by the Irish Temperance League. The returns show a small decrease in the membership.

Methodist New Connexion Conference.

This body discussed and adopted a programme of Methodist union to be submitted to the quarterly conferences. It adheres to the itinerancy and to the participation of the laity in all the church courts.

The Canadian Methodist New Connexion Conference held its annual session in Aurora, Canada. The increase in the number of members was reported as 220. The total membership in Canada is over 8,000. The question of Methodist union was left in the hands of the Executive Committee.

In the province of Tien Tsin, north of China, where this church has three missionaries, about 300 Chinese have professed conversion and abandoned heathenish practices. The Canada mission is prospering. The contributions are $600, and the membership has increased 22.

United Methodist Free Churches.

The Annual Assembly of this body met at Manchester. The reports showed a marked increase in the membership. A resolution approving the steps that have been taken in favor of union with the New Connexion was unanimously adopted after a lively discussion. This body adheres to free representation and the independence of the circuits. The subject was then remitted to the connexional committee with an express reservation in favor of these principles. The assembly made a decided expression in favor of total abstinence, and endorsed the principles of the United Kingdom Alliance in its efforts to abolish the sale of intoxicating liquors.

Union between the New-Connection and United Methodists.

At a conference between the members of the annual committee of the Methodist New Connection and of the connectional committee of the United Methodist Free Churches, held at Leeds, resolutions were adopted declaring the desirability of an organic union of the two denominations, and recommending the appointment of a sub-committee of three persons from each of the connectional committees in order to the removal of difficulties caused by the provisions of the "deeds" under which the churches were respectively constituted. The subcommittees have been appointed, and there is no doubt that the question will form an important feature in connection with the proceedings of the forthcoming conferences.

Primitive Methodists.—Theological Seminary in Canada.

The Primitive Methodist Conference of Canada resolved to establish a theological Seminary, and appointed a committee to carry out the matter in detail.

The Canada Primitive Methodist Conference have resolved to require a pledge of abstinence from the use of tobacco from all who in future enter its ministry.

A Primitive Methodist Theological Seminary is to be opened at Sunderland in June, 1868

Methodism in France.

There are now three districts in France, two of which report an increase, the third not having yet reported. The Southern district has more than 1,000 members, an increase of 132 from last year. There are 115 preaching places, with 11 itinerant and 75 local preachers. 1,200 Sunday scholars and 145 teachers. There are several educational institutions at Nismes.

The Wesleyan Reform Union on Clerical Titles.

The meeting of the representatives of the Societies of the Wesleyan Reform Union adopted a resolution against the use of any prefixes or affixes to the name of any person (minister).

Bible Christians on Union.

The annual assembly of the churches of this name adopted the resolutions of the New Connection Conference on Methodist Union.

Unitarians and Universalists.

British and Foreign Unitarian Association.

The British and Foreign Unitarian Association held its forty-second annual meeting this year. A prosperous condition of the denomination was reported. The Unitarian churches of Transylvania annually send over a student to complete his education at Manchester New College. The report gave an encouraging account of the condition of missions connected with the Association in the north of England and Scotland, referred to the formation of a theological library for the use of members and all free inquirers recommended by them, and to the distribution of books and tracts during the year.

"Liberal Christian" Conferences.

The organization of Unitarians, Universalists, and members of the Christian Connection into "Liberal Christian" is making progress.

Universalist Convention.

At the General Convention of Universalists this year a special committee reported adversely to propositions to amend the Constitution, and to a change of time of meeting, approving of the proposition to publish the Church History and recommending its reference to a committee consisting of Rev. Drs. Paige, Sawyer, and Thayer, and recommending the adoption of the following declaration, in reference to the meaning of the Winchester Confession:

That it was the evident attention of our denominational fathers to affirm the Divine Authority of the Scriptures and the Lordship of Jesus Christ; and in the judgment of this Convention those only comply with the prescribed conditions of fellowship who accept the Confession with this interpretation.

The Declaration was finally adopted, only one voting in the negative.

A resolution on the state of the country was adopted, affirming the principles of human brotherhood, and professing loyalty to the Government. A committee was appointed to report next year on the proper method of celebrating the centenary.

The Circuit System among the Unitarians.

A Committee on Christian Union, consisting of James Freeman Clarke, Hon. John G. Palfrey, and Rev. Eli Fay, in a report to the American Unitarian Association, have recommended a plan very like the old Methodist circuit system. The Committee says: "Our plan contemplates briefly this change. Instead of having a minister in every church, as now, let us have a minister presiding over several churches. In other words let us return to the origin of the episcopate, in which every church had its own officers chosen from among themselves, who were not clergymen but laymen; and one presiding overseer, who had the charge of several churches."

Progress of Universalism.

During the year over thirty churches have been erected, and over twenty are in progress and will be dedicated in a few months. Over forty societies have been reported in the papers as organized during the time. But the increase of ministers has not kept pace with that of societies and church buildings. There have been only five ordinations, not so many as there have been deaths in the ministry.

Western Unitarian Conference.

The Conference of the Western Unitarian churches met at Chicago on the 23d of October. The executive committee presented a report, from which we extract:

"We have assisted in the support of twelve pastors and missionaries and one theological student. Three new church edifices have been erected and paid for, in part, by our contributions. Preaching has been commenced at a number of new points, in several of which, new churches have already been organized. In no year of our existence has there been so much general missionary labor performed within our bounds, so many books, tracts and papers sold and distributed, and so large an amount of money collected for the various objects demanding our attention."

The conference at Buffalo had voted to raise $6,000 for the missionary fund during the year, but nothing has been contributed towards it. A resolution was adopted to raise $5,000 for the organization of societies in various parts of the West. A resolution for combining the Conference for missionary purposes with the American Unitarian Association, was reported by the committee on that subject, and laid over for consideration till next year. Cheering reports were received from the Meadville Theological school and Antioch college, and from most of the churches. The Conference adopted resolutions expressing gratification at emancipation, recommending the education of the freedmen, and approving the objects and action of the American Freedmen's Union Commission. Another resolution recommended the holding a Sunday School Convention in each State. A committee was appointed to see what opportunity there may be for organizing Liberal religious thought and feeling among the Germans, and in connection with the executive committee, to carry on whatever work may be deemed necessary till the next meeting of the Conference.

American Unitarian Association.

The forty-second annual meeting of this society was held at Boston on the 28th of May. The Treasurer's report showed receipts and disbursements to the amount of $177,526.22. The amounts of the trust fund are as follows: General fund, $26,400; Hayward fund, $20,060; Kendall fund, $2,000; Lienow trust fund, $3,300; Perkins fund, $8,000; balance of temporary investments, $23,000. During the year, the Association has aided 58 organized societies with money, had afforded preaching in 126 towns and cities where no Unitarian organization existed, employed 18 missionaries for three months or more, and 86 ministers for shorter periods, formed permanent organizations in 8 places, and had good prospects in 30 more. A mission has been opened at Wilmington, N. C., with a school of 112 pupils, an industrial school of 54 pupils, and a Sunday school of 98 pupils. The Indian mission has been aided by a general bequest, and is doing well, and a missionary has been commissioned to Buenos Ayres. The Association have published several new works, circulated 53,000 tracts, and given its publications to 38 public libraries. All the branches of its work were reported in a healthful condition.

Sandimanians.

The late Professor Faraday.

The late Professor Faraday belonged to a small sect called Sandimanians or Glassites, founded by Sandiman and Glass, both Scotchmen. Sandimanians profess very high Calvinism and have been decreasing in numbers and importance for many years past. Of late years, Faraday was an elder, and frequently preached in the chapel, Goswell road, London. A correspondent writes from Nottingham to a London paper: "I heard Faraday read the Holy Scriptures nearly forty years ago in the little Sandimanian chapel in Hound's Gate (now a warehouse), in this town, and was then struck by the simplicity of his manners and the clearness and impressiveness of his reading.

New Jerusalem Church.

The National Conference.

The National Convention of the New Jerusalem churches of the United States met at Cincinnati, May 31st. The reports of the State associations were very imperfect. The report of the Board of Publication showed that besides the *New Jerusalem Messenger* and the *Children's Magazine*, four new books have been published in New York. The Theological Institution at Waltham, Mass., has eight students.

The sixtieth General Conference of the English churches was attended by nine ministers and 29 representatives.

The proceedings of the Canada Conference show the church there to be in a condition of manifest growth and progress.

The Friends.

The English Yearly Meeting.

At the yearly meeting of the English Friends, the society again was anxious to sustain its testimony against war. It was the subject of annual inquiry whether all Friends had been consistent in this respect. In the United States, the testimony against war appeared to be carried out with more practical effect than among members of the society in England. Now that slavery had gone, the American Friends were resolved to make war the object of systematic and united attack. The claims of temperance on Friends were earnestly taken into consideration, one afternoon being devoted to the subject and it was decided to issue a minute, expressive of the concern felt by the yearly meeting on the subject.

Missions.

Hitherto, the peculiar missions, or "religious visits," constantly undertaken by devoted and earnest Friends have been of the nature of transient journeys through the country visited. Lately three members have been moved to go to Madagascar, for the purpose of taking up their abode in that country, to devote themselves to works of Christian beneficence as they may find opportunity. This movement has raised two important questions: In their own minds, how they shall act; in the minds of the Friends at home, how they shall be supported. A subscription of £1,500 answers the latter. As to the former, the three have declared that, in case they found it necessary to modify their previous habits, they wished to be left at liberty to act as "way might open," and "out of Christian consideration for their weak and lately pagan brethren, and, to avoid wounding their consciences or distracting their poor minds, not to interfere with customs already established by William Ellis and his brother missionaries."

In other words, they do not propose to form a separate "Friends' Meeting," or to organize a distinct society at all; but to do good in all the ways that piety and humanity shall dictate, and leave the religious order and practices of the people to the free determination of the people themselves, as they shall be guided by experience and the impulses of the Divine Spirit.

The Oneida Communities.

Peculiar colonies of Communists exist near and at Wallingford, Ct., and near Oneida, New York. Their economical features do not differ materially from those of the Shakers and other socialistic organizations. In religion, they have no formal creed, but claim to take the whole Bible as their guide, believe that the second coming of Christ took place at the fall of Jerusalem, that then there was a primary resurrection and judgment in the spiritual world; that a church on earth is rising to meet the approaching Kingdom in the heavens, and to become its duplicate and representative; that inspiration, or open communication with God, involving perfect holiness, is the bond of union between the church above and the church below, and the power by which the Kingdom of God is to be established and reign in the world. They have no religious service, or forms of worship, as they consider themselves perfect. They do not labor on the Sabbath, yet do not regard it as sacred. Their most peculiar notions are as to marriage, which they do not entirely repudiate, nor do they regard it as a permanent relation, nor entirely voluntary. They hold it to be assumed according to affinity, but to be regulated by the rules of the Society, and a certain respect to the judgment of the community. The children belong to and are cared for by the community, and not by their parents. The Oneida community was organized in 1848, has 215 members, and owns more than 500 acres of land. The Wallingford community was established in 1851, has about 45 members and 228 acres of land. There are also two other small families, in New Haven and New York.

Jews.

The Universal Israelite Alliance.

At the meeting of the Universal Israelite Alliance in Paris, held November 29th, 1866, the number of members was reported at 4,500, the receipts since May, 1865, 50,600 francs, and the expenditures 33 700. Protection and emancipation, instruction and education, religion and morals, are what the Alliance seeks to gain for its people. A Hungarian rabbi brought money to encourage emigration to colonize the Holy Land. It was accepted as a deposit, but Armenia was suggested as a preferable place. The President, M. Crémieux, told of his journey to Bucharest, and of his arguments in favor of liberty for Jews before a commission of sixty members of the chambers. His pointed question was, If the fathers had slain Jesus Christ, why must the children, 1833 years afterward, be made responsible? Surely, if God came upon earth again, they would not crucify him! Besides, if we take the Christian religion as it stands, that death is the pledge of salvation for all the world. The worship which people give themselves up to with so much happiness, is owing to the death of Christ. And yet 1600 years have done nothing to mitigate the accusation!

Synagogues in the East Indies.

A Hamburger, recently from Delhi, furnished the *Weekblad* of Amsterdam with an account of the Jews in the East-Indies. He states that in Delhi, Meirut, Agra, Lahore, Benares, Patna, Dinjapore, Cabul. Candahar, Poona, Bangalore. Mysore, Calcutta, Bombay, Madras, and other large towns. there are Jewish congregations. In the three last mentioned cities, there are a great number of European Israelites, while in the other places they are mostly natives, and cannot be distinguished from the Mohammedans by dress or manners, the only difference being in their religion.

The Israelitish Congress at Florence.

An Italian Jewish Congress met on the 30th of April last, at Florence, and completed its labors on May 5th. Twenty congregations were represented by as many deputies. Among other things, an annual grant of one thousand francs was again voted toward the publication of good books; it was further resolved to subsidize the Rabbinical college at Padua; the majority, moreover, passed a vote favorable to the convocation of a synod. An executive committee was then appointed, charged with carrying out the resolutions of the congress, after which the assembly adjourned.

Convention of American Jews.

A convention of Jews at Philadelphia in 1867, resolved against sending money to Palestine to be spent in almsgiving, proposing to devote money for that country to the development of agriculture and industrial pursuits there. It was resolved also to coöperate in measures for removing the Jews of Servia, Moldavia. Wallachia. Roumania, and the Barbary States to Palestine, and colonize them there.

Anti-Conversion.

The Universal Israelitish Alliance of Paris have determined to send out a messenger to counteract efforts to convert the Fallaohahs tribes of Abyssinia—supposed to be descendants of the lost tribes—to Christianity.

Jews in Office.

There are four Jews in the Prussian Parliament—all Liberals. There are five Jews in the Parliament and five Jewish magistrates in New South Wales, and one Jew in the Ministry of Van Dieman's Land. Seven Jews have been elected to the Italian Parliament, and three Jews have been elected from Prague to the Provincial Bohemian Diet.

The Jews in Roumania and Servia.

The Board of Delegates of American Israelites have called the attention of our Government to the persecution of the Jews in the Danubian principalities, with a view of procuring the exercise of its powerful influence in the interest of humanity, in behalf of their persecuted brethren. The Secretary of State has signified the compliance of our Government with the request of the Board of Delegates.

Jewish College.

A new Hebrew collegiate institution, to be located at Philadelphia, has been definitely determined on by the convention which met in that city last year.

The Jews in this country have already established educational institutions of different grades in New York, Savannah, Mobile, New Orleans, Cleveland, Albany, and other cities. This projected Maimonides College at Philadelphia is designed for a more advanced course of study than is pursued in any of the others, and of more thorough instruction in Hebrew than has ever yet been afforded in any theological seminary in America. "The conclusion has been formed," says *The Jewish Messenger*, "of not restricting the college course to Hebrew and theological studies, so that, instead of a divinity school, it is to be a college in the popular acceptation. It will have a faculty of science and letters as well as a faculty of Hebrew; it will furnish general instruction in classics, mathematics, and belles-lettres, as well as a special course for the future Hebrew minister and teacher. The plan is somewhat more grand and comprehensive than was first contemplated, but there appear to have been judicious reasons for its adoption."

The Tax on the Jews of Rome.

Dr. Philip, the Jewish Missionary in Leghorn, informs a correspondent of the *Evangelical Christendom* that there used to be a most important Hebrew colony in Venice, and that the printing press was much used among them. Almost all the old Jewish works bear either Amsterdam or Venice on their title pages, as the place of publication. Dr. Philip also mentioned a very interesting discovery he had made with regard to the Jews in Rome. It appears that every year the representatives of the synagogue humbly betake themselves to the Capitol, and deposit a sum of money in the hands of a lordly prelate who sits there. as officer of the Pope-King, at the receipt of custom. This annual tribute comes down from the time of Vespasian, who ordered that the contributions which the Romans were in the habit of bringing, in order to be forwarded for the Temple service in Jerusalem, should then and thereafter be changed into a perpetual tax of seven *denari* per Jew, to be paid to the government of Rome, in addition to all other taxes levied from Jew and Gentile alike. And to this day, and through all the intervening ages, from the time of the father of Titus, has this sum been exacted from the heads of the Jewish community.

Free Religious Association.

A meeting of persons of various shades of liberal belief was held in Boston on the 30th of May, 1867, "to consider the condition, wants, and prospects of Free Religion in America." Addresses were delivered by Universalists, Unitarians, Friends, Progressive Friends, Spiritualists, and persons of various shades of belief in doctrines commonly known as transcendental. Afterward a constitution was adopted for an association to be called a "Free Religious Association," the objects of which were declared to be to promote the interests of pure religion, to encourage the scientific study of theology, and to increase fellowship in the spirit; and to this end all persons interested in these objects are cordially invited to its membership. Each member of the Association is left individually responsible for his own opinion alone, and affects in no degree his relations to other associations. Any person desiring to coöperate with the association will be considered a member, with full right to speak in its meetings, but is required to contribute a small annual fee as a preliminary to the privilege of voting on questions of business. The association meets annually at Boston, one month's notice of the meeting being previously given. A permanent organization was effected, of officers and committees. The participants in the meeting were men and women of prominent rank in their respective spheres, and among them were persons of national fame as ministers, lecturers, and authors.

Positivism.

August Comte, author of the Positive Philosophy, was a Frenchman, of a Catholic family, born in 1798, and died in 1857. Rejecting the Catholic faith at an early age, he wrote a system of Positive Philosophy, the basis of which was science, rather than metaphysics or theology. He followed this by a treatise on Positive politics, in the composition of which he framed a system of Positive religion, to correspond with his other theories. His deity was a perfected Humanity, in which all mankind would be merged after death.

During the past year his followers in England have organized themselves into a church, under the leadership of Richard Congreve, formerly a clergyman of the Established Church. Eminent men who have contributed to the improvement of the race are objects of worship. Comte is an object of special reverence. It bases one of its claims for superiority over other religions on the fact that it sympathizes with the latest teachings of science, and utilizes them for the benefit of man.

A Positivist church has for some years existed in Paris, where M. Littré, an eminent French scholar, is the foremost representative of Comte's views. M. Littré has also begun the publication of a Positivist periodical. The organization of a Positivist community has been undertaken in this country at Modern Times, Suffolk county, Long Island, by Mr. Henry Edger.

Church of the Messiah.

This is a sect established in the United States a few years ago by G. M. Adams, formerly a lecturing Mormon Elder. In 1863, Mr. Adams appeared near Jonesboro, Maine, and there organized a congregation and established a periodical for the dissemination of his views. The only conditions of membership were immersion and belief in his apostolic character. Among the peculiar points of faith preached by Adams, is one that the members of the Church of the Messiah are of the tribe of Ephraim, and that, as the "curse is now taken off from Palestine," the time has come for the lost ten tribes to return to the land of their fathers. The re-establishment at Jerusalem of the throne of David, in greater than Solomonic splendor, is promised. In expectation of the near advent of the Messiah, 156 members of the sect from the State of Maine, in 1866 went to Palestine to establish a colony at Jaffa, the seaport of Jerusalem. Land had been secured for them in advance, and their settlement began under the most favorable auspices. But soon a large number of the colonists became dissatisfied with the management of "President" Adams, who was charged with dishonesty. The financial condition of the colonists was represented as most wretched.

The American Colony in Jaffa.

The agent sent out by the United States government, in the spring of 1867, to inquire into the condition of the Jaffa colonists, made a favorable report, but he must have been misled by those whom he saw, as the colonists on the 4th of July issued an appeal for help to return to their homes, which was endorsed by a committee in Palestine, at the head of whom was the American Consul. This stated that out of 151 of the original colonists, 54 had returned, 17 had died, and the remainder, except "President" Adams and thirteen others, desired to return. The steamer Quaker City, with a party of excursionists, stopped at Jaffa in the early fall, and took on board several of the colonists, whom it carried to Alexandria, Egypt, where they were furnished by contribution with means to pay their expenses to America. "President" Adams and a small number of the colonists yet remain in Palestine.

Free Congregations (Freie Gemeinden).

There are in Germany, and among the Germans in the United States, a number of societies under the above name. Their bond of union is the absolute freedom of inquiry for every individual on all subjects of religion and philosophy. Although not requiring a specific opinion on any other subject, all the societies, without exception, agree in rejecting a supernatural revelation. Some of the leading men were formerly deists; but it is understood that the rejection of the belief in a personal God is now the rule.

In Germany, the Union of Free Congregations numbers at present 121 congregations, with 25 000 members, and 6 periodicals advocate their views. Among the Germans of the United States, the Union (*Bund*) of Free Congregations embraces 5 congregations; namely, Philadelphia (since 1852); St. Louis (1850); Sauk Co., Wisconsin (3 branches); Dane Co., Wis.; Hoboken (1865). A periodical is published in Philadelphia. The Union acts hand in hand with the "Alliance of Freethinkers" (a German society in New York) and a number of "Free Men's Associations" in different parts of the country.

Similar Free Societies exist in France, Italy, Belgium, and Holland.

NATIONAL RELIGIOUS RECORD.

In this department we give some interesting facts of the history of the year 1867, which could not be given in the "Denominational Record," as they do not refer to any particular religion.

State Christian Conventions in the United States.

The American Christian Commission, in view of the numbers of the people who do not hear the gospel, and believing that many of them would gladly receive it when it was carried to them, appointed State Christian Conventions to be held in some of the Northern States.

Among the subjects discussed, were:

1. How can we best reach and influence those who habitually neglect public worship?
2. How shall the whole Church be interested and engaged in efforts for those who neglect the Gospel?
3. What can the laity of our churches do for Christ?
4. How can the unity of Christ's followers be better manifested to the world?
5. How can the Gospel be carried to neighborhoods remote from churches?
6. How can our devotional meetings be made more interesting and profitable to the unconverted?

and others of similar tenor.

The Convention at Indianapolis adopted resolutions recommending street preaching, preaching in halls and houses, cottage prayer-meetings, personal and household distribution of tracts and cards of invitation to the churches, that habitual attendants of churches come in plain attire, recognize strangers and invite them to come again; that ministers remember the poor in their prayers, and inquire if they sufficiently adapt portions of their discourses to the wants of the poor; that the laity interest themselves in Christian work, &c.

A State Convention for the State of New York met in New York city on the 13th of November. The discussions took a similar range to those in the other conventions. An address was adopted "to the pastors and members of the churches of Christ throughout the State," recommending the holding of County Conventions.

A Good Year for American Colleges.

The past collegiate year has been one of unexampled liberality toward the higher educational institutions. The colleges, old and new, have received the donations of their generous friends in such amounts as to inspire them with new vigor, while adding to their means of usefulness. Some idea of the aggregate amount of these benefactions may be gathered from the following table, which we find in the *Yale Courant*, and believe to be trustworthy. In this list no account is made of the amount given, in the way of land grants, to the Agricultural Colleges. The handsome gift of Mr. Cornell was made in 1865, but is given below, as it was not applied until within the last year:

Albion College, Albion, Mich	$ 25,000
Baldwin University, Berea, O.........	103,000
Beloit College, Beloit, Wis..........	18,000
Bowdoin College, Brunswick, Me......	27,000
College of New Jersey, Princeton......	20,000
Cornell University, N. Y.	760,000
Cornell College, Mt. Vernon, Iowa.....	25,000
Cumberland University, Lebanon, Tenn	35,000
Dartmouth College, Hanover, N. H....	35,000
Dickinson College, Carlisle, Pa........	100,000
Hamilton College, Clinton, N. Y.......	94,000
Hanover College, Hanover, Ind........	35,000
Harvard College, Cambridge, Mass ...	400,000
Kenyon College, Gambier, O....	35,000
Lafayette College, Easton, Pa..........	90,000
Lawrence University, Appleton, Wis...	30,000
McKendree College, Lebanon, Ill......	20,000
N. W. Christian Univ., Indianapolis, Ind	35,006
Norwich University, Northfield, Vt....	16,000
Oberlin College, Oberlin, O.	34,000
Otterbein University, Westerville, O...	30,000
Rutgers College, New Brunswick, N. J.	50,000
Shurtleff College, Upper Alton, Ill....	80,000
Tuft's College, Medford, Mass..........	309,000
University of Mississippi, Oxford, Miss.	35,000
University of Chicago, Chicago, Ill....	100,060
Wabash College, Crawfordsville, Ind..	46,000
Washington University, St. Louis, Mo..	100,000
Wesleyan University, Middletown, Ct..	98,000
Western University, Pittsburg, Pa.....	95,000
Yale College, New Haven, Ct.	206,000
Total of 31 colleges..............	$3,041,000

The South American Missionary Society.

At a late meeting of the South American Missionary Society of the Church of England, the Secretary said that the Society contemplated, among its objects of evangelistic labor, not only the aborigines, numbering six millions, and four millions of negroes, but a large English population settled in many districts, following mining, agricultural, and mercantile pursuits. British sailors, frequenting the South American ports and Chincha Islands in great numbers, formed another sphere of labor. The stations already opened were Panama, Callao in Peru, Coquimbo and Lota, with Araucania, in Chili, Paysandú in Uraguay, El Carmen in the North of Patagonia, and Keppel Island at the Falklands, with a mission vessel, the 'Allen Gardiner," named after the founder of the Society, for the work in Terra del Fuego.

Churches in British Guiana.

The London Missionary Society has now twenty churches, with nearly three thousand members, in British Guiana.

Protestantism in Mexico.

A Protestant Church of about thirty Mexicans has been organized in Monterey. A lot has been purchased, and efforts are being made to raise money to erect a building.

Sects in England.

The following is a list of denominations certified to the Registrar-General:—Apostolics, Arminian New Society, Baptists, Baptized Be lievers, Believers in Christ, Bible Christians, Bible Defence Association, Brethren, Calvinists, Calvinistic Baptists, Catholic and Apostolic Church, Christians, Christians who object to be otherwise designated, Christian Believers, Christian Brethren, Christian Eliasites, Christian Israelites, Christian Teetotallers, Christian Temperance Men, Christian Unionists, Church of Scotland, Church of Christ, Countess of Huntingdon's Connection, Disciples in Christ, Eastern Orthodox Greek Church, Etectics, Episcopalian Dissenters, Evangelical Unionists, Followers of the Lord Jesus Christ, Free Grace Gospel Christians, Free Gospel Church, Free Christians, Free Church, Free Church (Episcopal,) Free Church of England, Free Union Church, General Baptist, General Baptist New Connexion, German Lutheran, German Roman Catholic, Greek Catholic, Hallelujah Band, Independents, Independent Religious Reformers, Independent Unionists, Inghamites, Jews, Latter Day Saints, Modern Methodists, Mormons, New Connexion of Wesleyans, New Jerusalem Church, New Church, Old Baptists, Original Connexion of Wesleyans, Plymouth Brethren, Peculiar People, Presbyterian Church in England, Primitive Methodists, Progessionists, Protestants adhering to the Articles of the Church of England 1 to 18 inclusive but rejecting order and ritual, Providence Quakers, Ranters, Reformers, Reformed Presbyterians or Covenanters, Recreative Religionists, Refuge Methodists, Reformed Free Church of Wesleyan Methodists, Revivalists, Roman Catholics, Salem Society, Sandemanians, Scotch Baptists, Second Advent Brethren, Separatists (Protestants), Seventh Day Baptists, Swedenborgians, Testimony Congregation Church, Trinitarians, Union Baptists, Unitarians, Unitarian Christian, United Christian Church, United Free Methodist Church, United Brethren or Moravians, United Presbyterians, Unitarians Baptists, Welsch Calvinistic Methodists, Welsh Free Presbyterians, Wesleyan Methodists Associations, Wesleyan Reformers, and Wesleyan Reform Glory Band. (Many of the names in the above list do however not denot - different denominations, but are only different names of a particular denomination.)

Religious Societies of France.

The following are the principal Protestant Societies of France.

1. There are at Paris two *Biblical Societies*—the one called *Société Biblique de France*; the other *Société Biblique Protestante*. The one is orthodox, the other rationalistic.

2. The *Society of the History of French Protestantism* collects with care all which relates to the *old Hugenots*—their synodic deliberations, their sufferings, their heroic virtues, etc.

3. The *Society of Protestant Collections* addresses itself to the poor, and asks of each a subscription—of *one cent per week*.

4. The *Evangelical Society of France* is maintained by the members of independent congregations. Its design is to proclaim the Gospel to Catholics, and to open new places of worship wherever the number of converts has become considerable.

5. The *Sunday-school Society* deserves also to be mentioned. Many thousand children have been gathered in a large hall, called the *Cirque Napoleon*, and there pastors, elders and others have addressed brotherly words to the members of the rising generation. The children were attentive, interested, and more than once encouraged the speakers with their applause.

6. The *Evangelical Mission Society* established in France more than thirty years since. It has founded stations at Tahiti, at Senegal, at the Cape of Good Hope, etc. Its missions at the Cape have during the last year been attacked and grievously maltreated by the Boers, or Dutch settlers of that region.

7. *The Central Evangelization Society* is doing a work analogous to that of the *Evangelical Society*. But it turns its efforts and revenues entirely to the benefit of scattered Protestants, that is to say, of individuals, and families who have taken up their abode far from any place of worship, in the midst of Catholic populations.

8. The *Tract Society* (the Paris Religious Tract Society) moves in the same path as those of London, New York, Boston, etc.

9. The *Society of Primary Instruction* labors as its name indicates, to increase the number of the public schools, and to send good teachers into more humble villages.

10. The *Société des Diaconesses*, the *Société de la Colonie Agricole*, the *Maisons d'Orphelins d'Orphelines, de Vieillards* (Asylums of Orphans and the Aged) devote themselves especially to works of charity.

Deaconesses.

The Kaiserswerth Deaconesses' Institution had 139 stations during 1866. There were 491 sisters. At the present moment the number amounts to 500. The hospital has admitted 6?0 patients in the course of the year. The Orphan House in Smyrna was supplied with 20, the Servants' Refuge in Friedrichsdorf with 5, and the Hospital at Pesth with 3 sisters. Besides, there are a number of institutions under their care, schools, infirmaries, almshouses, etc.

Protestantism in Portugal.

A protestant congregation has been formed in the Azores. Another has been formed in Lisbon, of about 60 members, who meet secretly on Sunday, for fear of persecution.

Religious effects at the Paris Exposition.

A system of Bible and Tract distribution was organized for the grand Exposition at Paris, by the separate or conjoined efforts of several societies, some American. Agents of Sunday-school, Tract, and Bible Societies were in constant attendance, to converse with suitably disposed visitors, and to sell or give away their publications. The "Salle Evangelique" was visited daily. Every one who came received at least a Tract. Twenty-two thousand sheets were given away in this manner on one Sunday. The attempt to conduct stated religious services in the "Salle Evangelique" was not successful.

Evangelization in Venice.

The Evangelical work is prospering in Italy Four hundred and thirty-six persons attend th. services at Venice with more or less regularitye and are friendly to the preaching of the gospel. The evangelist hopes soon to open a class of catechism.

French Christian Associations.

A conference of Young Men's Associations was held in Paris during the year, under the Presidency of Mr. Paul Cook. It is pronounced successful, harmonious and fraternal. France, Switzerland, England, and America were represented on the list of Vice Presidents. Another general conference was appointed for 1879 at Amsterdam. A general conference of French Unions was also resolved upon to meet every three years.

Protestantism in Hungary.

The Protestant Church in Hungary has attained a development and influence which, considering the obstacles against which it had struggled are regarded by a writer in the *Christian Work* as little less than miraculous. It is divided into two branches, the Reformed (Calvinists) and the Lutherans. The Calvinists are nearly all Magyars, and are twice as numerous as the Lutherans. The characteristics of the Protestant Church in Hungary are: its indisposition to amalgamate its affairs with those of the state, or to subordinate the gospel to the state interest, the participation of the laity in all ecclesiastical functions except the administration of the sacraments, the solemnization of matrimony, and the ordination of ministers; and its consistent adherence to orthodoxy. The Bible and Hymn book are generally distributed, and "it is no rare occurence for poor and simple peasants to be so well versed in the Scriptures that they can put to shame many preachers." The Churches are generally well filled on Sundays. Many Associations for the promotion of a Christian Spirit have long existed in Hungary, and many have arisen in recent times where permitted by the laws, as conferences of preachers, circles of school teachers, Young Men's Unions, Auxiliary Unions for the poor; and an Association of Hungarian Protestant authors is contemplated. A movement has been made towards the dissemination of popular Christian books, and to extend the Gospel in Croatia and Danubian principalities. But very little has been done for missions to the heathen. Signs of a revival of greater religious activity are showing themselves.

Irish Societies.

The Hibernian Bible Society received for the year, ending last May £4.596, and issued 57,165 copies of the Scriptures. Its support has been chiefly drawn from the South and its benefits have been equally distributed all over the Island.

The Sunday-school Society reported 2525 schools, with 18 139 gratuitors teachers, and 194,172 scholars. It has issued over 50,000 Bibles and Testaments and other books. Since it was established, 56 years ago, it has supplied 1,527,105 Bibles and Testaments. and 367 518 portions of Scripture and Scripture reading books.

The Protestant Orphan Refuge supports 445 children, making a total of 1887 provided for since its foundation. Its receipts were £5,516.

The receipts of the Orphan Refuge were £1763.

The Church Education Society reports 1510 schools, with 68,277 children, and £45,619 income.

The Dublin Young Men's Christian Association has 553 members, with 47 affiliated societies, making the total membership 2500.

The receipts of other societies are as follows:

Irish Society	£ 8.460
Irish Church Missions	22,507
Protestant Orphan Society	5,518
Churc Missionary Society	6,059
Society for the Propagation of the Gospel	4,596
Colonial and Continental Society	41g

The Protestant Alliance of England.

The object of the Protestant Alliance is to maintain against all the encroachments of Roman Catholicism the doctrines of the Reformation, and the Principles of religious liberty. To this end it endeavors to awaken British Christians in the exercise of their constitutional privileges, to regard the interests of Protestantism as their paramount concern; to unite the Protestants of the empire in demands for the discontinuance of the national support and encouragement given to Roman Catholicism: and to extend sympathy and support to those in foreign countries who may be suffering oppression for the cause of the gospel. In accordance with this plan, its attention has been directed to various objects, such as preventing the introduction of sisterhoods into hospitals as nurses, keeping catholic influences out of schools, contending against the progress of ritualism, and the modification of acts of Parliament containing concessions to Roman Catholics, and preventing others from being passed. It has in hand the erection of a memorial to nine of the principal English Protestant martyrs, and another to Bishop Ferrar, of Wales. The receipts of the Society have fallen off on account of the stingency of the money market, and were for last year, £1823 14s 8d.

Protestantism in Italy.

A free Italian Church has been organized in Italy, with places of worship in Florence and other cities The sect of Plymouth brethren have succeeded in infusing their views into this movement.

The Vaudois, or Waldensian Church of Piedmont consists of six communities with a membership of 22,000. It has 23 principle stations, under its evangelistic agencies, mostly in Northern Italy, with some in Naples, Sicily, Elba, and France. It employs 19 pastors, 11 evangelists, and 29 teachers, and has 15 scholars in the theological school at Florence. The number of attendants upon public worship at these stations is reckoned at from 2000 to 2500; of communicants, 11,095. Income, £5611, Expenditure, £4911. The Synod, at its last meeting, resolved to employ a portion of the time of the evangelists in itinerating, so as to overtake, as much as possible, the calls for supplies.

The committee of evangelization connected with the Waldensian Church have also undertaking to open two schools in Venice, and had fifty children engaged and waiting the arrival of the teachers A new mission has been commenced by the Waldensians at Mantua.

APPENDIX TO THE DENOMINATIONAL RECORD.

On this page we give an account of some ecclesiastical meetings, which took place after the "Denominational Record" given on the preceding pages had been closed.

Lutheran.

Meeting of the "General Council."

The new ecclesiastical organization of those Lutherans who strictly adhere to the unaltered Confession of Augsburg as their standard of faith, was completed by the "General Council" which met at Fort Wayne, Indiana, on the 20th of November. The Council was organized by the election of Rev. G. Bassler, President, Revs. H. W. Roth and G. Fritschell, Secretaries, and Dr. H. H. Muhlenberg, Treasurer.

The following are the statistics of the Synods composing the Council: The Pennsylvania Synod, 125 pastors and over 50,000 communicants: the New York Ministerium, 50 pastors and above 12,000 communicants; the English Synod of Ohio. 12 pastors and near 2500 communicants; the Pittsburg Synod, 63 pastors and over 10,000 communicants; the Synod of Illinois, 32 pastors and nearly 4000 communicants; the Synod of Wisconsin, 51 pastors and about 15,000 communicants; the German Synod of Iowa, 52 pastors and 7000 communicants; the Michigan Synod, 13 pastors and above 3000 communicants; the Canada Synod, 23 pastors and over 7000 communicants; the Augustana (Swedish and Norwegian) Synod, 48 pastors and near 12,000 communicants; the Minnesota Synod, 22 pastors and 3000 communicants; the English District of the Joint Synod of Ohio, 40 pastors and 8000 communicants; in all about 550 pastors and 140,000 communicant members, embraced by 12 Synods. (According to the "Lutheran Observer" of Philadelphia, an organ of the General Synod these figures are too high. The Lutheran Almanac of Baltimore gives to the 12 Synods together 119,000 communicants.

A resolution was passed inviting those only, "who are in the unity of the faith with us, as set forth in the fundamental articles of this General Council," as "v siting brethren.".

The "Fundamental Principles" were then taken up. The New York Ministerium and the Wisconsin Synod, having passed amendments, it was decided, that inasmuch as ten Synods had adopted them without any change, they cannot now be subjected to amendment, except in accordance with the provision which they contain. Other parts of the constitution were then considered, amended and adopted. The ratio of representation was based upon the number of pastoral charges, ten of which are to be entitled to one clerical and one lay delegate, and more than five additional charges shall entitle a Synod to two more delegates.

The action of the Joint Synod of Ohio was presented, declaring the conditions upon which it could alone unite with the Council, viz: exclusion of congregations and ministers belonging to secret societies, the communion to be restricted to Lutherans, non-interchange of pulpits with other denominations, and the rejection of Millenarians. After much debate, a Committee was appointed, which reported certain principles by which the Council would be governedin deciding these questions, when regularly presented.

The Missouri Synod having addressed a communication to the Council, proposing a Conference with it, resolutions were adopted, laudatory of the fidelity of the Missourians to the faith of the Church, and expressing a willingness, at some future meeting of the Council, to meet them in a Free Conference.

The Iowa Synod presented a communication, containing its views on the subjects introduced by the Joint Synod of Ohio, on which a Committee reported, that the Council was not ready to endorse as correct the logical deduction and application of the negative part of our Confessional Books, "made by the Iowa Synod, and recommending that the matter be referred to the district Synods, in the hope that the Holy Spirit will enable them to see eye to eye in all the details of practice and usage." The resolution to publish the "Church book" prepared by a Committee of the Synod of Pennsylvania was adopted. The book is to contain as much of the Liturgy as will be needed for public worship, a collection of about six hundred hymns, the Unaltered Augsburg Confession, Luther's Small Catechism, and a collection of Family Prayers. A Committee was appointed, to correspond with Lutheran churches in the Danish West India Islands, and the Russian Possessions, when, after a vote of thanks to the people of Fort Wayne for their hospitality, the Council adjourned to meet in the English Lutheran Church of Pittsburg, at such time as the officers shall designate.

Presbyterian.

Southern Presbyterian General Assembly.

The General Assembly of the Presbyterian Church in the United States, or Southern General Assembly, met in Nashville, Tenn., on the 21st of November. Delegates were present from the Synods of Alabama, Arkansas, Georgia, Memphis, Mississippi, Nashville, North Carolina, South Carolina, Texas and Virginia. The Committee who had been appointed to confer with a Committee of the Cumberland Presbyterian Church on the subject of union, reported that they found all things favorable to union except that the Cumberland Presbyterians asked for modifications of doctrines, some of which were only verbal in their character, but others so fundamental as to require the deliberation of the General Assembly. A Committee from the "declaration and testimony" Synod of Kentucky presented the case of that body, which was admitted to the General Assembly. The Rev. Dr. Pressly of the Associate Reformed Presbyterian Church, addressed the Assembly to the effect that the body he represented declined the terms of Union tendered by the previous General Assembly. The report of the Church sustentation fund shows that 104 ministers representing perhaps 250 churches, have received aid from it. The foreign mission contributions of the churches were reported at $13,000. Eighty six thousand books and 335,000 copies of the *Childrens Friend* have been published during the year. The Book of Church order was reported rejected by a majority of the Presbyteries.

———o———

STATISTICAL DEPARTMENT.

---o---

The Creeds of the World.

It is, of course, extremely difficult to ascertain the numerical strength of religious denominations. The most trustworthy statistics of the class are those of the religious denominations which annually ascertain the number of their members. This is the case with most of the denominations of the United States, with most of the dissenters in England and with some of the free denominations on the Continent of Europe. In most of the European countries, the state governments, at the official census of the population, ascertain the population connected with each church. As a general rule it may be assumed, that the number of actual members multiplied by 2½ will be about equal to the number of population connected with a Church.

The collective name of Protestants has been retained in the following tables for all Christians who do not belong to either the Roman Catholic or the Greek or one of the other Eastern Episcopal Communions. The name is objected to by large portion of some of the denominations embraced under it, but no other name, that would be appropriate, has been proposed.

The following is the estimated summary of the aggregate population of the world, and of the total number of Roman Catholics, Protestants and Christians in general In the latter number are embraced, beside Roman Catholics and Protestants, the membership of the Greek and other Eastern religions. As we can only estimate, we leave out numbers smaller then one hundert thousand.

	Total Popul.	Rom. Cath.	Protestants.	Tot. Christ.
America	72,800,000	42,700,000	27,500,000	70,200,000
Europa	287,000,000	146,200,000	67,000,000	260,000,000
Asia	798,600,000	4,600,000	700,000	12,900,000
Africa	188,000,000	1,100,000	700,000	4,900,000
Australasia and Polynesia	3,800,000	400,000	1,000,000	1,400,009
	1,350,200,000	195,000,000	96,900,000	369,400,000

Ecclesiastical Statistics of America.

	Total Popul.	Protestants.	Rom. Cath.
United States of America	31,429,891	25,000,000	4,500,000
(with the late Russian America)	70,000	....	....
Mexico	8.218,080	5,000	8,200,000
Central America	2,500,000	....	2,500,000
U. S. of Colombia	2,791,473	4,000	2,790,000
Venezuela	1,565,000	....	1.560,000
Ecuador	1,040.371	....	1,040,000
Peru	2,500,000	1,000	2,499,000
Bolivia	1,987,352	....	1,987,300
Chili	2.084,945	10,000	2 070,000
Brazil	9 106,000	80,000	9,020,000
Argentine Republic	1,171,800	10,000	1.160,000
Paraguay	1,837.431	. ...	1,337,000
Urugay	240,965	3,000	237,000
Hayti and St. Domingo	900,000	10,000	880,000
Dominion of Canada (incl. Prince Edward Island and New Foundland) (1861)	3 295.706	1.750,000	1,485.000
Other British Possessions	1,140,000	600,000	150,000
French " (1862)	308,912	......	306,000
Spanish "	1.032,062	......	1.032,000
Dutch "	66.703	35,000	30.000
Swedish "	18,000	} 55,000	} 10,000
Danish "	48,111		
	72,873,402	27,583,000	42,793,000

At the usual rate of increase in the several countries o America since the last census, the aggregate population at the close of this year 1867, would amount to about 80.000,000, of whom 30,500,000 may be reckoned as Protestants and 46,500,900 as Roman Catholics.

---o---

Ecclesiastical Statistics of Europe.

	Total.	Protestants.	Rom Cath.
Portugal	4,349,966	7,000	4,340,000
Spain	16,302,625	10,000	16,280,001
France	38,067,094	1,600,000	36,000,000
North German Confederation	29,218,533	20,682,000	7,675,000
South German States	8.524.460	3,351,000	4,935,000
Austria	32,573,002	3,237,000	25,056,000
Italy	24,550,845	60.000	24,000,000
Papal States	690,000	1,000	6,680,000
San Marino	7.000	....	7,000
Switzerland	2,510,494	1,462,000	1,023,000
Holland (incl. of Luxemburg)	3,735 682	2,200,000	1,450,000
Belgium	4,893,021	25.000	4.8 0.000
Great Britain	29,591,009	23,000,000	6,000,000
Denmark	1,684,004	1,675,000	1,000
Sweden and Norway	5,614.366	5,800,000	5,000
Russia	67,701,176	3,918,000	7,081,000
Turkey	15,725,967	30,000	640,000
Greece	1,096,310	3.000	60,000
	287,066.174	67,051,000	146,230,000

The population connected with the Greek Church is about 70.000,000. The number of Jews is estimated at 3,300,000, and that of the Mohammedans at 4.800,000.

Ecclesiastical Statistics of Asia.

The total popoulation in the following column is taken from Brehm's *Geographisches Jahrbuch* (Vol. I. 1866.)

	Inhabitants.	Protestants.	Rom. Cath.	Tot. Chtsh.
Russian Dominions	9,327.966	40,000	10,000	4,500,000
Turkish Dominions	16.050,900	10,000	260,000	3,270,000
Arabia	4,000.000	......	......	......
Persia	5,000,000	2,000	10,000	70,000
Afghanistan and Herat	4,000.000	....	....	....
Beloochistan	2,000.000	....	....	....
Toorkistan	7,870,000	....	....	....
China and dependencies	477.500,000	20,000	700,000	750,000
Japan	35,000,000	1,000	10,000	11,000
India (incl. of British dominions in Farther India.)	157.694 323	} 500,000	} 1,600,000	} 2,200,000
Ceylon	1,919,187			
Farther India	21,109,000			
East India Islands	27,164.728	150,000	2.000.000	2,150.000
	793 635,504	723,000	4.580,000	12.951,000

To the East Asiatic religions a population of about 600,000,000 belong. The number of Mohammedans in Asia is estimated at 50,000,000. The number of Jews will hardly be more than about 500,000.

Ecclesiastical Statistics of Africa,

The total population of Africa is estimated in Brehm's *Geographisches Jahrbuch* (Vol. I. 1866) a standard authority in geographical matters, at about 188.000.000 divided as follows:

1. Eastern Africa 29,610,000
2. South Africa 15.813,000.
3. Islands in the Indian Ocean 3,838,000.
4. Islands in the Atlantic Ocean 114,000.
4. The Northern Coast 4,000.000.
6. Moham. Count. of Cent. Africa 61,100,000.
7. Western Africa 8.308,000.
8. Equatorial Territory 43,000.000.

The Statistics of the Christian population or rather the population under the influence of Christianity) are about as follows:

	Rom. Cath.	Protestants.	Tot. Christ.
British Possessions	140,000	650,000	800.000
French "	133.000	......	140,000
Portuguese "	439,000	......	439,000
Spanish "	12 000	......	12,000
Angola, Benguela, Mozambique	100.000	......	100,000
Algiers	185.000	10,000	200.000
Egypt	27,000	2,000	260,000
Abyssinia	30,000	......	3,000,000
Liberia	......	50,000	50,000
Morocco and Fez	200	......	......
Tunis and Tripoli	10,000	......	......
Madagascar	1,000	20,000	21,000
	1,077,000	732,000	4,992,000

Mohammedans are estimated at about 100,000,000: Jews in Morrocco, 340,000: also numerous in Abyssinia. The rest belongs to various pagan religions.

Ecclesiastical Statistics of Australasia and Polynesia.

	Total Population.	Protestants.	Rom. Cath.
New South Wales	376.935		
Victoria	574.331		
South Australia	140.416		
West Australia	18.780		
Tasmania	92.519		
New Zealand	175,357		
Queensland	59,712		
	1,439,050	1,050,00	350,000

The totol population of Australasia and Polynesia is about 3.854,000, of whom about 1,200,000 may be estimated as Protestants and 400,000 as Roman Catholics.
The following are detailed statistics of three of the Australian Colonies.

NEW SOUTH WALES.

	Numbers 1861.
Church of England	159.958
Presbyterians	34.692
Wesleyans	23.693
Congregationalists	5,411
Other Protestants	9,863
Roman Catholics	99,193
Hebrews	1,759
Mohammedans and Asiatic creeds	12,969
All others	3,393

There were at the same period, 270 churches and 447 chapels, or buildings used as such, providing accommodation for 119.075 people, that is, rather under one-third of the total population, having an overage attendance of 66,674, or under one-fourth of the population.

SOUTH AUSTRALIA.

	Numbers 1861.
Church of England	43,577
Roman Catholics	15,514
Wesleyan Methodists	14,3[illegible]2
German Lutherans	11,235
Independents	6,265
Church of Scotland	4,821
Bible Christians	4,216
Free Church of Scotland	4,137
Primitive Methodists	3.672
Baptists	3.454
Ch[illegible]ians	1,658
United Presbyterians	1,572
Other Christian Denominations	571
Unitarians	493
Hebrews	360
Moravians	217
New Church	192
Society of Friends	124
Mohammedans and Pagans	112
Not specified	1,391
Total	126,830

VICTORIA.

DENOMINATIONS.

	Numbers 1861
Church of Engl. and Episcop. Protest	205,695
Free Church	454
Protestants (not otherwise defined)	5,919
Presbyterian Church of Victoria	5,052
Church of Scotland	36,917
Free Church of Scotl. and Free Presb	21,219
United Presbyterian Church	16,734
Other Presbyterian Churches	346
Presbyterians (not otherwise defined)	6,635
Unitarians	1,430
Society of Friends	273
Calvinists and Calvinistic Methodists	650
Other persuasions	1,257
Roman Catholics	107.610
Catholics (no otherwise defined)	2,219
Greek Church	239
Israelites and Christian Israelites	395
Latter Day Saints or Mormons	108
Jews	2,903
Wesleyans, Wesl. Meth., and Method	40.799
Primitive Methodists	5,775
Wesleyan Methodists Association and Unit. Free Methodist Churches	1,446
Bible Christians	651
Other Wesleyan Methodists	140
Independents or Congregationalists	12.777
Baptists	9,001
Lutherans and German Protestants	10,043
Unsectarian, no denom. and Secularists	952
'No religion'	441
Mohammedans	189
Pagans (incl. of Chinese)	1,672
Chinese	24,551
Unspecified adults	2,391
" children	642
Objecting to State	11.535
Unenumerated migratory population	3,361
Total	540,322

Baptists.

1. ***Regular Baptists in the United States in 1866.***

States.	Assoc.	Church.	Tot. Pop.
Alabama, 1860	29	608	61,219
Arkansas, 1860	16	321	11,341
California	2	36	1,991
Connecticut	7	114	18,447
Delaware	—	5	609
District of Columbia	—	7	2,102
Florida, 1860	5	134	6,463
Georgia, 1869	39	994	81,567
Illinois	36	719	46,129
Indiana	30	450	29,103
Indian Territory, 1860	4	45	4,300
Iowa	17	278	14,377
Kansas, 1865	4	46	1,119
Kentucky, 1865	47	944	81,631
Louisiana, 1869	10	209	10,264
Maine	13	268	19,670
Maryland	1	39	4,348
Massachusetts	14	265	37,918
Michigan	13	239	15,376
Minnesota	6	122	3,434
Mississippi, 1860	22	598	41,610
Missouri	37	749	44,877
Nebraska, 1865	1	10	217
New Hampshire	7	84	7,718
New Jersey	5	129	21,094
New Mexico, 1864	—	1	49
New York	45	814	91,925
North Carolina, 1860	27	696	60,532
Ohio	30	482	33,869
Oregon	3	29	1,082
Pennsylvania	18	427	47,700
Rhode Island	3	56	8,537
South Carolina, 1860	18	473	62,984
Tennessee, 1860	24	663	46,564
Texas	22	456	19,089
Vermont	7	108	7,714
Virginia	22	622	116,526
West Virginia	8	220	12,774
Wisconsin	12	172	8,691
Germ. and Dutch Church	2	76	3,896
Swedish Churches	1	13	600
Welsh Churches, 1860	3	34	1,400
Tot. in the United States	609	12,955	1,094,806

The total number of ministers (reported at the dates above given in the several States) is 6,346, and of baptisms 92,075.

2.—*Baptists in the British Provinces of America.*

	Assoc.	Church.	Tot. Pop.
Nova Scotia	3	155	16,306
New Brunswick	2	119	8,755
Canada	11	275	15,091
West India Islands	4	101	22,261
Grand Tot. in N. America	22	650	62,415

These Provinces report 444 ministers and 2036 baptisms.

3.—*Other Baptist Denominations of America.*

	Assoc.	Church.	Tot. Pop.
Anti-Mission Baptists	184	1,800	105,000
Free-Will Baptists	147	1,264	56,258
Six-Principle Baptist, 1860	—	18	3,000
Seventh-Day Baptists	4	68	7,038
Church of God, (Winebrennarians.)*	10	360	32,000
Disciples (Campbellites)†	—	5,000	500,000
Tunkers, 1860	—	200	20,000
Mennonites, 1860	—	—	36,280

These denominations have 5,022 ministers.

4.—*Baptists in Great Britain.*

At the session of the (Particular) Baptist Union of England in April 1866, 2023 churches reported, 209,773 members, showing an increase from the year before of 130 churches and 4973 members. But 400 small churches are still unreported. Fifty-six new chapels were erected during the year, with sittings for about 25,000 persons, and 25 new churches were originated.

The following statistics of other Baptists in Great Britain are given by the census of 1851.

(In England.)	No. of Church.	No. of sitt'gs.
General Baptists	93	20,539
Seventh-Day Baptists	2	390
New connect. Gen. Bapt.	182	52,604
Scott. Bapt. (in Engl.)	15	2,547
Baptists in Scotland	119	26,076

The annual meetings of the Christian (Campbellite) Churches of England, Scotland, Ireland and Wales, which was held at Nottingham in August 1866, reported 505 additions. The present membership of the Churches represented is 4607. How many Churches were unrepresented, is not stated. The income for the year was £610 12s. 6d. The expenditures £462 0s. 11½d.

5.—*Baptist Benevolent Societies in the United States.*

The following are the names of the Baptist Benevolent and other societies, with the date of their organization, and amount of receipts for the year preceding the last report. ¶ American Baptist Missionary Union, organized 1814, last year's receipts, $191,714,000; ¶ American Baptist Publication Society, 1824, $240,165 68, and has published 171,037,050 18mo. pages during the year; ¶ American Baptist Home Mission Society, 1832, $176,899 04; American and Foreign Bible Society, 1838, $51,407 45; ¶ American Baptist Free Mission Society, 1843, $21,318 97; ¶ American Baptist Historical Society, 1843, $365 21, and 459 volumes added to the library.

6.—*Baptist Periodicals in the United States.*

Thirty-six Baptist Periodicals—24 weekly, 10 monthly, and 2 quarterly: are published in the United States, and 3 weekly periodicals in the British provinces. The Baptist educational institutions in the United States number 30 colleges and 14 theological institutions.

7.—*Baptist Missions on the Continent of Europe.*

	Church Dec. 1866	Memb. Dec. 1865	Memb. Dec. 1866
France	6	357	358
Germany	64	11,239	11,8[illegible]4
Denmark	16	1,702	1,726
Holland	1	36	52
Switzerland	1	269	292
France (Germ. miss.)	1	67	96
Poland	1	268	312
Russia	3	607	657
Sweden	183	6,489	6,875
Total	276	21,064	22,402

* The estimates of this denomination vary from 25,000 to 40,000. The figures here given are a medium.

† There are supported by this denomination 11 Colleges and Universities, 27 Female Colleges and seminaries, and 26 periodicals; viz. 6 weekly, 2 semi-monthly, 16 monthly, and one quarterly periodical.

There are 1300 stations and outstations connected with the European missions, and about 300 preachers and assistants. Baptisms last year, 2280. Exclusive of the Swedish, these churches contributed 40,599 Prussian thalers to he missionary fund.

8.—*Asiatic Missions.*

The Asiatic Missions are in Burmah and the neighboring kingdoms, Siam and China. They embrace 16 stations where missionaries reside, and 400 outstations with 90 American missionaries, and 300 native preachers and assistants, and about 16,000 members.

The Mission Press at Rangoon printed during the year ending September 30., 1865, 171,900 copies of books and tracts (mostly in native languages), giving a total of 8,573,200 pages.

9.—*Baptists in Australia.*

There are 3424 Baptists in South Australia, and 9601 in Victoria.

10.—*Mennonites in Europe and Asia.*

The number of Mennonites in Europe and Asiatic Russia was computed in 1860 at 10,000, and an estimate made at this time gave the total Mennonite population of the world (not members but the entire population connected with the Congregations) at 222,237.

Methodists.

1.—*Methodist Episcopal Church.*

The following table presents the present *membership* and the *increase*, by Conferences, in both the ministerial force and the laity:

Conferences.	Travelling Preachers.	Members.	Increase.
Alabama	46	9,341	9.341
Baltimore	107	15 768	1.721
Black River	213	20,933	dec. 566
California	106	5.766	1,284
Central German	90	9 592	438
Central Illinois	170	21,736	1,332
Central Ohio	128	20.067	923
Cincinnati	157	31,008	208
Colorado	10	524	193
Delaware	40	9.024	809
Des Moines	90	12,682	793
Detroit	174	19,368	2,228
East Baltimore	231	38.306	1,404
East Genesee	203	23,858	438
Eastern German	29	2.659	231
East Maine	91	10,052	dec. 625
Erie	258	31.873	1.603
Genesee	130	9,465	194
Georgia	40	10,235	10,235
Germany and Switzerl'd	43	5 928	578
Holston	[illegible]	23·720	5.509
Illinois	193	32.835	2.205
India Mission	24	358	93
Indiana	133	28.740	1.317
Iowa	110	19.186	1,641
Kansas	74	7,046	1 119
Kentucky	61	13.997	7,101
Liberia Mission	19	1.376	dec. 54
Maine	120	12,538	401
Michigan	166	19.993	1,929
Minnesota	101	8 790	48
Mississippi	31	7,899	5,207
Missouri and Arkansas	161	20 416	7,708
Nebraska	30	2,106	109
Nevada	11	367	122
Newark	159	27,465	8,210
New England	206	22.266	1,255
New Hampshire	127	12 620	597
New Jersey	152	27.588	dec. 182
New York	257	37.446	939
New York East	215	35.312	1.430
North Indiana	137	30 079	1.822
North Ohio	123	16,371	1,125
Northwestern German	85	6,523	564
Northwest Indiana	107	16,016	444
Northwest Wisconsin	40	3.351	161
Ohio	157	31,849	684
Oneida	188	19,697	413
Oregon	59	4 218	673
Philadelphia	280	57,887	103
Pittsburgh	232	44.049	869
Providence	131	17,419	1,184
Rock River	205	21 033	583
South Carolina	29	9,668	6,531
Southeastern Indiana	64	17,713	dec. 429
Southern Illinois	127	22.238	1,081
Southwestern German	94	7 557	557
Tennessee	61	6.110	2,934
Texas	17	1,564	1,589
Troy	218	27 585	1.124
Upper Iowa	138	16.669	1,598
Vermont	138	13,275	202
Virginia	14	671	671
Washington	75	17,463	4.251
West Viginia	107	26.783	7,675
West Wisconsin	77	8.200	798
Wisconsin	155	12.333	1.507
Wyoming	118	17,033	191
Total	7,969	1,144,763	....
Last year	7.576	1,032,164	....
Increase	413	112,579	....

Of *Annual Conferences* there are 68, an increase of four over the previous year. This increase has been obtained by extending the work in the South. The new conferences organized are: Virginia and North Carolina, organized January 3.; Texas, January 3.; Georgia, October 10.; Alabama, October 17.—The number of *Churches* (houses of worship) is 11,138, being an increase for the year of 676; number of parsonages, 3,570, an increase of 256. The total value of these church edifices and parsonages is $41,012,479, being an increase for the year of $6,997,516. The increase in *parsonage property alone is nearly a million of dollars.* Full reports of the centenary returns had not been made up to November. Thirty-seven conferences had reported a total of $6,141,027. The returns from the remaining conferences it was expected would swell this amount to over *seven millions of dollars.*

The Statistics of the Principal Societies of the Church during the year 1866 were as follows:

Missionary Society of the Methodist Episcopal Church organized in 1819. Receipts last year, $671,090 66. Appropriations for 1867, $1,030,978 00. It supports 2341 missionaries and ministers to 75,754 members.

Church Extension Society organized 1864. Receipts in 1866, $60,000. It has assisted during the year in building 139 churches.

Sunday School Union. Contributions $19,853 89. Sunday Schools, 13,845: officers and teachers, 162.000; scholars, 980,706; volumes in libraries 2,619,215. All show an increase from last year. Pages printed 589,711 621.

Tract Society. Receipts. $14.571 24, an increase of $1007 63 from last year. Disbursements $12,316 63. Pages printed last year. 3.830,000. Add *Good News* reduced to 12mo pages. and we have 22,018 000. One thousand dollars have been granted to Germany, and smaller amounts to India and other fields.

There are under charge of the Methodist Episcopal Church, twenty-three Colleges and Universities, five Theological Seminaries, and 82 Seminaries, Female Colleges and Academies.

The *Book Concern* of the Methodist Episcopal Church belongs to the General Conference and is under its control. It has two publishing houses at New York and at Cincinnati, under the charge of separate committees and separate publishing agents, and depositories in Boston, Chicago Pittsburgh, Buffalo, St. Louis, and San Francisco. The Book Agents publish over nineteen hundred different bound volumes, and the unbound and tract list embraces about one thousand, the tracts varying from two to sixty-four pages each. The books and tracts are in English, German, Welsh, Swedish, Danish, and French. The sales for 1866 were, at New York, $775,513 19; at Cincinnati, $628,453 66; total $1,303,966 92,

Sixteen *Periodicals*: 1 quarterly review, 1 monthly, 9 weeklies, one German weekly, 1 missionary journal, 2 sunday school papers, and 1 paper in the interest of the M. E. Tract Society are published by direction of the General Conference.

The *Comparative Progress* of the Methodist Episcopal Church during the first century of its existence is shown by the following table:

Years.	Trav. Preach.	Memb.
1767	....	....
1776	24	4.021
1786	117	20,689
1796	293	56,664
1806	452	130,560
18'6	695	214.235
1826	1.416	360,800
1836	2.928	650.109
1846	3 682	*644,223
1856	5.877	800.327
1866	7,576	1,032,184

* By the withdrawal and separation of Southern conferences in 1844, organizing the Methodist Episcopal Church, South, the Methodist Episcopal Church lost 1,345 traveling preachers and 495,288 members, and yet, so rapid was her growth during the decade, that at its close (two years after the separation) there was a net gain of 751 preachers, and a lack of only 5.874 members of making up the number lost.

2.—*Methodist Episcopal Church, South.*

The following statistics were published in the Southern Methodist Almanac for 1860. No official statistics of the Church have been published since the beginning of the war.

Conferences.	Trav. Preach.	Members in Society. Whites.	Col. and In.	Total.
Kentucky	81	17,737	5.196	23,228
Louisville	88	22,068	4 160	26,540
Missouri	84	17,566	1,915	19,725
St. Louis	103	22,074	1,069	24,065
Kansas Mission	24	590	156	782
Tennessee	190	37,339	7,794	45,704
Holston	110	44,977	4.642	50,144
Memphis	152	32,153	7,960	40,662
Mississippi	124	16,157	15,655	34,150
Louisiana	68	8,368	5,061	13,612
Virginia	174	38,086	7.007	45.473
Western Virginia	57	10.337	295	10,767
North Carolina	117	31,435	13,195	41,946
South Carolina	150	37.095	46.740	84.201
Georgia	197	53.863	25.166	79,831
Alabama	202	45,640	24.086	70,481
Florida	77	9,585	7.778	17,569
Texas	130	13,990	3.663	17 983
Eastern Texas	80	14,166	2.398	16,843
Arkansas	53	12,178	1.174	13.266
Wachita	66	9,532	2,400	13,160
Indian Mission	34	88	3,787	3.964
Pacific	49	2,667	14	2.708
Total	2,408	499,694	191,915	699,164

Superannuated preachers, 163; local preachers, 4964.

At the General Conference of 1866, the number of Conferences represented was 25; Alabama having been divided into Montgomery and Mobile, Texas into Texas and Rio Grande, and the Baltimore Conference (part of the Baltimore Conference of the Methodist Episcopal Church, being admitted.

In 1867 several "Christian Union Churches" of Illinois were organized into the Illinois Conference.

The Church has suffered a large decrease in its colored membership. A number of Annual Conferences have not reported their statistics] and no official statement of the aggregate membership can therefore be given.

The session of the Annual Conferences for 1867 began in September. The return of the Tennessee Conference show an increase of 3,400 white members; decrease of colored members, 390; preachers received on trial, 21; readmitted 3; located, 5; increase of local preachers, 69.

The West Virginia Conference reports an increase of 3,000 members, and 7 preachers received on trial. Forty-five preachers were stationed.

The new Illinois Conference has about 40 preachers.

In 1867, there were 30 Annual Conferences:

Kentucky	Mississippi	South Georgia
Louisville	Louisiana	Florida
Missouri	Montgomery	West Virginia
St. Louis	Mobile	Virginia
Indian Mission	Texas	North Carolina
Arkansas	East Texas	South Carolina
Little Rock	Northw. Texas	Baltimore
Tennessee	West Texas	Columbia (Oreg.)
Holston	Trinity (Texas)	Pacific (Califor.)
Memphis	North Georgia	Illinois

Official Papers were in 1867 published at Nashville, Macon, Richmond, Memphis, St. Louis, New Orleans, Little Rock, Galveston, San Francisco, and independent papers at Baltimore, Raleigh, Jackson, Catlesburg.

The Church sustains a mission in China.

The number of colleges in 1860 was 12, of female colleges, high schools and academies about 80.

3.—*Methodist Protestants.*

The main body of the Methodist Protestants comprising the conferences in the Northern States held in 1866, a "union convention" which was to effect a union between Non-Episcopal Methodists. The name of the new body was to be simply the "Methodist" Church. But this plan of union was repudiated by all save the Methodist Protestants and the new "Methodist" Church is sustantially identical with the former Methodist Protestant Conferences of the Northern States. The complete statistical report made in 1867 is approximately, not fully, as follows: Annual Conferences, 19; Ministers, 625; local preachers, 430; communicants, 50,000; churches, 480; parsonages, 104; property value, $1,150,000. Contribution for missions in 6 months were less than $600.

Their Book Concern has real estate, valued at twelve or fifteen thousand dollars only.

The number of Methodist Protestants in the North and South together is estimated at about 100,000. The present membership in the Maryland district is between nine and ten thousand; itinerant ministers, 75; local preachers, 45; and Sunday-school children about 10,000.

The "Methodist" Church publishes a weekly paper at Springfield, Ohio, and the Southern Methodist Protestants have an organ at Baltimore. In both these cities there are book concerns.

4.—*The Wesleyan Connection.*

At the "Union Connection" held in 1866 to effect a union with the Methodist Protestant and other Non-Episcopal Churches, the following annual Conferences were represented: Central Ohio, New York, Iowa, Indiana, Miami, Michigan, Rochester, Alleghany, and Syracuse.

The membership of the denomination is about 25,000. There is a denominational Book-Concern at Syracuse.

5.—*Free Methodist Churches.*

This Church, in Oct. 1866, reported the following statistics:

Annual Conferences	Preach.	Memb.	Church Pr'ty.
Genesee	31	2,025	$46,050
Illinois	25	1,278	42,550
Susquehana	21	1,104	7,349
Michigan	8	482	——
Total	85	4,839	$95,949

6.—*Primitive Methodists.*

The following statistics were reported in 1865: 42 Sabbath-schools; 3,018 teachers and scholars; 20 traveling preachers; 14 parsonages, and 36 churches valued at $43,200 (indebtedness $3000). Members about 2000, mostly in Wisconsin and Illinois.

7.—*Evangelical Association.*

The statistics of this denomination, for 1867, not reaching us in time, for insertion here, we expect to give on another place.

8.—*African Methodist Episcopal Churches.*

Of these there are two, generally called the "African Methodist Episcopal Church" and the "African Methodist Episcopal Zion Church". Both have of late largely increased in membership in the Southern States.

The former, in 1867, had 10 Conferences, 550 preachers, including 5 bishops, but exclusive of 1500 local preachers, and about 200,000 members, nine-tenths of whom live in the southern states. They have Church property to the amount of four millions of dollars, a Book Concern in Philadelphia, a weekly newspaper, and a college in Ohio.

The second organization reports more than 60,000 members, with nearly 300 traveling and many local preachers.

9.—*Methodist Churches of Canada.*

The Canadian M. E. Church suffers a small decrease. The Niagara Conference, at its late session reported a total of ministers and members of 7,294, showing an increase of 62; the Ontario Conference reported 5,376, a decrease of 315; and the Bay of Quinte Conference 6,267, an increase of 63. From the foregoing it will be seen that the aggregate increase in the first and last named amounts to 125, but the large decrease in the Ontario Conference over-balances the increase in the other two by 190.

For the statistics of the other Methodist bodies which are in connection with the Methodist Churches of Great Britain, see the latter.

10.—*Wesleyan Connection of Great Britain.*

I. British Conference:	Memb.	Incr'se.	Decr'se.
Great Britain	326,076	5,887	
Ireland, and Irish Missions	19,657		178
Foreign Missions	61,794	1,898	
II. French Conference	1,890	191	
III. Australasian Conf.	49,433	1,738	
IV. Canada Conference	55,078	1,124	
V. Conference of Eastern British America	14,873,		402
Totals	539,795	10,838	580
Last year	529,537		580
Net Increase	10,258	10,258	

Connexional Institutions.

1. *Home Mission and Continent Fund.* Instituted 1756, remodelled 1856. Increase £22,000. Has assisted during the year in building 65 chapels, costing £109,970, and accomodating 28,147 persons.

2. *Wesleyan Chapel Committee.* Instituted 1818, reinstituted 1854. Receipts (from subscriptions and collections) £7,417 7s. 6d.

Amount expended on Wesleyan trust property during the year, £295,594. Amount actually raised and paid, ...£215,760
To which add grants from Connexional Funds.................................. \8,550

Total...£224,360
An increase from last year.................. £32,406

3. *Childrens Fund.* Instituted 1818.

This is a fund desired to equalize the assessment on the circuits for the support of ministers children. It is so divided that for a certain number of members in the circuit (90 in 1856) the circuit shall contribute 60 guineas a year, the allowance for each child.

4. *Wesleyan Education Committee.* Institnted 1837, has charge of Sunday-schools and Day-schools.

5. *Auxiliary Fund.* The Connexion supports an Auxiliary Fund for the support of worn out preachers.

6. *Publication House, Theological Institutions &c.* There are under the charge of the Conference, a Book-room in London, a theological institution with branches at Richmond, Surrey, and Didsbury, near Manchester, schools at Kingswood and Wood House Grove, a Normal Institution at Winchester, a college at Sheffield, and a collegiate institution at Taunton.

Wesleyans Missions.

	Missionaries and Assist.	Memb'rs and Probationers	Sunday and Day Scholars	Attendants on Public Preachings
France, Switzerland and Corsica (17 stations)............	31	1 876	2,114	10,195
Germany (5 circuits)..	8	1,807	200	4,481
Italy (2 circuits)..	3	20	183	
Spain (Gibraltar and Malta)................................	2	5	204	600
North and South Ceylon (22 circuits)...................	31	2,003	3,582	8,365
India (21 stations and circuits)	34	558	3.625	
China (6 stations)	9	58	225	218
Cape of Good Hope (9 circuits)...........................	8	1'701	2,703	6,889
Graham Town (14 circuits)..................................	19	6 907	5,295	20.530
Incenstown (12 circuits).....................................	10	3.381	1,511	13,800
Bechnaner (9 stations).......................................	9	1,088	1,196	52.110
Natal (10 stations)...	15	1,613	1,286	12.840
Siena Leone, Gambia, and Gold Coast (14 circuits)........	23	7,923	5,127	26,713
Antigua, St. Vincent, and British Guiana (24 circuits)....	45	20,496	11,193	65,290
Jamaica, Honduras, Bahama, and Hayti (36 circuits).....	38	19,479	8.160	45,429
Ireland (24 circuits)....	30	2,165	1,748	7,125
Australasia and Polynesia (164 circuits)..................	282	57,183	51,607	251,526
British America (298 circuits)................................	381	35,316	13,957	140,499

11.—*Statistics of the Primitive Methodists,* 1867.

		Increase.
Traveling Preachers..............	891	11
Local Preachers....................	13,865	138
Connexial Chapels.........	3,118	126
Rented Chapels and Rooms.......	3,192	9
Sabbath-schools....................	2,984	68
Sabbath-scholars.	234,794	7,318
Sabbath-school Teachers..........	41,191	988

This does not include these in the United States, but includes those in the Home Missions and the Colonies.

Primitive Methodist Missions.

	Missionaries.	Members.
Home stations......	101	7,772
Ireland, Scotland, and Channel Island..........	13	818
Australia, N. Zealand, and Tasmania............................	37	1,904
Canada.	39	2.919
Total...........	100	13,413

12.—*Statistics of the United Methodist Free Churches.*

Ministers, 288, increase, 5; local preachers, 3,368; leaders, 4,420; members, 67,478, increase, 1,721; on trial, 5,962, increase, 717; chapels, 1,173, increase 33; other preaching-rooms, 398; Sunday-Schools, 1,121, increase, 46.

United Methodist Free Churches Missions.

	Itinerants.	Members and Probationers.	Sunday and Day Schol'rs
Australian District (10 circuits)..	12	612	1,431
Jamaica District (7 circuits)......	9	1,795	498
Eastern Africa and China........	4	6	
Siena and Leone..................		2,618	563
Total..........................	25	5,030	2,771

There are 125 local preachers and 229 leaders at all these stations. There is an increase of preachers and leaders from last year, but a decrease in members and Prebationers of 441.

13.—*Methodist New Connexion.—Statistics.*

The Statistics of this body show a total of 3270 members. The increase in England is 85. But there has been a decrease in Canada of 300, making a net decrease of 215.

Methodist New Connexion Missions.

	Circuit and local preachers.	Members and probationers.	Sunday scholars.
England	50	952	2,316
Ireland	12	681	819
Canada	215	8,110	5,190
China	10	108	6
Australia	12	147	240
Total	299	9,998	8,571

14.—*Wesleyan Reform Union Statistics.*

		Increase.
Members	9,175	243
Preachers	602	
Chapels	285	
Schools	182	
Scholars	17,691	704
Teachers	782	

United Brethren in Christ.

Conferences.	Number of Societies.	Number of Members.	Itinerent Preachers.
East Pennsylvania	165	4.915	28
Pennsylvania	119	4,477	29
Alleghany	154	4,380	25
*Virginia	95	3,500	10
Parkersburg	91	2.905	20
Western Reserve	102	2,520	24
Erie	93	1,629	33
Canada	48	1,121	11
Kansas	86	1,918	34
Missouri	101	2,382	28
Muskingum	77	2,735	20
California	19	271	9
Oregon	33	832	6
White River	125	4,989	29
Indiana	125	4,575	21
Miami	85	3.814	25
Auglaize	154	3,761	24
Sandusky	163	6,161	45
Scioto	219	7,315	37
Michigan	119	3,026	21
North Michigan	111.	1,813	28
St. Joseph	158	4,064	47
Upper Wabash	99	3,440	26
Lower Wabash	142	4,029	32
Illinois	110	3.120	26
Central Illinois	82	2,265	29
Rock River	94	1,971	29
Wisconsin	57	1,293	15
Fox River	29	480	12
Minnesota	41	502	15
North Iowa	61	1,336	20
Iowa	63	1,497	15
East Des Moines	67	1,450	25
West Des Moines	65	1,427	20
Ohio German	62	1,253	19
Tennessee		209	9
Kentucky	—	402	6
Cascade	3	106	4
Total for 1867	3,444	97,982	837
Total for 1866	3,297	91,570	789
Increase	148	6,413	

There are 4,428 preaching places, 2042 Sunday schools, with 94,180 scholars and 14,003 officers and teachers. The collections were: for preachers salaries, $213,369 27; Missions, $26,999 47½; Conference Collections, $3,957 57; Sunday-schools, $25,054 04; Bible Course, $4,416 55, &c. The total of all collections was $418,720 11, an increase of 7,440 20 from last year.

The Church supports seven colleges and universities, a female college and a classical seminary. It has a printing house at Dayton, Ohio, where is published an official organ, a Sunday-school, and a missionary paper. The bishops are five in number, and are elected at every session of the General Conference.

The following are the *mission statistics* of the United Brethren: During the year ending May, 1867, three missionaries employed in the foreign field, eighty-one on the frontier, and one hundred and twenty-seven in the home fields. These received from the missions they served, as salary, $41 903 55; and they were paid from the missionary fund $29,566 69, making a total of $71,470 24, and an average salary of $338 72.

Number of missions, 200; appointments, 1,049; members, 13,787; collected for missions, $3,220 69; meeting houses, 130; Sunday-schools, 368; teachers, 987; scholars, 14,798.

Moravians.

The Moravian Churches embraces two American Provinces (Northern and Southern), a British Province, a Continental Province embracing missions in Germany, Switzerland, France, Denmark, Norway, Sweden and Russia and the Foreign Mission Field.

There are 25 churches, and 18 missions in the Northern Province. The number of communicants in the churches is 4327, and the total of souls (including non-communicants and children) is 7,550. The number of communicants in the missions is 893, and the total 1,730. Total of communicants in the Northern Province, 5,220, and of souls, 9,280.

An English and a German Periodical are published by the Moravian Book Store and Publication Office at Bethlehem, Pa.

The number of communicants in the *Southern Province* is 1,042, so that the whole number of communicants in the two Provinces is 6,262, and the whole number of souls, 11,033. The whole number of ministers in active service, in both Provinces, is 64. Number of boarding schools, 6; of pupils, 875. In the Theological Seminary there are 3 students; in the college, 30.

There are 71 communicants and 172 souls under the care of the Church in the Indian missions. The whole number of Sunday-school scholars in the Northern Province, including the Indian missions, is 4,836. The statistics of the other provinces are as follows:

*Estimated.

	Commun.	Total
Continental Province (1865)	5,104	7,120
British " (1865)	3,239	5,402
Americ. Northern and Southern,	6,262	11,033

In the Foreign Missions there are 70,235 souls in connection with the church.

Congregationalists.

1. *America.*

States, etc.	Churches.	Members.	Sabbath School Scholars.
Maine	243	19,237	21,215
New Hampshire	183	18,513	22,585
Vermont	191	17,149	17,008
Massachusetts	463	74,955	87, 107
Rhode Island	23	3,414	4,390
Connecticut	286	45,555	20,992
New York	225	22,004	23,924
New Jersey	8	1,332	1,492
Pennsylvania	60	3,582	1,490
Delaware	1	14	—
Maryland	1	48	60
District of Columbia	1	174	—
North Carolina	1	20	—
Ohio	165	13,204	14,932
Indiana	24	788	1,151
Illinois	222	15,297	17,941
Michigan	150	6,969	10,201
Wisconsin	158	9,868	13,110
Minnesota	58	2,203	2,410
Iowa	166	7,248	9,157
Missouri	29	844	1,747
Tennessee	1	70	80
Louisiana	1	28	—
Nebraska	10	190	195
Kansas	33	891	1,302
Colorado	4	75	150
Washington Territory	1	15	50
Utah Territory	1	18	—
Oregon	8	320	530
California	32	1,428	4,025
Foreign Missionaries	—	—	—
Totals, U. S.	2,780	267,353	286,275
Canada	96	4,311	5,907
Nova Scotia, etc,	13	424	402
New Brunswick	6	372	429
Jamaica	5	415	320
Totals, American	2,900	272,975	293,333

The following table exhibits the growth of the Congregationalists in Churches, Ministers, Members, and Sunday-school scholars in the last 10 years.

Year.	Churches.	Ministers.	Members.	Sund.Sch'l Scholars
1857	2,479	1,795	232,549	128,772
1858	2,619	1,810	239 586	162 815
1859	2,670	1,927	257,634	206,441
1860	2,734	1,953	260 389	250,690
1861	2,756	1,906	259,119	246,547
1862	2,774	1,960	261,474	255,257
1863	2,828	1,906	264,313	260,492
1864	2,865	1 966	268,015	286,798
1865	2,840	1,054	269,662	279 059
1866	2,900	2,015	272,975	293,333

The total number of ministers in the United States, in the pastoral work and not in it, is 2919. The number in the British Provinces (Canada, Nova Scotia, New Brunswick, Jamaica, etc.) is 90, making a total for America of 30,009. The number of admission by profession in the United States is 11,249, the total for America, 11,485.

Great Britain and Colonies.

	County Associat., or Unions.	Church.	Minist.
England	43	1,923	1,829
Wales	16	788	405
Scotland	8	105	105
Ireland	1	27	25
Colonies	8	278	317
Channel Islands	—	13	—
Foreign lands	—	—	202
Total	76	3,135	2,782

The Congregationalists have 6 theological seminaries, with 28 professors and 258 students. There are 17 colleges and 20 theological colleges etc., in the British Islands and Colonies. They have no official organ, but several periodical and weekly papers are published by Private Congregational enterprise.

Reformed Dutch Church.

Classes.	Communicants.	Sunday School Scholars.	Benevolent Contributions.
Albany	2,007	1,890	$17,329 11
Arcot	341	—	2,262 10
Bergen	1,177	1,882	3,708 98
South Bergen	2,578	2,533	14,617 20
Cayuga	863	724	4,016 12
Geneva	1,621	1,006	3 626 97
Greene	1,488	957	2,248 68
Holland	2,028	585	6,419 13
Hudson	1,314	965	3,180 45
Illinois	1,128	1,161	1,341 30
Kingston	1,712	1,387	2,283 04
North Long Island	2,179	2,025	5,671 43
South Long Island	3,495	3,012	29,113 66
Michigan	431	680	69? 48
Monmouth	923	522	905 46
New Brunswick	1 861	1,291	6,672 11
New York	4,419	4,602	98,863 45
South New York	2,300	2,175	16,059 00
Orange	2 966	2,074	5,081 37
Paramus	2 376	1,390	4,758 64
Passaic	1,339	916	1,865 79
Philadelphia	2 650	2,625	5,605 86
Poughkeepsie	2,108	1,255	7,181 53
Raritan	2 418	2,187	4 617 10
Rensalaer	1,669	1,228	4,095.23
Saratoga	1,412	970	2,224 60
Schenetady	2,067	1,645	2,826 00
Schoharie	1,028	539	917 14
Ulster	1,610	1,051	5,548 37
Westchester	1,468	963	9,391 94
Wisconsin	1,373	617	3,705 75
Total	57,846	46,411	$377,209 10

Domestic Missions.

The receipts of the Board of Domestic Missions for the last year were $25,208 28. They have extended their care to 86 churches and stations with 4213 families and 5839 communicants, 96 Sunday-schools, and 5652 scholars. The number of domestic missionaries and missionary pastors is 76.

Foreign Missions.

The receipts of the Boards of Foreign Missions were $119,530 89.

Missions at Amoy, China: Missionaries and assistants, 6: members, 626; contributions, $6379.

Mission at Arcot, India: Missionaries and assistants, 14. Members in Congregations 1525: communicants, 330; scholars in vernacular schools, 312 boys, 55 girls.

A mission has been established in Japan, in which 6 missionaries and assistant missionaries are engaged.

German Reformed Church.

The following are the *General Statistics* of the German Reformed Church in 1866 as given by the "Almanac of the Reformed Church for 1868."

1 General Synod, 3 Subordinate Synods, 29 Classes, 485 Ministers, 1,183 Congregations, 103,925 Members, 70,432 Unconfirmed Members, 11,115 Baptisms, 6,845 Confirmations, 2,421 Received by Certificate. 91,547 Communicants, 196 Excommunicated, 1,244 Dismissed, 4,207 Deaths, 939 Sunday-schools, $60,977 46 Benevolent Contributions.

The statistics of the three Synods, composing the General Synod, are given as follows in the German Almanac of the German Reformed Church for 1868.

	Preachers.	Congreg.	Commun.
Eastern Synod	275	703	67,635
Ohio Synod	130	300	17,444
Germ. North W. Syn.	83	162	7,726
Total	488	1,165	82,815

The Church has *six colleges*, at Lancaster, Mount Pleasant, Meyerstown, and Mercersburg, Pennsylvania, Tiffin, Ohio, and Newton, North Carolina; *one college institute*, at Reimersburg, Pennsylvania; 2 theological Seminaries at Mercersburg, Pennsylvania, and Tiffin, Ohio and a Mission House, at Howard Grove, near Sheboygan, Wisconsin.

The Board of *Home Missions* in 1867 had 70 stations under their care. Over $11,000 were contributed to this object, and upwards of $12000 for Church Extension.

The Church has 5 English *papers*, (1 quarterly, 2 monthlies, 2 weeklies), and 6 German (1 quarterly, 2 monthlies, 1 semi-monthly, 2 weeklies).

Presbyterians.

1.—*Old School Presbyterian Church.*

Synods.	Ministers.	Commun.
Albany	96	10,448
Alleghany	86	12 846
Baltimore	105	11,445
Buffalo	96	5,205
Chicago	104	7,473
Cincinnati	105	11,829
Illinois	110	9,361
Indiana	68	6,939
Iowa	55	3,981
Kansas	22	1,118
Kentucky	63	7,441
Mississippi	5	173
Missouri	82	6,936
Nashville	8	482
New Jersey	245	26 948
New York	224	22,663
North Carolina	7	1,970
Northern India	22	352
Northern Indiana	60	6,085
Ohio	100	11,453
Pacific	42	1,666
Philadelphia	245	20,816
Pittsburg	117	19 292
St. Paul	33	1,617
Sandusky	29	3,677
Southern Iowa	57	4,271
Wheeling	109	16,980
Wisconsin	41	2,861
Total	2,302	247,350

There are no reports from the Synods of Alabama, Arkansas, Georgia, Memphis, South Carolina, Texas, and Virginia.

Synods in connection with the General Assembly, 54; Presbyteries, 176; Ministers, 2,302; Churches, 5,622; total of baptisms, 15 295. Number of persons in the Sunday-schools, 195,623. Amount contributed for the boards, $27,473; whole amount of contributions, $3,731,164.

Board of Domestic Missions. Missionaries in service, 626; members of churches, 27,492; Sunday-schools, 481, with 4269 teachers and 30,644 scholars. Baptisms 3311. Receipts, $96,977 81, total resources, $120,622 09.

Foreign Missions. The Board of Foreign Mission report that they have missions among the Jews and the Indian tribes, in this country, the Chinese of California, the Roman Catholics in Brazil and the United States of Columbia, in China, Japan, Siam, Candia, Liberia, Corisco (Africa), Italy, France, and Belgium. Missionaries, 70; native Ministers, 20; assistants, 174; churches 44; stations, etc., 60; children in schools, over 7000; receipts, $244,667 80.

Board of Publications. The Board of publication have issued 500,400 copies of publications during the year, and 13,208,188 since its organization. It has sold during the year 226,623 volumes and 374,700 pages of tracts and has printed 14,697 volumes and 179,54 pages. Receipts $145,701 52.

Disabled Ministers Fund. Receipts, $27,740 28.

Committee on Freedmen. Appropriations, $40,160 97. During the year this committee have had in commission 104 Missionaries, of whom 47 were colored.

Theological Seminaries. The theological Seminaries under the care of this Church are four in number.

Board of Education. Receipts, $4,720 41. Candidates passing their studies, 261.

Board of Church Extension. Receipts, $37,623 30. Available means for the year, $96,624 51.

2.—*New School Presbyterian Church.*

Synods.	Ministers.	Communic'ts.
Albany	80	8,337
Utica	81	7,573
Onondaga	88	8,919
Geneva	101	9,857
Susquehanna	38	3,591
Genesee	138	13,919
New York and N. Jersey	284	32,172
Pennsylvania	113	16,342
West Pennsylvania	30	3,709
Michigan	116	10,472
Western Reserve	96	6,887
Ohio	50	4,569
Cincinnati	58	3 814
Wabash	36	3,280
Indiana	42	4,143
Illinois	87	5.764
Peoria	103	6,556
Wisconsin	44	1.640
Iowa	90	2,733
Minnesota	34	1.668
Missouri	41	1,506
Tennessee	20	2.858
Alta California	29	1,210
23 Synods	1,870	161,538

Number of Presbyteries, 100; of Churches, 1560; of Baptisms, 9.175; of persons in Sunday-schools, 163,242.

Foreign Missions. Contributions, $110,349. The Missions are located in Western Africa, South Africa, Turkey, Syria, etc., Southern and Eastern Asia, Pacific Islands, and among the North American Indians. The number of Missionaries is 43.

Home Missions. Receipts, $128,500; Missionaries, 419; Conversions 2500; Additions, 3000.

Church Erection Fund. Contributions, $16,762 78; total receipts, $24.298; Grants, $20 700.

Publication Committee. Sales, $45,190 73; Books and Catalogues, 357; Donations received, $8,128 49; value of books given away, $5500 95.

Education Committee. Receipts, $22,270 42; Students assisted, 145.

Presbyterian House. Receipts, $22,482.49.

Ministerial Relief Fund. Receipts, $9647 09; persons assisted, 137.

3.—*United Presbyterian Church.*

Synods.	Ministers.	Communicants.	Sunday-School Scholars.
New York	71	13.546	8,819
1st Synod of the West	72	11.883	4,353
Pittsburgh	53	12,746	3.581
Ohio	33	6.442	1,853
2d of the West	52	7,641	3,681
Illinois	53	6,350	3,748
Iowa	37	4,469	1,729
Missionary Presbyteries	9	412	130
Total	380	63,489	27,894

Total number of Presbyteries in 1867, 54; Missionary Presbyteries, 3; Congregations, 736; Foreign Missionaries and teachers, 26; Home Missionaries, 125; Baptisms, 4111; Contributions to Church Funds, $108,265; total Contributions, $631,688; average per member, $10.

Foreign Missions. Contributions, $45,730. Receipts including balance at the beginning of the year, $72,809 75; expended $68,252 78. The missions are in Trinidad, Syria, India, Egypt, China, and Italy.

Contributed for Home Missions, $30,548.

Board of Publication. Sales, $23 740.

Board of Education. Contributions, $3210; Appropriations, 5050 00; Persons assisted, 40.

Board of Church Extension. Contributions, $9,389.

Missions to the Freedmen. Contributions, $14,252; Total resources. $22,241 71.

4.—*Presbyterian Church, Southern.*

The *Central Presbyterian*, of Richmond, gives from the "Minutes of the General Assembly for 1867," the following statistical exhibit of the Southern Presbyterian Church.

General View of the Presbyterian Church during the year ending November, 1866.

Synods	10
Presbyteries	46
Licentiates	41
Candidates for the Ministry	40
Ministers	829
Churches	1.290
Members added on examination	4,674
Members added on certificate	2,094
Total number of communicants reported	66,629
Adults baptized	1,637
Infants baptized	1,072
Children in Sabbath-schools and Bible Classes	21.094
Domestic Missions	$14,226
Foreign Missions	4,089
Sustentation	8,519
Education	9,058
Publication	8.633
Commissioners and Contingent Fund	6.982
Congregational purposes	334,165
Miscellaneous	23,610

"There are," says the *Central Presbyterian*, "340 churches, including four whole presbyteries from which no report of members is made. If all the churches had been reported there is no doubt that our membership would have been found to exceed 70,000, and probably to approach near 80,000.

These are the first minutes since 1868, and also since the union with the United Synod in 1864, which contain statistics, compiled from the Presbyterian reports.

5.—*Reformed Presbyterian Church, Old Side.*

This Church is composed of 8 Presbyteries, 66 ministers, and 91 congregations, with a membership of 8.324. During the year, 530 members had been received on profession of their faith, and in all ways 877, the net gain being 406. The congregations raised—for Foreign Missions, 9,107 35, for Home Missions, $2,478 02; for the Freedmen, $5,116 79; for Seminary endowment, $2,548 74 for Church erection, $23,193 02; for Pastors salaries, $47,163 49; for miscellaneous purposes, $33,336 42; making a total of $123 007 34, or an average of between fifteen and sixteen dollars per member. It has a Theological Seminary with 16 students and an Endowment Fund of $23,113 05.

6.—*Cumberland Presbyterian Church.*

This Church had, in 1860, 927 ministers, 1188 churches and 84,349 communicants. The number of Presbyteries was 96. There are official boards on publications, missions and other objects. Number of Educational publications, 24, weekly papers were published, in 1867, at Waynesburg, Pa., Alton, Ill., and Nashville, Tenn.

7.—*Other Presbyterian Churches in the United States.*

	Minist.	Comm.	Collect.
Associate Reformed Synod of New York	16	1,631	$7,102
Assoc. Ref. Pres. Ch. South	68		
Assoc. Synod of N. Amer.	11	776	190
Ref. Presb. Church, Synod	63	5,821	9,484

8.—*Presbyterian Churches in Great Britain.*

The Church of Scotland. Has 16 Synods, 84 Presbyteries, and 1243 congregations. The contributions at the last session of the General Assembly, from 838 congregations, the others not having reported, were:

For Home Missions	£69,665 5s 6d
Educational purposes	23,850 16
Endowments	27,000
Foreign purposes	17,000 17 3
Total	£136,516 18s 5d

The Free Church of Scotland has 16 synods, 71 Presbyteries, 861 churches, 3 theological schools, with 226 students. Funds received in 1866—7.

Building Fund	£ 48,735
Sustentation Fund	132,337
Congregational Fund	12,024
Education	20,358
College	6,797
Missions, home and foreign	36,816
Total	$369,104

A decrease of £14,467 from previous year.

Reformed Presbyterian Synod (Cameronians), 6 Presbyteries, 45 Churches, 2 professors in divinity, 41 Ministers.

United Presbyterian Church. 31 Presbyteries, in England and Scotland, 584 Ministers, 596 Churches. Also a theological hall, with 4 Professors.

Presbyterian Seceders. 4 Presbyteries, 25 Congregations.

Presbyterian Church in England. 7 Presbyteries, 105 Churches. 1 theological college, with 3 Professors. There are also 15 Presbyterian Churches in England formed into 3 Presbyteries in connection with the Church of Scotland.

Presbyterian Church in Ireland. 50 Ministers, 60 Churches.

9.—*Presbyterians in Australasia.*

The following are the Presbyterian statistics of Australasia, as far as they can be obtained.

New South Wales .... Members 18,156
Amount received from State Funds....... £3,527

Queensland. Free Presbyterians, 7 churches, 1650 sittings.

United Presbyterian Church of Scotland. 1 Church, 200 sittings.

South Australia. Free Church of Scotland.................4,137 Members.
United Presbyterians...........1,572 "

Victoria. Presb. Church of Vict. 5,052 Members.
Church of Scotland.........36,917 "
Free Church of Scotland and Free Presbyterians............ 21,219 "
United Presbyterians...........16,734 "
Other Presbyterians............ 7,181 "

Lutherans.

1.—*America.*

Statistical View of the Evangelical Lutheran Church in North America.

Synods connected with the General Synod of the United States.

Synods.	Ministers.	Churches.	Communic'ts.
1. Synod of New York	16	16	2,200
2. Hartwick Synod, (N. Y.)	27	31	4,300
3. Franckean Synod, (N. Y.)	20	29	2,500
5. Synod of New Jersey	8	10	1,500
5. Synod of East Pennsylvania	56	82	9,900
6. Susquehanna Synod (Penn.)	14	28	3,500
7. Synod of West Pennsylvania	50	93	12,520
8. Synod of Central Penn	34	78	6,800
9. Alleghany Synod, (Penn.)	45	96	6 606
10. Synod of Maryland	35	35	8,307
11. Melanchthon Synod, (Md.)	18	46	4,300
12. Synod of Texas	10	23	2,800
13. East Ohio Synod	40	60	3,700
14. Wittenberg Synod, (Ohio)	37	57	3,306
15. Miami Synod, (Ohio)	35	44	3,500
16. Synod of North. Indiana	28	65	3,00
17. Olive Branch Synod, (Ind.)	22	42	1,809
18. Synod of Northern Illinois	23	55	2,000
19. Synod of Southern Illinois	19	16	1,200
20. Synod of Central Illinois	12	17	2,00
21. Synod of Iowa	22	23	1,200
	570	944	86,933

Synods of the "General Council."

1. New York Ministerium, etc.	49	47	12,000
2. Synod of Penn. etc	125	300	50,500
3. Pittsburg Synod, (Penn.)	67	300	8,300
4. English Dist- Synod of Joint Synod of Ohio	34	58	7,000
5. English Synod of Ohio	11	26	1,700
6. Synod of Illinois, etc	32	40	4,600
7. Synod of Wisconsin	50	90	11,000
8. Synod of Michigan	14	35	3,061
9. Synod of Iowa	52	75	7,0[illegible]
10. Synod of Minnesota	10	35	2,5[illegible]
11. Scandinavian Augustana Synod	50	100	10,000
12. Synod of Canada	24	64	1,500
	258	1010	119,100

Synods connected with the (Southern) General Synod of North America.

1. Synod of Virginia	30	61	3,200
2. Synod of South-West Virginia	21	40	2,179
3. Synod of North Carolina	18	34	3,716
4. Synod of South Carolina	33	44	4,817
5. Synod of Georgia	6	10	1,200
6. Holston Synod, (Tenn.)	12	25	2,000

Synods, not connected with any General Synods or General Council.

1. Joint Synod of Ohio, etc.	109	227	30,500
2. Joint Synod of Missouri, etc	250	304	37 000
3. Norwegian Synod, Wis., etc.	50	200	20,000
4. Tennessee Synod	32	85	5,800
5. Eilson's Synod	9	25	2,000
6. Union Synod. (Ind.)	15	20	2,210
7. Buffalo Synod, (N. Y.)	30	40	5,000
8. German Synod of N. Y., etc.	10	10	1,800
9. Synod of Mississippi	7	11	2,000
10. Missionary Synod of the West	11	30	700
	523	944	109,010

GrandTotal—49 Synods, 1,750 Ministers, 3,112 Congregations, 332,155 Communicants.

Under the Patronage of the Lutheran Church are 14 literary and theological schools, 19 colleges, 11 academies, 9 female seminaries, and 15 elemosynary institutions. Other benevolent institutions are:

The Parent Education Society	organized 1837
Foreign Missionary Society	" 1837
Home Missionary Society	" 1845
Church Extension Society	" 1853
Publication Society	" 1851
Historical Society	" 1845
Pastors Fund	

The Lutheran Periodicals are 11 English (4 weekly, 2 semi-monthly, 4 monthly, and 1 quarterly), 10 German (4 semi-mothly, 3 monthly, and 2 not defined), and Swedish and Norwegian (1 weekly, 2 semi-monthly, and 3 monthly.)

2. *Europe.*

1. *Germany.*—In Prussia and a number of other States the Lutheran and the Reformed churches have been fused into the "United Evangelical Church". This new denomination is viewed by some as an entirely new denomination, absorbing Lutheran and Reformed Churches, while others consider it merely as a confederation, which leaves the Lutheran or Reformed character of the several congregations unimpaired. By far the larger portion of the United Evangelical Church were formerly Lutherans, and many of these desire the repeal of the union and the reconstruction of a strictly Lutheran church. In those states where the United Evangelical Church legally exists, it is impossible to ascertain the number of the persons who still regard themselves as Lutherans. We give, on that account, for the several German States, the statistics of the Lutheran, Reformed, and United Evangelical churches together.

A number of the German State Churches are clearly, more or less, under the influence of the Liberal ("Rationalistic") party, which lays no claim to the name or character of a distinctly Lutheran, Reformed, or United Evangelical Church, and considers itself bound to no standard of faith. These churches, on the whole, would sympathize most with the Unitarian Church in the United States. The Liberal party is at present in the ascendancy in Baden, Hesse-Darmstadt, Hamburg, Saxe-Weimar, Saxe-Coburg-Gotha, Saxe-Meiningen, and is largely represented in a number of other states.

From all these reasons, it is extremely difficult even to estimate the number of Lutherans in Germany.

As far as they can be ascertained, the statistics of the Lutheran, Reformed, and United Evangelical churches of Germany are as follows:

Prussia Proper (that is, without the states annexed in 1866), had a "Protestant" or "Evangelical" population of 11,592,451. Of these, about 40,000 are "Independent Lutherans," who have refused to be incorporated with the United Evangelical Church, and have obtained permission to form an independent organization. There is also a considerable number of "Reformed" congregations which have not joined the Union, but the independent Lutherans and Reformed count together a population less than 100,000 souls, leaving all the remainder nominally connected with the "United Evangelical Church." The numerical proportion of the Lutherans and the Reformed element in the United Evangelical Church, may be seen from the fact that in 1816, a year before the union, there were 5,873,146 Lutherans, and only 391,114 Reformed.

The ecclesiastical statistics of the countries annexed, in 1866, to Prussia, were as follows:

Hanover—Total population, 1,923,492; Lutherans 1,581 767, Reformed 98,010.

Hesse Cassel—Total population, 745,063; Protestants about 618.000. Most of the Lutherans and Reformed now belong to the United Evangelical Church. Before the introduction of the Union, the number of Lutherans was 144,000.

Nassau—Total population, 468,311; United Evangelical 241,354.

Frankfort—Total population, 91,074; Lutherans about 48,000, Evangelical 1,600, German Reformed 1,000, Calvinists 700.

Schleswig-Holstein—Total population, 918,392; nearly all Lutherans.

The ecclesiastical statistics of the other German States are as follows (the total population, if not otherwise stated, being that given in the official census of 1864):

Anhalt—Total population, 193,046; nearly all United Evangelical; before the Union a majority was Reformed.

Baden—Total population, 1,429,199; United Evangelical Church 472,258.

Bavaria—Total population. 4,774,454; Protestant population about 1,300,000, of whom 980,000 are Lutherans, 5,000 Reformed, and 316,000 United Evangelicals.

Bremen—Total population, 104,091; Lutherans 50,000, Reformed 45,000.

Brunswick—Total population, 293,388; Lutherans 285,934, Reformed 1,676.

Hamburg—Total population, in 1866, about 251,000; about 220,000 Lutherans, 7,000 Reformed.

Hesse-Darmstadt—Total population, 816,902; Protestants 558.559. Before the union there were about 400.000 Lutherans and 170,600 Reformed Most of both now belong to the United Evangelical Church.

Lippe-Detmold—Total population, 111,336; Lutherans 8,000; Reformed 100.000.

Lubeck—Total population, in 1862, 50,614; Lutherans 49,000, Reformed 500.

Mecklenburg-Schwerin—Total population, 552,612; Lutherans 548,457, Reformed 184.

Mecklenburg-Strelitz—Total population, in 1866, 99,060; almost all Lutherans.

Oldenburg—Total population, 314,416; Lutherans 198,122, Reformed 1,196, United Evangelical 26,020.

Reuss-Greitz—Total population, 43,924; nearly all Lutherans.

Reuss-Schleiz—Total population, 86,472; nearly all Lutherans.

Saxony—Total population, 2,343,994; Reformed 5.239.

Saxe-Weimar—Total population, 280,201; Protestants 269,007, of whom about 260,000 are Lutherans, and 9,000 Reformed.

Saxe-Meiningen—Total population. 178,065; Protestants 175,083; all Lutherans, with the exception of about 400 Reformed.

Saxe-Altenburg—Total population. 141,839; Lutherans 141,212, Reformed 79, United Evangelical 218.

Saxe-Coburg Gotha—Total population, 164,-527; Lutherans about 145,000. 3,000 Reformed.

Schaumburg-Lippe—Total population, 31,382; Lutherans 26,000. Reformed 5,000.

Schwarzburg-Rudolstadt—Total population, 73,752; Lutherans 73,457; Reformed 28.

Schwarzburg-Sondershausen—Total population, 66,189; Protestants 65,914; nearly all Lutherans.

Waldeck-(in 1867 united for a term of 10 years, with Prussia) total population, 59,143; Evangelical 57,036; nearly all Lutherans before the union.

Wurtemberg—Total population, 1,748,328; Protestants 1,200.363, almost all Lutherans.

2.—The Lutheran Church is the State Church in all the Scandinavian States—*Sweden, Norway*, and *Denmark*. In Sweden, the Church has 1 Archbishop, 11 Bishops, 3,200 pastors. The population, which, in 1865, amounted to 4,114,141. was all Lutheran, with the exception of about 10,060. Norway has 5 Bishops, 336 pastors; population, in 1865. 1,701,478; with a still smaller number of non-Lutherans than Sweden. Denmark has 10 Bishops, 69 Provosts, 1,100 parishes, and 1,200 pastors; the population (1,608,095, and in the dependencies 124,020) are Lutherans, with the exception of 12,907 members of other creeds.

3.—*Austria* has 1,218,750 Lutherans.

4.—*France* has 44 consistories, 232 parishes, 199 annexes, 302 temples, 658 schools, 263 official pastors, 40 vicars, and in Algeria the Reformed and Lutheran (mixed) consistory of Algiers has 12 parishes. 59 annexes, 71 places of worship, 12 schools, 16 official pastors. The Lutheran population is about 500,000, mostly in the Alsace.

5. *Russia*.-The Lutheran Church is the predominant church in the Baltic provinces and in Finland, It has, in *Russia Proper*, 8 consistories, 431 churches. 566 ministers. The Lutheran population of Poland is 382,000, and of Finland 1,787,000.

6.—In *Holland* there are two organizations of Lutherans; the one, the "Evangelical Lutheran," is supposed to be under the influence of the Liberal (Rationalistic) party, and has a population of about 66,000 souls; the other, the "Reformed Lutheran," adheres to the symbolical books, and numbers about 10,000 souls.

7.—In the *Other Countries* of Europe there are but few Lutherans.

3. *Asia, Africa, and Australia.*

The Lutherans sustain missions in India China, and several parts of Africa, for which we refer to the table of the Foreign Mission Societies.

There are about 10,000 Lutherans and German Protestants in Victoria, and a number in the other Australian Colonies.

Reformed Churches.

1.—The statistics of the (*Dutch*) *Reformed Church* and the *German Reformed Church of the United States* have been given before.

2.—*Germany*. The *Reformed Churches of Germany* have mostly been absorbed by the United Evangelical Church. For their statistics as far as they can be ascertained see Lutheran Church.

3.—*France*. The *Reformed Church of France* had in 1860. 105 consistories, about 1045 congregations, 826 church-buildings, 1139 schools; a theological faculty at Montauban. A large number of the ministers are "Liberals" (Rationalists) in theology.

4.—*Holland*. The *Reformed State Church of Holland* had in 1860. 1,800 000 members, 1272 congregations, 1511 clergymen.the overwhelming majority of whom are "Liberals" ("Rationalists"). The number of classes 43, forming 10 provincial synods. The General Synod meets annually. There are theological schools at Leyden, Utrecht, Groningen, beside the Atheneums at Deventer and Amsterdam.

The *Free Reformed Church* has 28 classes, from 50 to 70,000 members, and a theological school at Kampen.

5.—*Belgium*. Before the union of Belgium with Holland, Belgium had only 4 Reformed Congregations. The number increased during the Dutch rule. In 1838, all the Protestant Congregations which receive support from the state, formed the "Protestant Union", which united under one Directory several evangelical denominations. The majority of the Congregations are Reformed Total number in 1859, 16.

6.—*Switzerland* had in 1860, a Protestant population of 1,417,754, who with the exceptions of a few thousand Lutherans, and Mennonites and Independents, are members of the Reformed Church. In some cantons, especially in Geneva and Vaud there are Free Reformed Churches beside the National Reformed Churches.

7.—*Russia*. The Reformed Church has a population of about 200,000 souls, about one-half of whom live in Lithuania, where they are divided into 4 districts.

8.—*Austria*. The Reformed Church of Austria or as it is there called the Church of the Helvetic Confession numbered according to the last official census, a total population of 1,869,516 of whom 1,453,009 were in Hungary and 297,419 in Transylvania.

9.—*Africa*. The *Dutch Reformed Church* has a considerable number of congregations in the countries of South Africa, (Cape Colony, Transvaal Republic, Orange Free State etc.) The Dutch Reformed Synod of the Cape Colony has for years been considerably disturbed by the Rationalistic Controversy.

United Evangelical Church.

1.—*Germany*. The statistics of the *United Evangelical Church* have been given, together with those of the Lutheran Churches, under the head of Lutheran Church.

2.-*United States of America*. The *Church Union of the West* (*Kirchenverein des Westens*) is a branch of the United Evangelical Church of Germany. It has about 4000 members.

Anglican Church.

The main branches of this church are: 1. The Protestant Episcopal Church of the United States.

2. The Established Church of England and Ireland. 3. The Scotch Episcopal Church.

1.—*Protestant Episcopal Church of the United States.—General Statistics.*

Dioceses.	Clergy.	Parishes.	Commc'ts
Alabama	31	44	1,950
California (1866)	30	33	———
Connecticut	147	123	15 022
Delaware	22	27	1,347
Florida	10	12	512
Georgia	31	27	2,2.4
Illinois	90	82	3,960
Indiana	31	29	1,832
Iowa	36	48	1,460
Kansas (1866)	12	15	
Kentucky	38	35	2 796
Louisiana	42	48	1,864
Maine	16	19	1,527
Maryland	157	136	11,120
Massachusetts	120	62	10,427
Michigan	63	73	4,890
Minnesota	37	26	1,720
Mississippi	28	41	982
Missouri	28	29	1,856
New Hampshire	26	23	1,224
New-Jersey	115	110	8,846
New York (1866)	407	328	33,790
North Carolina	50	68	2,832
Ohio	103	101	7,686
Pennsylvania	219	179	16,160
Pittsburgh	44	45	2,629
Rhode Island	39	35	4,280
South Carolina	62	72	2,710
Tennessee	35	24	1,996
Texas (1866)	21	29	950
Vermont	24	37	2,260
Virginia	112	172	6,522
Western New York	169	161	14,855
Wisconsin	63	44	3,823
Total	2,600	2,370	178 102

The number of Baptisms was 34,436, and of Confirmations, 19,616 The increase of Communicants in 23 dioceses is 10,244. There are 19,897 Sunday-school teachers, and 180,152 scholars. The total of contributions for missionary and church purposes was $3,859,296 02. The missionary dioceses are in Arkansas, Oregon and Washington, Nebraska, Dacotah, Colorado and New Mexico, Nevada and Arizona. Montana, Utah and Idaho, Western Africa, China, and Japan, and there is a mission at Greece. Some foreign congregations, at Paris, Rome, Port au Prince, Hayti, and St. Croix, in the West Indies, are under the care of this church.

General Institutions.—General Theological Seminary, New York. Whole number of students from the foundation, 968; *Domestic and Foreign Missionary Society.* In the Domestic Department: 4 missionary bishops and 213 missionaries. In the Foreign Department: 2 missionary bishops 16 missionaries, and 31 assistants.

Sunday school Union and Church Book Society. Historical Society. Society for the Promotion of Evangelical Knowledge. Society for the increase of the Ministry. American Church Missionary Society. Christian Unity Society. University of the South, Sewanee, Tenn.

2.—*The Established Church of England and Ireland and the Scotch Episcopal Church.*

Statistics.	Bishops.		Clergy.
England (incl. 2 Archbishops)	28	about	17,000
Ireland " "	12	"	2,200
Scotland	8	"	162
The Colonies (incl. India, Melanesia and Sandwich Islands.)	51	"	2,000
America	41	"	2,538
Retired Bishops	6		
Total	149		23 900

In England there are 5,764,513 Church-sittings; in Scotland, 165 churches, and 94 schools.

Eastern Churches.

1.—*The Greek Church.*

The Greek Church consists of 10 different groups which in point of administration are independent of each other, namely:

1.—The *Patriarchate* of Jerusalem; it has 13 Sees, (Metropolitical and 1 Archiepiscopal) 2. Antioch, 6 Metropolitical Sees. 3. Alexandria, 4 Metropolitical Sees. 4. Constantinople, 135 Sees (90 Metropolitical and 4 Arch episcopal). 5. Russia, 65 Sees (5 Metropolitical, 25 Archiepiscopal). 6. Cyprus, 4 Sees (of which 1 is Archiepiscopal). 7. Austria, 11 Sees (2 Metropolitical). 8. Mount Sinai, 1 Sec. 9. Montenegro, 1 Metropolitical See. 10. Greece, 24 Sees. (The Archbishop of Athens is *ex officio* President of the Holy Synod.

The long struggle between the Government of Roumania (the united Danubian principalities of Moldavia and Wallachia) and the Greek Synod of Constantinople, terminated, in 1866, in the formal recognition of the entire independence of the church in the principalities, by the Patriarch of Constantinople and his Synod. This would therefore be an 11th Independent Group of the Greek Church. There are 4 Bishops in Wallachia, and 3 in Moldavia. The people of Servia and those of Bulgavia desire for their bishops a similiar independence of Constantinople.

Since the annexation of the Ionian Islands to the kingdom of Greece, the Government of Greece has naturally been desirous to unite, the 7 bishops of the islands who formerly were under the jurisdiction of the Patriarch of Constantinople, with the Holy Synod of Greece. The Church of the Ionian Islands showed itself however opposed to such a union.

The statistics of the Greek Church, reported in 1867, were as follows:

Russia. (in Europe 51,000,0000; in Siberia 2,650,000; Caucasus, (total population 4,257,000) not reported total about	55,000,000
Turkey. (Incl. of the Dependencies in Europe and Egypt) about	11,500,000
Austria	2,921,000
Greece. (Incl. of Ionian Islands)	1,220,000
United States of America. (Chiefly in the territory purchased in 1867 from Russia)	50,000
Prussia	1,500
China	200
Total	69,692,700

2.—*The Armenian Church.*

The total number of Armenians scattered all over the world is according to Dr. Petermann about 2,500,000. Of these about 100,000 are connected with Rome United Armenians, 15,000 are Evangelical Armenians, and all the others belong to the National (or Gregorian) Armenian Church. Russia, according to an official report of the Ministry of Popular Enlightenment, had, in 1851 22,253 Catholic (united) Armenians, and

172,535, "Gregorian" (non-united) Armenians. The Armenian population of Turkey is estimated at 2,000,000. Persia has about 30,000 Armenians. The highest bishop of the Armenian Church resides at Etchmiatsin (in Asiatic Russia). The bishops of Sis and Aghthamar have also the title of Catholicos.

3.—*The Nestorians.*

They have a patriarch at Diz (Mosul), in Turkey, and 18 bishops. In 1833, their number was reported as 10,054 families, or 70,000 souls. Other statements give higher figures. The number of Nestorians in Persia is estimated at 25.000.

Since 1833 the American Missionaries have labored among the Nestorians, and formed a number of Evangelical Congregations. Those Nestorians who have united with Rome, are generally called Chaldeans. They have a patriarch, bearing the title of Patriarch of Babylon and residing at Bagdad, archbishops at Amadia and Seleucia, in Asiatic Turkey, four bishops in Turkey and 2 in Persia.

In India, the Nestorians are commonly known under the name of Christians of St Thomas of whom there are about 70.000. About 150.000 are united with the Church of Rome.

4.—*The Jacobites.*

They have a patriarch, with the title, Patriarch of Antioch at Caramit (Diabekir), a maphrian (head of the Eastern Jacobites), in a convent near Mosul. Besides, there are said to be 21 bishops in Asiatic Turkey. The number of families in Turkey is variously estimated from 10,400 to 34,000. It is said that there are about 200,000 Jacobites living in East India (in Malabar and Travancore. Of late, the Roman Catholic Church has made progress among the Jacobites in Syria.

5.—*The Copts and Abyssinians.*

The Copts in Egypt.—A patriarch of Alexandria residing at Cairo, and the head of the entire church, with jurisdiction also extending over Nubia and Abyssinia, and the right of consecrating the Abuna (patriarch) of the latter country; 16 bishops, churches and convents 146. Population variously estimated from 150,000 to 250,000, of whom about 10.000 in Cairo. Of the Copts about 13,000 have united with the Roman Catholic Church (United Copts.) The Abyssinians number about 3,000,000.

Roman Catholic Church.

1.—*Pope and Cardinals.*—The Pope, Pius IX., formerly Giovanni Maria di Mastai Ferretti, was born at Sinigaglia on the 13th of May 1792; elected Pope on the death of Gregory XVI., in 1846, and crowned on the 21st of June of that year.

There are 59 Cardinals, of whom 6 are Cardinal Bishops, 44 Cardinal Priests, and 9 Cardinal Deacons. Thirty-nine are Italians by birth, 8 French, 4 Spanish, 4 Germans, 1 Croatian, 1 Belgian, 1 Portuguese, and 1 Irish.

2.—*Archbishops and Bishops.*—The number of Archbishops in authority was, in 1867, as follows: In the United States 7; British North America, 3; Mexico, West Indies, Central and South America, Turkey, 4; Ireland, 4; Portugal, 2; Prussia, 12; Italy, 47; Austria, 16; France, 17; Spain, 9; Bavaria, Russia, Greece, 2 each; Belgium, Holland, England, Baden, Poland, Malta, 1 each; Asiatic Turkey, 10; Spanish possessions in Asia; 1; Portuguese do., 1; Africa, 2. There are in the world 692 bishops.

3.—*Monastic orders.*—The following are the statistics of some of the Monastic orders: *Male:* Franciscans, 50,000; School Brethren, 16,000; Jesuits, 8000; Congregations for nursing the sick, 6000; Benedictines, 5000; Dominicans, 4000; Carmelites, 4000. Trappists, 4000; Lazarists, 2000; Piarists, 2000; Redemptorists, 2000. There are about 190.000 members in Female orders, of whom 162,000 are in Europe, 20,000 in America, and the rest in the other parts of the world.

4.—*Roman Catholics in the United States.*—There are 7 provinces in the United States, comprising 44 dioceses and 3 vicariates apostolic, as follows: *Province of Baltimore* comprises the Dioceses of Baltimore, Charleston, Erie, Philadelphia, Pittsburg, Richmond, Savannah, and Wheeling, with the Vicariate Apostolic of East Florida, and extends over the District of Columbia, and the States of Maryland, Pennsylvania, Delaware, Virginia, North and South Carolina, Georgia, and the *eastern* section of Florida. *Province of Cincinnati* embraces the dioceses of Cincinnati, Cleveland, Covington, Detroit, Fort Wayne, Louisville, Marquette and Vincennes, including the States of Ohio, Indiana, Michigan, and Kentucky. *Province of New Orleans, La.*, comprises the dioceses of New Orleans, Galveston, Little Rock, Mobile, Natchez, and Natchitoches, and includes the States of Louisiana, Alabama, Mississippi, Texas, and Arkansas. *Province of New York* includes the dioceses of New York, Albany, Boston, Brooklyn, Buffalo, Burlington, Hartford, Newark, and Portland, and includes New England, New York, and New Jersey. *Province of Oregon City* includes the dioceses of Oregon City, Nesqualy, Vancouver Island, and the vicariate of British Columbia. *Province of St Louis* comprises the dioceses of St. Louis, Alton, Chicago, Dubuque, Milwaukee, Nashville, Santa Fé, St. Paul, the vicariates apostolic of Kansas, and the Indian Territory, and Nebraska, and embraces Missouri, Tennessee, Illinois, Wisconsin, Iowa, Kansas, Nebraska, Minnesota, Dacotah, New Mexico, Colorado, Arizona, and the Indian Territory. *Province of San Francisco* comprises the dioceses of San Francisco, that of Monterey and Los Angelos, and the vicariate apostolic of Marysville, and embraces the States of California and Nevada, and all the territory east to the Rio Colorado.

These have in all about 4000 churches, chapels and stations, 2700 priests, 74 theological Seminaries and colleges, over 1400 academies and schools with over 30,000 pupils, and upwards of 150 convents and monasteries. The total Catholic population of the United States is estimated at from 4,000,000 to 5,000,000.

5.—*Roman Catholics in British America.*—There are three provinces in British America (Quebec, Halifax, and Oregon), with 18 dioceses and 2 vicariates apostolic, with nearly 1000 priests, and a catholic population of about 300,000.

6.—*Roman Catholics in Great Britain.*—The Roman Catholics have in England, 1415 priests, 1014 churches, chapels and stations, 63 male communities, 204 convents, and 11 colleges. In Scotland there are 4 bishops, 193 priests, as many churches, 16 convents, and 2 seminaries. There are 26 Roman Catholic peers. The number of bishops in England is 16. The number of Roman Catholics in England and Scotland is from 1 500,000 to 2,000,000. In Ireland are 4 provinces, 31 archbishops and bishops, 1070 parishes, 3120 priests of all kinds, 67 male and 189 female communities, and 4,490,583.

7.—For statistics of Roman Catholicism in other countries, see tables of ecclesiastical statistics of America, Europe, Australasia, and creeds of the world.

Unitarians.

1.—*America.*

The Unitarian Yearbook for 1867 gives the following statistics of American Unitarianism. Number of societies about 294, number of ministers about 359.

The National Conference of Unitarian and other Christian Churches, (organized 1865) is composed of such delegates, elected once in two years not to exceed three from any one Church, including the minister, who shall officially be one as any of the churches may accredit to it by a certificate of their appointment. The "American Unitarian Association" of Boston, the "Conference of the Western Churches," and other Unitarian organizations, are also entitled to representation in it.

They support a mission in India, under the charge of Mr. Dall, who superintends five schools —a school for useful arts, a vernacular school, a native girl's school, the Mary Carpenter or ragged school, and another separate school—and the Rev. Mr. Roberts, who is laboring at Madras. There are also schools at Salem and Secunderabad, receiving assistance from the Unitarian Asociation and from Mr. Dall.

No statistics of members are given. They have been variously estimated from 13,000 to 30,000.

2.—*Europe.*

In England there are about 300 Unitarian ministers who have charge of Congregations In Ireland there are three Presbyterian bodies, which in point of doctrine are regarded as Unitarians, namely: the Presbyterian Synod of Antrim, the Remonstrant Synod of Ulster, and the Synod of Mescucter. Together they form the "Non-Subscribing Presbyterian Association of Ireland," which meets annually. In the English Colonies the Unitarians have chapels. On the Continent of Europe the Unitarians exist as a separate denomination only in the Austrian Province of Transylvania, where they number a population of over 50,000.

Universalists.

The Universalist Register in 1868 gives the following statistics:

Conventions.	Associa'ns	Societ's.	Minis'rs
Maine	6	68	39
New Hampshire	3	35	15
Vermont	5	46	35
Massachusetts	6	115	115
Rhode Islands	6	6	5
Connecticut	3	14	14
New York	16	168	112
New Jersey		5	2
Pennsylvania	6	18	2C
Ohio	13	95	52
Michigan	4	24	1F
Indiana	4	33	15
Illinois	6	36	37
Wisconsin	3	23	18
Minnesota		13	9
Iowa	4	24	15

In most states, there are annual "State Conventions". A "General Convention of the United States" meets annually.

There are also a few societies and ministers in the other States.

There are 11 Literary Institutions, colleges, and Theological Seminaries under the care of denomination. Periodicals are published, in Maine, 1, Vermont, 1, Massachusetts, 4, New York, 2, Ohio, 1, Illinois, 2, Alabama, 1, Missouri, 1.

Nova Scotia, 2 ministers, 2 societies, 2 meeting houses; *New Brunswick*, 2 societies, 1 minister; *Canada West*, (Ontario) 3 societies, 3 meeting houses, 2 ministers; *Canada East*, 2 ministers.

The Universalists, in 1860, had only three Congregations in England. But their distinctive view of universal salvation has a number of adherents among the members of the Protestant Churches of Great Britain, Germany and other countries.

Christians, (Christian Connection.)

The statements concerning the statistics of this denomination greatly vary. Belcher, in his work on *The Religious Denominations in the United States* (1854), gives to them 607 organized churches, 469 ministers, and 34,000 communicants. In 1859 they claimed 1500 churches and 1000 ministers, and 150,000 communicants. In the late slave states they number about 100 ministers, 140 Churches, and about 10 000 members. The denomination has spread in England and the English possessions. Their institutions of learning are Christian Union College, at Merom, Ind.; Graham College, in North Carolina; and academies at Wolfborough, N. H., and Starkey, N. Y. They are to commence a Biblical School, and have fixed its location at Newark, N. Y. More than sixty Conferences have been organized in the United States and Canada, which meet annually. The General Conference meets every fourth year. At the last, held in 1866, 40 annual Conferences were represented.

Jews.

The statistics of Judaism in 1867, according to the best authorities were about as follows: Portugal, 3000; Russia (European), 1,300,000; France, 80,000; Great Britain and Ireland, 36,000; Austria, 853,000; Prussia, 250,000; Other German States, 192,176; Netherlands, 70,000; Belgium, 1,336; Denmark, 4,143; Sweden and Norway, 815; Switzerland, 3,000; Italy, 40,000; Greece, 8,000; Turkey (European), 70,000; Syria and Asiatic Turkey, 52,000; Morocco and North Africa, 610,000; East Asia, 500,800; America, 400,000. The total number of Jews is from 6 to 7 millions.

Evangelical Association.

(The Almanac published by this denomination did not reach us in time, to put the latest denominational statistics in its proper place among the statistics of American Methodism.)

According to the Almanac of the Evangelical Association for 1868", there are 13 Annual Conferences 11 in the United States, 1 in Canada, 1 in Germany), with 478 preachers, 382 local preachers and 60,241 communicants. (an increase, over 1866, 5 preachers, 27 local preachers and 3394 members.)

The number of Sunday-schools is 800, of schoolars, 40,655, and of officers and teachers, 8266. The contributions for the Sabbath school and teachers union were $1676.70, and the total receipts for mission purposes were $42,104 16.

Free-Will Baptist.

(The "Free-Will Baptist Register for 1866" not having reached us in time, we have to give the statistics of the denomination out of their people place under the head of Baptist.)

This denomination, in 1867, 29 yearly meetings, 148 quarterly meetings, 1276 Churches, 1100 ordained preachers 59,211 communicants. The "Free-Will Printing Establishment at Dover, N. H., publishes a quarterly Review, 1 weekly paper, and a Sunday-school paper. Another weekly was established in 1867, in Chicago.

The educational institutions are a Biblical School at New Hampton, N. H., 3 colleges and 10 seminaries and academies. The "Free-Will Baptist Foreign Mission Society" supports a mission at Orissa, in India.

The Friends.

1.—In the United States, the Friends number 100,000, belonging to 8 yearly meetings. A yearly meetings has also recently been organized in Canada. Two weekly papers are published in Philadelphia.

The separate organization of the "Hicksite" (Liberal) Friends numbers about 10 members in 6 yearly meetings. They have a weekly paper in Philadelphia.

The most important of the yearly meetings of "Progressive Friends" is that at Longwood, Chester Co., Pennsylvania. There are others, (or were some years ago) at Waterloo, N. Y., North Collins, N. Y., Wabash, Ind.

2.—The Friends in England numbered in 1867, 13,786 members, an increase of 11 over the preceding year.

The New Jerusalem Church.

The "General Convention of the New Jerusalem Church in the United States" is composed of 9 Associations (Illinois, Maine, and New Hampshire, Maryland, Massachusetts, Michigan and Northern Indiana, New York, Ohio, Pennsylvania) 9 isolated Societies, and Members by Eelection. The total number of organized Societies in the United States, is 67.

In England, Scotland and Ireland, 56 Societies are in connection with the "General Conference" and 10 Societies not in full connection.

In Germany, there are 12 places where there are known to be "receivers," in Switzerland 4 places, in France 4 places, in Italy 2 places, in Australia 8 places.

Other Denominations in the United States.

The *Shakers* have 18 Societies with about 4500 members.

The *Adventists* have about 30,000 members and publish papers in Boston, New York, and Battle Creek, Mich.

The *River Brethren* have an Annual Conference in Pennsylvania and another in Canada. Ministers from 50 to 60.

The "*Bible Christians*" have 1 Congregation in Philadelphia.

The *Irvingites* (Catholic Apostolic Church) have Congregations in New York, Philadelphia, Potsdam, N. Y., and perhaps a few others. They have also a few Congregations in England, Germany and other countries.

The *Mormons* number about 60,000 in the United States; 20,000 in Europe, and a small number in several other countries.

The *Oneida Communists* had in December 1867, communities at Oneida (210 members) Wallingford (45 members) New Haven, New York.

ALPHABETICAL INDEX.

W. WATERS & SON,

BOOK AND PAMPHLET BINDERS,

118 William St.,

NEW YORK.

UNION PRINTING HOUSE.

79 JOHN STREET.

NEW YORK.

C. S. WESTCOTT & CO.

Book, Pamphlet, Plain and ornamental Printing of every description.

PETTINER & CARR

ELECTROTYPERS

AND

STEREOTYPERS,

74 Ann St.,

NEW YORK.

JOHN SMITH,

PRACTICAL JOB

Book Binder,

24 ANN STREET,

Near Nassau, NEW YORK.

All kinds of Book Binding done at the shortest notice and lowest trade prices. Also photograph Albums neatly repaired.

☞ Special attention paid to the Binding of Music, three days time required. Newspapers, Blank Books, Pamphlets, &c., bound to order. All orders promptly attended to.

Published by FRDR. GERHARD, New York, and for sale by all the Newsdealers:

THE AMERICAN FARMERS ALMANAC FOR 1868,

Price 30 Cents.

AND

THE AMERICAN FAMILY ALMANAC FOR 1868,

Price 30 Cents.

The former (besides the usual number of Calendars) contains over hundred and twenty pages of reading matter, including an excellent story of South Western Border Life, and remarks and hints on various subjects of domestic and agricultural economy. The second contains likewise over hundred and twenty pages of a miscellaneous character, including two excellent stories, and a number of short articles, stories, essays, notes of interesting facts, and hints on domestic economy. The articles in both are well chosen, and make the books good things to have about, aside from their value as Almanacs.

OUR NEW

FAMILY SEWING MACHINE.

The superior merits of the "Singer" Machines over all others, for either Family use or Manufacturing purposes, are so well established and so generally admitted, that an enumeration of their relative excellences is no longer considered necessary.

THE LETTER "A" FAMILY MACHINE,

Hitherto manufactured by this Company, has gained and maintained, the world over, and for years past, an unparalleled reputation and sale. But notwithstanding the excellence of this Machine, we now have to announce that it has been superseded by our

NEW FAMILY MACHINE,

Which has been over two years in preparation, and which has been brought to perfection regardless of TIME, LABOR, OR EXPENSE, and is now confidently presented to the public as incomparably the BEST SEWING MACHINE IN EXISTENCE.

The machine in question is **simple, compact, durable, and beautiful.** It is quiet, light running, and **capable of performing a range and variety of work** never before attempted upon a single Machine,—using either *Silk, Twist, Linen, or Cotton Thread*, and sewing with equal facility the very finest and coarsest materials, and anything between the two extremes, in the most beautiful and substantial manner. Its attachments for *Hemming, Braiding, Cording, Tucking, Quilting, Felling, Trimming, Binding, etc.*, are *Novel* and *Practical*, and have been invented and adjusted especially for this Machine.

New designs of the *Unique, Useful, and Popular Folding Tops and Cabinet Cases*, peculiar to the Machines manufactured by this Company, have been prepared for enclosing the new Machine.

A faint idea, however, can at best be conveyed through the medium of a (necessarily) limited advertisement; and we therefore urge every person in quest of a Sewing Machine by all means to examine and test, if they can possibly do so, all the leading rival Machines before making a purchase. A selection can be made there understandingly. Branches or agencies for supplying the "Singer" Machines will be found in nearly every city and town throughout the civilized world, where Machines will be cheerfully exhibited, and any information promptly furnished. Or communications may be addressed for Circulars or otherwise, to

THE SINGER MANUFACTURING COMPANY,

458 BROADWAY, NEW YORK.

☞ Circulars describing and illustrating the MANUFACTURING MACHINES made by this Company, as also the truly wonderful and only practical BUTTON HOLE MACHINE ever yet devised, will be sent post free on application.

PRINCIPAL DOMESTIC BRANCHES.

Boston, 69 Hanover St.
Philadelphia, 810 Chestnut St.
Baltimore, 159 Baltimore St.
Chicago, 50 Clark St
St. Louis, 312 N Fourth St.
Cincinnati, cor. Fourth and Race Sts.
Indianapolis, 48 E Washington St.
Detroit, 60 Woodward Av.
Milwaukee, 17 Newhall House.
St. Paul, 250 Third St.
Newark, 273 Broad St
Brooklyn, 326 Fulton St.
Albany, 564 Broadway.
Troy, 4½ Franklin Square.
Rochester, 31 Buffalo St.
Buffalo, 253 Main St.
New Haven, 219 Chapel St.
San Francisco, 139 Montgomery Street.
New Orleans, 7 Camp St.

Fam. 15

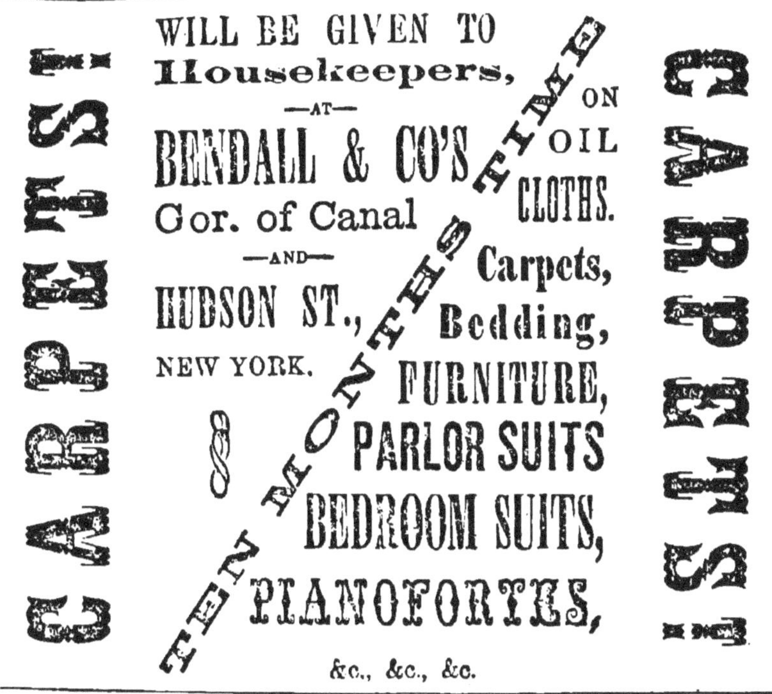

STATEN ISLAND

FANCY DYEING ESTABLISHMENT.

NOS. 5 & 7 JOHN STREET, NEW YORK.

Branch Offices, { 748 BROADWAY, NEW YORK.
269 FULTON STREET, BROOKLYN.
47 NORTH EIGHTH STREET, PHILADELPHIA.

All kinds of Dress Goods dyed, in the piece or in garments.

Ladies' Dresses, Cloaks, etc., cleaned, and Gentlemen's Coats, Overcoats, Pants, Vests, etc. dyed or cleaned without ripping.

Kid Gloves and Feathers dyed or cleaned.

Goods received and returned by Express.

BARRETT, NEPHEWS & CO,
Nos. 5 & 7 John Street, New York.

A. D. F. RANDOLPH.

770 BROADWAY COR. OF NINTH ST., N. Y.

BOOKS FOR CLERGYMEN.

BOOKS FOR SUNDAY SCHOOLS, embracing Selections from all Unecceptionable Sources.

DEVOTIONAL BOOKS.

BOOKS FOR CHILDREN AND YOUTHS, in great variety.

Particular attention paid to the selection of Libraries, for the Parish and Sunday School.

All American Publications, sent by Mail prepaid on the receipt of the price; and Catalogues of publishers sent on application.

EXPOSITION UNIVERSAL.

PARIS, 1867.

The Howe Machine Co.—Elias Howe, Jr.,—699 Broadway, New York, awarded, OVER EIGHTY-TWO COMPETITORS, the

Only Grand Cross of the Legion of Honor,

AND GOLD MEDAL,

given to American Sewing Machines, as per Imperial Decree, published in the "Moniteur Universel" (Official Journal of the French Empire), Tuesday, 2d July, 1867.

THE GREAT PRIZE:

THE ONLY

Grand Cross of the Legion of Honor and Gold Medal,

Awarded to AMERICAN SEWING MACHINES at the Paris Exposition of 1867, was given to us as per Imperial Decree, published in the "Moniteur Universel" (Official Journal of the French Empire.) Tuesday, July 2d, 1867.

The HOWE Sewing Machines,

MANUFACTURED BY

THE HOWE MACHINE CO.,

ELIAS HOWE, Jr., President,

699 BROADWAY, NEW YORK.

FOR FAMILIES AND MANUFACTURERS.

They are celebrated for doing the best work, using a much smaller needle for the same thread than any other machine.

The New Improved Family Machine is without a rival, and cannot be surpassed,—a Hemmer, Feller, Braider, Quilter and Guide go with each Family Machine free of charge.

Every Machine is as near perfection as the best machinery in the world can make it.

They are adapted to all kinds of Family Sewing, and Manufacturing of every description, making a beautiful and perfect Stitch, alike on both sides of the articles sewed, and will neither rip nor ravel.

The parts being exactly alike, if any part needs to be replaced, the operator can replace it Loss of time and expense of sending to a machine shop rarely occurs.

The best Machines in the World. Send for Circular.

THE HOWE MACHINE CO., Manufacturers and Sole Proprietors of THE HOWE SEWING MACHINE, 699 Broadway, N. Y.

Independent, Fraternal, Loyal, and Progressive.

THE METHODIST:

AN

Eight-Page Weekly Newspaper.

RELIGIOUS AND LITERARY.

THE METHODIST

throughout this year will Publish Sermons delivered by

NEWMAN HALL, D. D. **HENRY WARD BEECHER,**

AND

The **BISHOPS** and other representative **MINISTERS** of the **METHODIST EPISCOPAL CHURCH.**

These Sermons are reported verbatim expressly for its columns and are in every respect reliable. Those by Rev. Newman Hall were delivered during his recent tour in this country, and those by Mr. Beecher are by his own Authorized Reporter.

THE METHODIST

is progressive in its character and is the Advocate of Lay Representation in the Councils of the Church. It is edited, as heretofore, by

REV. GEORGE R. CROOKS, D. D.,

assisted by the following able corps of

EDITORIAL CONTRIBUTORS.

REV. ABEL STEVENS, L L. D., REV. JOHN McCLINTOCK, D. D., LL. D.
PROF. A. J. SCHEM.

Its Department of Religious Intelligence is of special interest to Members of all Christian Denominations of whatever name. It is prepared by Prof. A. J. Schem, the Editor of the "Ecclesiastical Almanac" and is unsurpassed in point of completeness and accuracy. It contains, also, vigorous Editorials, ample Correspondence, News, a Children's Story every week, etc.

Terms to Mail Subscribers, Two Dollars and Fifty Cents per Year, in advance; to Ministers, for their own Subscription, Two Dollars. Postage prepaid at the Post-Office where received, Twenty Cents per year. Twenty Cents must be added by Canada subscribers, to prepay postage.

Any one sending Three Subscribers and $7 50, will receive a fourth copy free for one year.

Subscription received at any time during the year.

Liberal Cash Commissions or Premiums allowed to those getting up Clubs of Subscribers.

Specimen Copies sent free on application.

Address

The Methodist,

114 Nassau Street,

New York.

H. W. DOUGLAS,

Publishing Agents.

Have been familiarly known to the American Public for upw
three-quarters of a Century.

THEY SPEAK THEIR OWN PRAISE WHEREVER PLAN

DEALERS IN SEEDS,

Whether Country Merchants, Booksellers, Druggists, or regular
men, not already customers of the subscribers
are invited to become such.

OUR WHOLESALE PRICE LI

Published to the TRADE ALONE, will be mailed to all DEALERS who a

MARKET GARDENERS,

to whom seeds of undoubted worth are of vital importance, and
Families, who aim to raise vegetables of high quality ONLY, a
reside remotely from merchants that vend our seeds, will be s
by mail, or express.—Catalogues of approved varieties on applic

LANDRETH'S RURAL REGISTER, 1

Containing numerous Hints on Horticulture, will be mailed to all applica
enclose a two-cent stamp, with their address plainly written.

DAVID LANDRETH & SON,

Nos. 21 and 23 South Sixth Street, Philade

www.ingramcontent.com/pod-product-compliance
Lightning Source LLC
Chambersburg PA
CBHW031120160426
43192CB00008B/1063

* 9 7 8 3 3 3 7 3 3 6 5 9 2 *